RESTAURANT
FINANCIAL BASICS

RESTAURANT
FINANCIAL BASICS

Raymond S. Schmidgall

David K. Hayes

Jack D. Ninemeier

JOHN WILEY & SONS, INC.

For general information on our other products and services or for technical support, please contact our Customer Care Department within the United States at (800) 762-2974, outside the United States at (317) 572-3993 or fax (317) 572-4002.

Wiley also publishes its books in a variety of electronic formats. Some content that appears in print may not be available in electronic books.

Library of Congress Cataloging-in-Publication Data:

Schmidgall, Raymond S., 1945–
    Restaurant financial management basics / Raymond S. Schmidgall, David K. Hayes, Jack D. Ninemeier.
        p. cm.
    ISBN 0-471-21379-9
    1. Hospitality industry—Finance.   2. Restaurant management.   I. Hayes, David K. II. Ninemeier, Jack D.   III. Title
    TX911.3.F5 S36 2002
    647.94′068′1—dc21

                                                                                2002003460

Printed in the United States of America

10 9 8 7 6 5

The authors dedicate this resource to their past, present, and future hospitality business students. Some have (will be) enrolled in our accounting courses reluctantly; others were (will be) very anxious to learn about the basic concepts of financial management. All eventually realize that an understanding and application of this information is critical to the success of their hospitality operation. It is our hope that restaurant operators (who, with their wisdom and experience, could also be their teachers) will benefit from this primer on the application of accounting and financial management principles to the restaurant business.

CONTENTS

PREFACE

Restaurant managers often see themselves as "people" persons. They enjoy the satisfaction that comes from serving guests and doing their personal best to exceed their guests' expectations. Consistently producing and serving quality food and beverage products increases the level of job satisfaction of most managers. However, managers in today's environment need to know much more than just how to serve good food and drink at reasonable prices. In addition to numerous other tasks, they must also know how to "report" or "account" for the activities and costs related to managing their restaurants.

Systems used to report the revenue, expenses, "bottom-line profits," and overall financial health of a business involve accounting processes and procedures. The term "accounting" is a variation of the word "account," which is defined as "a report, record, description or explanation related to the finances of a person or business." Restaurant managers must know the basics of restaurant accounting for the sake of their constituents and themselves:

- **Guests:** Understanding accounting basics allows a manager to monitor costs involved in providing outstanding guest service at a price that ensures the restaurant is profitable. In addition, guests who pay by credit card or advance deposit deserve to know that their payments will be properly credited to their bills. Proper accounting procedures help ensure that this occurs. Thorough understanding of the restaurant's financial condition helps managers to make operating decisions that positively influence their guests' dining experiences.

- **Employees:** Employees are the focus of many accounting procedures. Payroll taxes, wages and salaries, and benefits are just a few of the employee-related areas that must be accounted for. If a restaurant is to provide employees with steady jobs and competitive wages, its managers must be very knowledgeable about accounting.

- **Vendors/Suppliers:** The individuals and organizations that sell the products and services managers need to run their businesses need to know about the creditworthiness of the restaurants with which they do business. Questions regarding the operation's financial health must be answered using standard financial reports that can easily be understood and interpreted by outside groups such as vendors.

- **Owners/Investors:** If managers work for a publicly held company (one that is owned by stockholders) its investors will require that the financial information they receive be timely and accurate. Data must also conform to commonly accepted financial reporting standards to clearly and fairly present the financial condition of the business. This is the only way investors can monitor the value of their investment. Banks and other lending institutions also require the use of standard accounting procedures. If they did not, a business could misrepresent its financial strength to acquire more loan proceeds than it is qualified to receive. Such a business might then be unable to repay its loans, and the funds of the bank and its depositors would unfairly and needlessly be at risk.

- **Governmental Agencies:** There are numerous federal, state, and local governmental agencies that require the reporting of financial information. From employee wage reports needed to compute payroll taxes to the reporting of food and beverage revenues used to determine sales taxes, governmental agencies require the regular and precise reporting of a wide range of financial data. The taxes paid on the restaurant's profits are determined in large measure by financial operating results presented annually in a manner acceptable to the Internal Revenue Service (IRS). Foodservice managers whose operations have nonprofit status (e.g., schools, hospitals, military institutions) must also submit reports to comply with governmental regulations.

■ *The Hospitality Industry:* One of the advantages to the use of generally accepted accounting principles is that the results obtained can be compared to the operating results of other, similar foodservice operations. For example, food, labor, rent, and utility costs can be compared when the operators of two (or more) units consistently use the same accounting procedures to report results. The National Restaurant Association (NRA) regularly publishes financial data about the restaurant industry that managers can best interpret if they record their own financial data in a comparable way.

■ *Managers Themselves and Their Careers:* Future employers evaluate a prospective manager's past success to predict future success. Applicants for management positions may be asked about their previous impact on the revenue, costs, and profits in the operations they have managed or helped to manage. They must be able to speak knowledgably about accounting-related aspects of their performance. In addition, restaurant managers' compensation and bonuses are usually tied to the restaurant's financial performance. A thorough understanding of basic accounting procedures helps to ensure that managers can monitor and influence aspects of the restaurant's operation that relate to their personal financial and career success.

BACKGROUND INFORMATION

Some restaurant managers may believe the tasks of accounting and financial management are too complex and "should be left to an accountant." In fact, a manager must interact with others as accounting systems are designed and as systems/procedures to collect financial data are developed. Effective managers must be able to discuss their needs with professional accountants and understand the accounting information that is provided. As well, they must be able to ask the right questions about the meaning of financial information. None of these or related activities can occur unless the manager has a good working knowledge of the basics of a managerial accounting system.

The manager who understands the basic information provided in this book will be able to:

- Know what information is needed for the short- and long-term control of the restaurant
- Understand information reported in financial statements
- Take corrective action(s) as necessary to improve the restaurant's profitability
- Make operating decisions with full knowledge of their potential impact upon the restaurant's financial status

This book also recognizes that restaurant managers are very busy. The authors have attempted to separate the "must know" from the "nice to know" information. Both the depth and breadth of the discipline of accounting has been narrowed to focus on what the manager must know and be able to do in everyday operations. Accounting will be placed within the context of the full range of duties and responsibilities of the restaurant manager. The accounting information provided will be easy to read, easy to understand, and easy to apply.

CONTENT OF BOOK

This book focuses on providing restaurant managers with a clear and up-to-date survey of financial management issues important to the successful completion of their jobs. Each chapter focuses on a specific topic and provides a comprehensive discussion of relevant issues. The book can be used in two different ways:

- It can be read cover-to-cover in chapter sequence. Using this approach, managers can begin to acquire the comprehensive background of accounting and financial information relevant to their restaurant's operation.

- Chapters (or even partial chapters) can be read (consulted) on an as-needed basis. If, for example, a manager wishes to use break-even analysis to consider whether entertainment should be added on a weekend evening or if he/she has questions about procedures for developing/analyzing data from an operating budget, these specific chapters/sections can be reviewed.

The book is divided into two basic units. The first provides an overview of financial management and then reviews the basic elements of a restaurant's two most important financial statements, the balance sheet and income statement. It then provides information about how to interpret them. Additional background information is provided relative to cash flow, understanding cost concepts, establishing menu selling prices, and developing/using operating budgets. The second part of the book addresses issues that begin when planning activities conclude. Operating concerns relating to food and beverage controls, payroll and equipment accounting, and revenue and cash control are addressed, always with a focus on the information most critically required by busy restaurant managers.

Book elements include:

1. *Manager's Brief:* A short overview of what will be covered and why it is important begins each chapter.

2. *Internet Assistant:* Readers will be directed to Internet addresses throughout the book that can provide more information.

3. *Manager's Tools:* Where appropriate, recordkeeping/accounting forms and control procedures are provided that can be used "as is" or modified to meet the needs of a specific restaurant.

4. *Manager's 10 Point Effectiveness Checklist:* Each chapter concludes with a checklist of activities that can be undertaken by the reader to improve operations and/or knowledge. For example, a section of the book related to cash flow includes a TACTIC item that advises the manager to monitor cash flow on a monthly basis.

This book has been carefully developed to help practicing restaurant managers understand the concepts and procedures needed to accurately analyze, understand, and report the financial status of their business (or an operation they might invest in or purchase). There is a significant difference between simply recording and summarizing financial data and analyzing and effectively using that data. This book teaches managers how to undertake all of these essential managerial tasks and shows them how to do them both well.

The creation of a book such as this one is truly the work of many individuals, as well as the authors. Thus, we wish to express our appreciation, first to our families and friends for their support, and second to Ms. Debbie Ruff and Ms. Rosa Soliz for their technical assistance.

The authors wish all readers the very best as they learn and apply the accounting principles so critical for continued success in the exciting field of hospitality. We offer this publication in the hope that it will help them and their businesses prosper.

Raymond S. Schmidgall
David K. Hayes
Jack D. Ninemeier

1

INTRODUCTION TO
FINANCIAL MANAGEMENT

MANAGER'S BRIEF

In this chapter you will begin the study of procedures to effectively manage and document your restaurant's finances. You will be introduced to the accounting process and its four specialty areas. In addition, you will see how the various users of accounting information will count on you to follow special accounting principles and practices that have been standardized for use by businesses in general and restaurants more specifically. As you use these specialized principles other businesses and government agencies that may be required to review your financial documents will be able to understand and use them.

There are several restaurant management and staff positions that may assist you in managing the money you earn and spend in your operation. This chapter introduces you to each of them and the important roles they can play in the financial management process.

Restaurant managers are not accountants; however, in this chapter you will learn how the financial control processes necessary for success are interrelated with the accounting process and the work of the accountant. Finally, you will review the characteristics of an effective working relationship among the restaurant manager, owner, and accountant.

If you own or manage an existing restaurant the accounting system is already established. It may be a cost-effective system that yields high-quality, usable information or it may be a less-than-adequate system that is not cost-effective. A new manager beginning work in the restaurant must know the basics of effective financial accounting systems to know, first, if the current system provides meaningful and helpful information, and second, what to do if it does not. Alternatively, if you are going to own or manage a new restaurant that is "on the drawing board," you may be asked for input on the design of the basic accounting system, or at least on the development of source documents and basic record-keeping procedures. If a system is being proposed (for example, by an accounting service you have hired for the task) you should be able to evaluate its potential worth to your new restaurant. Regardless, then, of the restaurant you will manage (existing or not-yet-opened), you will need to know about the standards that make up a good accounting system. A good restaurant manager must be aware of *what* is needed, *why* it is needed, *how* information can most effectively be collected, and *when* accounting-related activities must be undertaken.

FINANCIAL MANAGEMENT: WHAT IS IT?

FINANCIAL MANAGEMENT The process of organizing, analyzing, interpreting, recording, summarizing, and reporting financial information in ways that are meaningful for owners, managers, and other internal users and for lenders, government agencies, and other external users. Also referred to as accounting.

Restaurant managers use financial information to manage activities involving money that is earned and spent in the operation of their business. Financial information that summarizes these activities must be organized and expressed in ways that are meaningful. Analysis and interpretation of data is necessary, and the results must be recorded, summarized, and reported to those needing to know about the economic health of the restaurant. As will be seen, users will be both internal—owners and managers, for example—and external—including lenders and government agencies.

Financial management is *not* the same as **bookkeeping:** There is a big difference! Financial management includes organizing, analyzing, interpreting, recording, summarizing, and reporting financial information. By contrast, a bookkeeper's primary task is to analyze and record transactions. In very large restaurants, a bookkeeper may handle only one type of transaction, such as sales, accounts receivable collections, or payroll. The accountant then summarizes the bookkeeper's work and further interprets the results for management.

> **BOOKKEEPING** The task of analyzing and recording financial transactions of a specific type (for example, sales, collection of revenue, and payroll).

ACCOUNTING SPECIALTIES

There are several specialized areas within the accounting profession. For example, **financial accounting**—the topic of this book—involves the overall process of developing and using accounting information to make business decisions; the "deliverables" of financial accounting are such financial statements as the balance sheet, income (profit and loss) statement, and the statement of cash flows—all of which are discussed in this book. These are among the most important reports that managers, owners (investors), government agencies, financial institutions, and others use to learn about the financial status of the restaurant.

> **FINANCIAL ACCOUNTING** The process of developing and using accounting information to make business decisions, which involves organizing and presenting financial information in financial statements. The major focus is on the past.

Auditing

Auditing is another accounting specialty. Auditors review the internal controls of restaurants to assess measures taken to safeguard cash and inventory. They study the accounting system to ensure the proper recording and reporting of financial information. Auditors evaluate whether the restaurant's financial statements fairly present the financial position, operating results, and cash inflows and outflows by activity, and whether generally accepted accounting principles are consistently applied from period to period.

> **AUDITING** The accounting specialty that involves studying the restaurant's internal controls and analyzing the basic accounting system to assure that all financial information is properly recorded and reported.

Managerial Accounting

MANAGERIAL ACCOUNTING
The process of using historical and estimated financial
information to help man-
agers plan for the future.
The major focus is on
the future.

Managerial accounting uses historical and estimated financial information to develop future plans. Managerial accountants may help managers make decisions by assessing the financial impact of alternatives being considered. For example, should the restaurant open or close on a specific day or for a specific meal period? A managerial accountant can study actual and estimated information and provide managers with recommendations.

One way to view the difference between financial accounting and managerial accounting is to focus on the reports they produce. Statements stemming from financial accounting are of particular interest to parties external to the restaurant (investors, creditors, etc.). By contrast, reports stemming from managerial accounting are mainly designed for managers and other internal users. Likewise, they are generated more frequently (weekly or daily) than statements from financial accounting (monthly). Examples of managerial reports are inventory values (separated by product: food and beverage), listings of food and beverage products received, sales history records, and operating reports. Operating reports typically include actual operating results and budget estimates for the period.

Tax Accounting

As the name implies, **tax accounting** is concerned with the tax consequences of business decisions and the preparation of (often) quite complicated tax returns. Accounting methods restaurants use for tax purposes may differ from the methods they use for financial reporting. For example, **depreciation** may be calculated using a method that results in a faster write-off of a piece of equipment for tax purposes than for financial reporting purposes. (This may be preferred because taxable income is lowered, taxes are reduced, and cash is conserved.)

TAX ACCOUNTING The accounting specialty that involves planning and preparing for taxes and filing
tax-related information with
government agencies.

DEPRECIATION The allocation
of the cost of equipment and
other tangible assets as an
expense for a series of accounting periods according to
the useful life of the assets.

You can see, then, that the accounting field is broad; restaurant managers who must be well versed in diverse areas such as food preparation and service, marketing, personnel management, layout design, and

---

WWW: Internet Assistant

For more information on the Hospitality Financial & Technology Professionals (formerly the International Association of Hospitality Accountants), visit their web site at http://www.hftp.org

---

equipment and systems maintenance must also be able to organize and use accounting data and procedures to make the best possible management decisions. They may, as well, need to rely on accounting experts as financial systems are designed and as special accounting-related issues arise.[1]

USERS OF ACCOUNTING INFORMATION

We have already emphasized that restaurant managers need accounting information to help evaluate the daily, intermediate (monthly), and long-range success of operations. Other users of accounting information include:

- **Owners.** Those who have invested in the business. Owners may include one person in a sole proprietorship, two or more people in a partnership, or up to thousands of people in a corporation. All owners want to know how their investment is doing.

- **Boards of directors.** Large restaurants or foodservice chains may have corporate stockholders who elect persons to represent them in the management of the business. They need accounting information to evaluate the effectiveness of the managers who operate their restaurants.

- **Creditors.** Those who lend money (lenders) or provide products and/or services (suppliers) want to know the likelihood that payment obligations will be met.

---

[1]Note: Managers might find it helpful to contact Hospitality Financial & Technology Professionals (HFTP), a professional association for financial and management information systems (MIS) specialists in the hospitality industry. It has over 4,000 members and provides services such as continuing education, seminars, and certification.

- *Government agencies.* Income is taxable by the federal government, most states, and many communities. Accounting information is based upon the type of tax assessments that are made. For example, the Internal Revenue Service (at the national level), state revenue departments, and local taxing authorities have an ongoing interest in accounting records. Also, the Securities Exchange Commission (SEC) is required to review audited financial statements as it approves prospective information developed by large restaurant organizations wishing to issue securities to the public.

- *Employee unions.* Accounting information is used by union officials and membership in unionized restaurants to assess the abilities of the business to meet wage and benefit demands.

- *Financial analysts.* Persons outside of the restaurant, such as staff members of mutual investment and insurance companies, may desire accounting information about a restaurant for their own or their clients' purposes.

GENERALLY ACCEPTED ACCOUNTING PRINCIPLES (GAAPs)

> **GENERALLY ACCEPTED ACCOUNTING PRINCIPLES (GAAPS)** Standards that have evolved in the accounting profession to ensure uniformity in the procedures and techniques used to prepare financial statements.

> **ASSET** Something of value that is owned by the restaurant. Examples include cash, product inventories, equipment, land, and building(s).

A set of standards called **Generally Accepted Accounting Principles (GAAPs)** constitutes the framework against which accounting procedures and techniques are measured.

GAAPs include:

1. *Business entity.* The restaurant is distinct and separate from its owners; it generates revenues, incurs expenses by using **assets,** and makes a profit, suffers a loss, or "breaks even" by and for itself. The impact of this principle occurs when income is measured as it is generated by the business (there is an increase in owners' equity), not when it is distributed to owners. Likewise, an obligation

owed by the business is considered a **liability.** It may be owed to a vendor to pay for products received, or the liability may be an obligation (such as a loan to the business) which the owners owe to themselves!

2. *Historical cost.* The value of an asset is its agreed-upon cash equivalent. When a transaction occurs (for example, an asset such as an equipment item is sold), the price paid normally reflects its **current fair value.** Over time, the value may change (for example, inflation may increase the value of land or buildings). However, the historical cost—not the current fair value—normally represents the asset's value in accounts and in financial statements.

3. *Going concern.* An accountant assumes—unless there is reason to believe otherwise—that the restaurant will exist in the indefinite future. If, for example, the restaurant were to cease operation, certain liabilities would be due immediately. Likewise, assets might need to be sold at a considerable loss. When accountants assume that the business will continue (and this is the normal assumption), there is no need to write down assets to a liquidation value or to reclassify long-term liabilities as being due immediately.

4. *Periodicity.* Statements of the restaurant's financial condition, including the income statement, should be developed periodically. For example, income tax regulations require the annual filing of tax returns. Owners and others desire monthly statements about the economic health of their organizations. Tax authorities require annual reports.

5. *Expenses matched to revenues.* **Expenses** that are incurred must be matched with, and deducted from, **revenues** that are generated in

> **LIABILITIES** Obligations (money owed) to outside entities. Examples include amounts owed to suppliers, to lenders for long-term debt such as mortgages, and to employees (payroll that has been earned by but not paid to the restaurant's staff members).

> **CURRENT FAIR VALUE** The market value of the asset at the date of the financial statements. For example, assume a building (structure and land) cost $5,000,000. At the time of purchase, the cost would equal the fair value. Two years later the current fair value may be $6,000,000, yet the financial statements would reflect the historical cost of $5,000,000.

> **EXPENSE** A decrease in a resource (such as food inventory) that occurs when the restaurant sells a product or service.

REVENUE An increase in a resource (such as cash) when a product or service is sold by the restaurant (often referred to as "sales").

ACCOUNTS RECEIVABLE Money owed to the restaurant, generally from guests, that has not been received.

ACCOUNTS PAYABLE Money owed by the restaurant to suppliers and lenders that has not been paid.

CASH ACCOUNTING SYSTEM An accounting system that treats revenues as income when cash from operating activities is received and expenditures as expenses when cash is paid.

ACCRUAL ACCOUNTING SYSTEM An accounting system that matches expenses incurred with revenues generated. This is done with the use of accounts receivable, accounts payable, and other similar accounts.

an accrual accounting system that recognizes revenues and expenses without concern about when cash is received or paid by the restaurant. Amounts owed to the restaurant are called **accounts receivable;** amounts owed by the restaurant to suppliers are referred to as **accounts payable.** Small restaurants may use a **cash accounting system** (which treats revenues as income when cash is received and expenditures as expenses when cash is paid). However, GAAPs require an **accrual accounting system,** and this system will be used as the basis for the accounting discussion throughout this book.

6. *Conservatism.* This GAAP requires that all losses be shown in financial records if there is a reasonable chance that a problem will occur; gains and related financial benefits, however, should not be reflected in financial records until they are realized. For example, assume a restaurant had a lawsuit for negligence filed against it. If the restaurant's legal advisor indicates that the restaurant is likely to lose and can reasonably estimate the amount, the conservatism principle dictates the recording of the loss rather than waiting for the judge's decision. This principle is important, since many accounting decisions do not have a single "right answer." This concept guides the accountant confronted with alternate measurements to select the option that will yield the least favorable impact upon the restaurant's profitability and financial position within the current accounting period.

7. *Consistency.* The same procedures used to collect accounting information should be used each fiscal period; if this GAAP were not used, restaurant managers would not have an accurate information base upon which to make decisions.

8. *Materiality and practicality.* The significance of fina
pacts the financial viability (long-term operation) c
Experience and judgment are necessary to determine wₕₑ.
practical to report "minor" financial events and/or matters related to
confidential information.

The above and other GAAPs help form the basic foundation upon which
accounting systems and procedures must be developed. They provide reasonable requirements but still permit discretion as financial accounting systems are
designed for specific restaurants. They help chart the development of accounting systems for restaurants and other businesses. GAAPs taken in concert with
three important characteristics of effective accounting systems provide the basic
"prerequisites" for useful information:

- Accounting information must be relevant; it must be useful to the specific situation. For example, reports can be produced with greater
  or less frequency and can be very detailed or less so depending
  upon the manager's needs. Cost/benefit concerns (whether the information gathered is worth more than the cost to collect it) are of great
  importance.

- Accounting information must be current; "old" data is generally of little or no assistance as decisions are made in today's fast-paced restaurant operations. Information needed to monitor daily performance
  must be generated daily. Many managers, for example, develop and analyze food costs and revenues daily; they find the results to be worth
  the efforts expended to collect the information.

- Accounting data must be accurate. Given the restraints of cost/benefit
  already discussed (data must be worth more than the costs needed to
  collect it) the financial information generated must reasonably "tell"
  (reflect) the financial aspects of the activities measured.

POSITIONS WITH ACCOUNTING RESPONSIBILITIES

Someone must be responsible for developing accounting information for line
managers. (According to personnel management principles, **line positions** are

LINE POSITION A job held by an employee who is in the chain of command; for example, the restaurant manager, department heads such as chef and head bartender, and other decision-makers.

STAFF POSITION A job held by a technical specialist such as an accountant, who provides information to but does not make decisions for line personnel.

held by employees such as managers, department heads, supervisors, and others who are in the chain of command. By contrast, **staff positions,** held by accounting, personnel, and purchasing department employees, provide specialized and advisory assistance to line officials.)

In a small restaurant, the manager (who is likely to be the owner) develops some of the financial information needed for decision-making. However, because of the increasingly complex process needed to generate financial data, especially for tax accounting purposes, the manager/owner of the small restaurant will likely need the services of an external accountant. As restaurants increase in size, some or all of the accounting responsibilities assumed by the manager of the small operation fall to other employees. Here are some examples:

- *Bookkeeper.* As noted above, bookkeepers are involved in some of the processes by which financial transactions of the restaurant are recorded and summarized. Frequently, bookkeeping services are used

SOURCE DOCUMENT A record from which financial information is initially drawn and entered into an accounting system.

  by restaurant managers who supply **source documents** (schedule of hours employees worked, delivery invoices, sales data from electronic registers, etc.) to external bookkeepers who develop records, reports, and financial statements for the manager.

- *Accountant.* Accountants in large restaurants often work under the controller (see below) and perform duties that include designing and monitoring the data collection system and source documents, summarizing information in financial statements, developing management reports, coordinating budget development, collecting information required by tax authorities, and completing required external reports.

- *Controller.* This official is generally the chief accounting officer (CAO) in a large restaurant organization and oversees the development and implementation of the accounting system. The controller may supervise many employees in large firms (if so, accounting-related activities are generally only part of the responsibilities of the position).

- *Food and beverage controller.* Moderate- and large-sized restaurants may employ a food and beverage controller who is responsible for developing a wide variety of routine operating and control reports. Likewise, for control purposes, product receiving, storing, and/or issuing activities and responsibilities are frequently assumed by this official. (A basic principle [standard] of control involves the need to separate tasks to make it difficult [at least without collusion] for employees to commit fraudulent acts. If products are purchased by a staff purchasing agent and come under the control of production personnel [chef and bartender] after issuing, the control process is tightened when these intermediate tasks [receiving, storing, and issuing] are the responsibility of the controller.)

- *Internal auditor.* Very large restaurants and foodservice chains may employ internal auditors to evaluate the operating effectiveness of the accounting information system. As companies grow into multiunit organizations, corporate-level personnel are often asked to audit records and systems of specific properties.

- *External accounting positions.* There are at least two types of external accounting personnel used by restaurants. An accountant (frequently a Certified Public Accountant—CPA) performs services for a fee as an independent agent rather than as an employee. In this role, he/she may develop and monitor accounting systems and procedures used by the restaurant. External auditors can be used to render an opinion as to whether financial statements reflect fairly the financial position of the restaurant and whether the statements are prepared in accordance with generally accepted accounting principles (GAAPs) and on a consistent basis with the prior year.

ACCOUNTING AND CONTROL ARE INTERRELATED

The relationship between the management task of control and accounting activities is important. To control any resource (food and beverage products, labor, revenue, energy, etc.), the restaurant manager must use a five-step process:

1. Performance standards (expectations) must be established. (This is done as the operating budget is developed.)

2. Actual financial information must be collected to measure the results of operation.

3. Comparisons must be made between expected performance (Step 1) and actual performance (Step 2).

4. Corrective action must be taken when necessary to bring actual results (Step 2) in line with expected performance (Step 1). Generally, an investigation of alternative causes of problems (negative variances) and their assumed impact on standards is required.

5. Evaluation of the results of the corrective action procedures is necessary.

Collecting actual information (Step 2 above) is done through the formal process of accounting. This provides a clear example of the relationship between financial accounting (with its emphasis on external communication) and managerial accounting (which focuses upon internal management communication).

Generally, the restaurant's accounting system yields information useful for both external and internal purposes. As data is collected for one purpose (financial statements) it can also be used for another (for example, operating reports used by managers). Suppose the manager establishes a budgeted food cost percentage. (If all goes well, a specified percentage of revenue generated from food sales will be used to purchase the food required to generate more food revenue.) Actual operating results (the assessment of dollars actually spent to purchase food) will be measured through the use of an accrual accounting system. (This will require calculating cost of goods sold: Changes between beginning and ending inventory values along with the cost of purchases during the fiscal period and various adjustments that consider employee and promotional meals and transfers between the food and beverage departments will likely be made.) The difference between the budgeted food cost and actual food cost suggests the extent to which operating procedures may need to be revised. Note that actual food costs developed through the formal accounting system could be used both for information on the financial statement and for routine operating control.

RELATIONSHIP BETWEEN MANAGER AND ACCOUNTANT

The most effective relationship between the manager and the accountant has already been noted; the accountant serves in a staff (advisory) relationship to the manager and provides specialized help to the manager as needed. Sometimes, however, managers are much more passive, because they are unfamiliar with either accounting principles and/or the development/use of accounting systems. These passive managers believe their role in the financial management of the restaurant is to:

- "Do what the accountant says" and provide and accept information using systems and procedures suggested by the accountant.

- Believe that accounting information, regardless of how it is collected, analyzed, or reported, is correct. (In fact, the failure to consider the accuracy of accounting information can be a significant impediment to problem-solving.)

- Use accounting information regardless of how it is presented in formal financial statements. Many managers make decisions with information from various reports and statements that they neither helped to design nor understand. When this occurs, managers often make misinformed decisions.

- Defer to the accountant all or much of the responsibility for making decisions about financial matters. This practice violates the basic distinction between line and staff relationships.

- View the accountant as a "necessary evil" rather than as a partner and helpful provider of useful information.

Each of the above perceptions frequently arises when the role of the accountant in the restaurant operation is not properly understood. In practice, remember that the manager should be the expert who makes decisions. While managers need financial information provided by the accountant, they must determine the meaning of the data themselves. Therefore, a more proper relationship between the manager and the accountant should include the following essentials:

- The manager must know, at minimum, the information required for short- and long-term control of the restaurant's operation. Once the manager has identified what information he or she needs, the accountant can offer advice about the best ways to gather that information.

- Information needed for internal control purposes should be combined with that used to assemble required financial statements. In this way, there is a "dovetailing" effect; the need to keep two sets of books is minimized.

- After receiving input from the manager, the accountant should design an information collection system that assembles information required for both management and accounting purposes.

- After information is developed into financial statements, the accountant can assist the manager in analysis and make corrective action recommendations, if necessary.

- Wise restaurant managers carefully consider the advice of the accountant. They recognize, however, that it is their responsibility, not the accountant's, to make operating decisions.

- The manager should ask questions when fiscal information supplied by the accountant is analyzed. For example, he or she might ask: "How were values of revenues and expenses derived?" "What do the figures mean?" "What are the consistencies and inconsistencies in the way information was collected between fiscal periods?"

The overriding point here is that the manager should be in charge of the restaurant. This means assembling all available talent including that of the accountant to make the best management decisions. Ultimately, the manager—not the accountant—must make decisions. The relationship between the manager and accountant is, then, a team effort. The manager makes use of accounting-related resources to maximize attainment of the restaurant's goals.

MANAGER'S 10 POINT EFFECTIVENESS CHECKLIST

Evaluate your need for and the status of each of the following financial management tactics. For tactics you judge to be important but not yet in place, develop an action plan including completion date to implement the tactic.

TACTIC	DON'T AGREE (DON'T NEED)	AGREE (DONE)	AGREE (NOT DONE)	IF NOT DONE WHO IS RESPONSIBLE?	IF NOT DONE TARGET COMPLETION DATE
1. Manager has purchased an up-to-date hospitality financial management resource to use as a management aid.	❑	❑	❑		
2. Management thoroughly understands the difference between bookkeeping and accounting.	❑	❑	❑		
3. Manager knows all individuals and organizations that will use the financial information produced by the restaurant's management team.	❑	❑	❑		
4. Manager has an effective system in place for administering accounts receivable.	❑	❑	❑		
5. Manager has an effective system in place for administering accounts payable.	❑	❑	❑		
6. Manager recognizes the importance of protecting the integrity of source documents and has systems in place to do so.	❑	❑	❑		
7. Manager understands the difference between line and staff assistance in financial management of the restaurant.	❑	❑	❑		
8. Manager clearly understands the difference between financial management and accounting.	❑	❑	❑		
9. The restaurant's financial management system incorporates Generally Accepted Accounting Principles (GAAPs).	❑	❑	❑		
10. Manager has established a schedule of regular meetings with the restaurant accountant.	❑	❑	❑		

2

DEBITS AND CREDITS—THE MECHANICS OF ACCOUNTING

MANAGER'S BRIEF

In this chapter you will be introduced to the single accounting equation that describes what a restaurant owns compared to what it owes:

$$\text{Assets} = \text{Liabilities} + \text{Owners' Equity}$$

This basic equation drives all financial records relating to the restaurant.

You will also learn how the accountant or bookkeeper creates "T" accounts to permit the easy recording of changes in assets, liabilities, and owners' equity. Increases and decreases in these accounts are achieved by adding to or subtracting from each account. You will learn how and why this is done as you examine the concept of debiting and crediting T accounts to keep them in balance.

Additional procedures used by an accountant to maintain aspects of the accounting equation are presented so you can learn how sales levels, inventories, depreciation of assets, and other financial aspects of the restaurant are accounted for. In addition, the concept of posting (recording) financial information to the variety of summary account records (ledgers) used in a restaurant will be discussed.

Finally, you will review the accounting cycle: the entire process of recording all bookkeeping entries that affect the basic accounting equation and then preparing financial statements based on these entries.

Financial statements prepared by the accountant are the end product of a process, comparable to plated food prepared by the chef. If the food is not liked by a guest, future sales to this guest are doubtful. Likewise, if financial statements do not yield relevant and useful information, they will likely be ignored in the future.

Many important details must be addressed as accounting systems are designed and as financial statements are developed. This can be complicated, and in the case of tax regulations, ever-changing. The purpose of this book, and specifically this chapter, is *not* to make the busy restaurant manager a professional accountant. Rather, it is to review the basics of accounting that comprise only one aspect of the manager's responsibilities. These basics should be incorporated into the restaurant's procedures for collecting, assembling, reporting, and using financial information.

TYPES OF BUSINESS TRANSACTIONS

BUSINESS TRANSACTION The act of exchanging something (such as money in the form of cash, check, credit card, or promise of future payment) to purchase food products, employee labor, or resources needed by the restaurant during the conduct of business.

Every day, innumerable business transactions occur in restaurants. There is an exchange of cash to purchase food from suppliers, and guests use credit cards or cash to pay for their meals. These are simple **business transactions.** A business transaction generally involves some type of an exchange. In the examples just presented, one exchange involved cash and another involved a credit card. All transactions must be recorded in accounting records, and each transaction must be carefully analyzed to determine its effect on the business. After analysis, the transaction must be properly recorded in the accounting records of the restaurant.

Certain events occur that change the value of the business but don't involve transactions. For example, as an equipment item wears out, periodic accounting adjustments called **depreciation** are made. Likewise, **accounts receivable** that cannot be collected require an accounting adjustment for bad debt expense. The job of the accountant is to record transactions and other events that result in the changes in the "value" of the business.

DEPRECIATION The allocation of the cost of equipment and other depreciable assets according to their useful life.

ACCOUNTS RECEIVABLE Money owed to the restaurant by guests that has not been collected.

BASIC ACCOUNTING EQUATION

The "things" owned by a restaurant are called assets and commonly include cash, accounts receivable, equipment, land, buildings, food/beverage inventories, and investments. Some assets are given to the restaurant by its owners; other assets might be obtained by borrowing money from a bank or other lenders. There are, then, two groups who have claims to the restaurant's assets—owners and lenders. Broadly speaking, claims to assets are called **equities.** Therefore, the assets of the restaurant equal its equities.

Equities are commonly divided into two groups:

EQUITIES The claim against the restaurant's assets by those who provided the assets.

OWNERS' EQUITY Assets minus liabilities; the financial interest of the restaurant owner(s).

STOCKHOLDERS' EQUITY A claim to the assets of a restaurant corporation by the "owners" (stockholders) of the corporation.

- Ownership claims to assets are called **owners' equity** if the restaurant is unincorporated. If the restaurant is a corporation, the term **"stockholders' equity"** is used. (One owner of an unincorporated business may be referred to as "proprietor"; two or more owners may be called "partners.")
- Claims of outside parties such as financial institutions and suppliers are referred to as **liabilities.** The sum of owners' equity and liabilities (external parties' equity) must equal assets.

LIABILITIES Obligations (money owed) to outside entities. Examples include amounts owed to suppliers, to lenders for long-term debt such as mortgages, and to employees (payroll that has been earned by but not paid to the restaurant's staff).

LUIS'S RESTAURANT

To illustrate basic accounting techniques, let's look at Luis's, a small (100 seat) restaurant that its owner, Luis Alvarez, is just opening. His cash investment is $5,000. This is shown in the accounting equation:

Assets	=	Owners' Equity
Cash $5,000		Luis Alvarez, Capital $5,000

Note: In an unincorporated business like Luis's, the ownership claim to assets is recognized by the owner's name followed by the word "Capital." If the business had been incorporated, the term "common stock" would have been used instead of "Luis Alvarez, Capital."

Assume that Luis pays the first 3-months' rent of $2,250 for building space. Prepaid rent (an asset) must be accounted for as well as the $2,250 reduction in cash. The effect of this transaction on the basic accounting equation is:

Assets	=	Owners' Equity
Cash $2,750 + Prepaid rent $2,250		Luis Alvarez, Capital $5,000

Assume Luis acquires used equipment for $10,000. Since he only has cash of $2,750 available, he pays $1,000 cash and finances the rest of the equipment purchase with a one-year note of $9,000 (notes payable). The basic accounting equation now is:

Assets		=	Liabilities	+	Owner's Equity	
Cash	$ 1,750		Notes payable $9,000		Luis Alvarez, Capital	$5,000
Prepaid rent	2,250					
Equipment	10,000					
Total	$14,000	=	$9,000	+		$5,000

Note that claims against assets (liabilities and owners' equity) always equal assets. A balance sheet prepared after these three transactions is as follows:

Balance Sheet

Luis's Restaurant

ASSETS		LIABILITIES	
Cash	$ 1,750	Notes payable	$ 9,000
Prepaid rent	2,250		
Equipment	10,000	OWNERS' EQUITY	
Total Assets	$14,000	Luis Alvarez, Capital	5,000
		Total Liabilities and Owners' Equity	$14,000

Now all elements in the basic accounting equation have been presented: assets, liabilities, and owners' equity. The basic accounting equation is:

$$\text{Assets} = \text{Liabilities} + \text{Owners' Equity}$$

If the debts of a restaurant (liabilities) are subtracted from its assets, the result equals owners' equity. Liabilities represent the first claim to assets. When they are subtracted from assets, owners' equity (the residual claim to assets) remains. We can rearrange the basic accounting equation to show this:

$$\text{Assets} - \text{Liabilities} = \text{Owners' Equity}$$

A basic financial statement of the restaurant (the balance sheet) reflects the fundamental accounting equation; assets must equal (balance against) the liabilities and owners' equity. (Balance sheets will be discussed in detail in chapter 3.)

REVENUE AND EXPENSES IMPACT OWNERS' EQUITY

The restaurant's goal is to generate profit. Profit (net income) results when revenues exceed expenses. Revenues increase owners' equity; expenses reduce owners' equity. Assume that a dinner is sold for $15.00 in cash and that related expenses (food costs, labor costs, supplies, etc., are purchased with $10.00 in cash). The net result is an increase in cash of $5.00 ($15 − $10 = $5) and an increase in owners' equity by $5.00. The sales transaction by itself would be an increase in both cash and owners' equity of $15.00. The purchase (expense) transactions would reduce both cash and owners' equity by $10.00 each.

These transactions would be reflected as follows in the basic accounting equation:

Assets		= Liabilities	+ Owners' Equity
Cash		Notes payable $9,000	Luis Alvarez, Capital,
$1,750 + $15 − $10 = $ 1,755			$5,000 + $15 − $10 = $5,005
Prepaid rent	$ 2,250		
Equipment	$10,000		
Total	$14,005	= $9,000	+ $5,005

Note that owners' equity has increased by the amount of profit of $5. (Revenue of $15 less expenses of $10 equals profit of $5.) The increase in assets of $5 is in the cash account since both transactions involved cash. Also note that the balance between assets and claims to assets remains intact.

TYPES OF ACCOUNTS

ACCOUNT   A device that shows increases and decreases in a single asset, liability, or owners' equity item.

All transactions affect the basic accounting equation and are recorded in accounts. An **account** is a device for recording increases and decreases in a single asset, liability, or owners' equity item. The T account, named for its shape, is a simple way of illustrating an account as follows:

Name of Account

(Left side)	(Right side)

Asset accounts are increased by entries on the left side of the account and decreased by entries on the right side. The reverse is true for equity accounts; liability and owners' equity accounts are increased by entries on the right side of the account and decreased by entries on the left side. This may be shown as follows:

ASSET ACCOUNT		LIABILITY ACCOUNT		OWNERS' EQUITY ACCOUNT	
Increases	Decreases	Decreases	Increases	Decreases	Increases

Asset Accounts

- **Cash on hand.** This account includes house funds (such as petty cash) and cash register banks.

- **Cash on deposit.** This account is the restaurant's bank account. If more than one bank account is used (example: one for general disbursements and another for payroll) separate accounts should be established for each on the books of the restaurant.

LUIS'S RESTAURANT

We'll use Luis's first three transactions, (1) his initial investment, (2) the payment of three months' prepaid rent of $2,250, and (3) the purchase of $10,000 of equipment, to illustrate how the T accounts reflect transactions:

Cash		Prepaid Rent		Equipment	
(1) 5,000	(2) 2,250	(2) 2,250		(3) 10,000	
	(3) 1,000				
Bal. 1,750		Bal. 2,250		Bal. 10,000	

Notes Payable		Luis Alvarez, Capital	
	(3) 9,000		(1) 5,000
	Bal. 9,000		Bal. 5,000

Each account is balanced, and the sum of the asset balances (cash = $1,750; prepaid rent = $2,250; and equipment = $10,000) of $14,000 equals the sum of the equities (notes payable = $9,000; Luis Alvarez, Capital = $5,000) of $14,000.

- **Accounts receivable.** This account is mainly used to record amounts due from guests. Amounts due from officers and employees, rentals, and commissions are also receivables but should be maintained in separate receivable accounts.

- **Allowance for doubtful accounts.** This account provides a reserve for probable losses when receivables are not collected.

- **Notes receivable.** Promissory notes from officers and employees are included in this account.

- **Inventories.** A separate account should be maintained for each type of inventory. Food inventory consists of the cost of food on hand in the storeroom, pantries, kitchens, freezers, etc. Beverage inventory consists of stock at the bars, in the storeroom, etc. Separate inventory accounts should be maintained for other merchandise for sale and for cleaning, office, and other supplies.

- **Marketable securities.** This is an account for recording investments made on a temporary basis using surplus cash. Investments of a permanent nature should be recorded in an account called "investments."

- *Prepaid expenses.* A separate account should be established for each prepaid expense item such as rent, licenses, and unexpired insurance.

- *Investments.* This account is used to record assets that are not readily liquidated. Examples include long-term stocks and bonds, which are usually reported at cost.

- *Land.* This account is used to record land purchased that is used in the business.

- *Building.* This account is used to record the purchase of buildings used by the restaurant.

- *Equipment.* This account is used to record the purchase of equipment.

- *Furniture.* This account is used to record the purchase of furniture.

- *China, glassware, silver, and linen.* This account is used to record the purchase of china, glassware, silver, and linen. (Alternatively, many restaurants expense these items when purchased.)

- *Accumulated depreciation.* This account is used for recording depreciation over the useful life of an asset such as equipment.

- *Deposits.* Deposits with utility companies for water, gas, etc., should be recorded in this account.

Liability Accounts

- *Accounts payable—trade.* This account is used to record amounts due to suppliers of goods and services in the restaurant's ordinary course of business.

- *Accounts payable—others.* Amounts due concessionaires representing collections from guests or extraordinarily large open accounts (such as might result from equipment purchases) are shown in this account.

- *Notes payable.* This account is used for short-term notes owed by the restaurant.

- *Taxes payable.* This group of accounts (one for each type of tax) is established to record taxes due to government authorities. Examples include federal, state, and city withholding payables, FICA (social security) payable, sales taxes payable, and federal and state income taxes payable.

- *Deposits on banquets.* This account is used for recording deposits made by guests for future banquets/parties.

- *Accrued expenses.* This group of accounts is maintained for recording the amounts payable for expenses incurred at or near the end of an accounting period, including accrued payroll, utilities, interest, and rent.

- *Dividends payable.* This account is for recording dividends payable based on formal declaration of dividend action by the board of directors. Note: This account is not applicable to unincorporated businesses.

- *Long-term debt.* This group of accounts is to record debt that is not due for 12 months from the balance sheet date, including mortgage payable, notes payable, and bonds payable. A separate account is established for each debt.

Equity Accounts

For Sole Owner (Proprietorships) or Multiple Owners (Partnerships)

- *(Name of Proprietor or Partner), Capital.* This account shows the owners' net worth in the restaurant. The initial investment less withdrawals and operating losses plus operating profits results in the balance. If the business is organized as a partnership, a separate account is maintained for each partner.

For Corporations

- *Capital stock.* This group of accounts is used for recording each type of stock issued.

- *Paid-in capital in excess of par.* This account is used for recording proceeds from sale of capital stock in excess of the par value. A separate account should be established for each type of stock.

- *Retained earnings.* The amount of earnings retained in the restaurant is recorded in this account.

Revenue:

Food sales	Other sales	Dividend income
Beverage sales	Interest income	

Expenses:

Cost of food sales	Uniforms	Cleaning supplies
Cost of beverage sales	Laundry	Guest supplies
Payroll	Linen rental	Bar supplies
Employee benefits	China and glassware	Menus
Payroll taxes	Silverware	Provision for doubtful
Dry cleaning	Electricity	accounts
Contract cleaning	Fuel	Painting/decorations
Flowers and decorations	Water	Repairs expense
Automobile expense	Waste removal	Rent
Freight	Office supplies	Real estate
Parking	Postage	Capital stock tax
Licenses and permits	Telephone	Interest expense
Professional entertainers	Data processing costs	Depreciation
Piano rental	Insurance	Amortization
Newspaper advertising	Professional fees	Income taxes
Direct mail	Franchise fees	
Outdoor signs	Collection fees	
Donations	Kitchen fuel	

Revenue and Expense Accounts

Revenue and expense accounts are really temporary owners' equity accounts, because they are closed out each period to the permanent owners' equity accounts. These accounts are extremely important for collecting financial information for management decisions. The accounts are generally self-explanatory, and some of the many accounts that can be used by restaurants are listed above.

DEBITS AND CREDITS

It is awkward to say "record on the left side of a T account" or "record on the right side of a T account." Therefore, the accounting concepts of **debits** (abbreviated "Dr.") and **credits** (abbreviated "Cr.") have been established. For example, when cash is increased by $10, rather than say "record $10 on the left side of the cash account," one can just "debit cash for $10."

> **DEBIT** An entry made on the left side of a T account.

> **CREDIT** An entry made on the right side of a T account.

Definitions

Debit simply is an entry on the left side of an account, while credit is simply an entry on the right side of an account. Debits are increases to some accounts but decreases to others; credits increase certain accounts but decrease others.

The effect that debits and credits have on the major categories of accounts follow:

ASSETS		LIABILITIES		OWNERS' EQUITY		REVENUES		EXPENSES	
+	−	−	+	−	+	−	+	+	−
Dr.	Cr.	Dr.	Cr.	Dr.	Cr.	Dr.	Cr.	Dr.	Cr.

Note that debits increase asset and expense accounts but decrease liability, owners' equity, and revenue accounts. On the other hand, credits increase liability, owners' equity, and revenue accounts but decrease asset and expense accounts.

All transactions are recorded with at least one debit and one credit entry, and in all cases, the total of debits must equal the total of credits for an entry. When Luis purchased his equipment, he paid $1,000 in cash and signed for a notes payable for $9,000. The debit of $10,000 to the equipment account is equal to the sum of the credits of $1,000 to the cash account and $9,000 to the notes payable account.

Types of Accounting Transactions

There are nine possible types of accounting transactions that affect the three major types of accounts: assets, liability, and owners' equity. Illustrations of these nine types of transactions follow.

1. *Increase one asset and decrease another asset.*
   Example: Equipment is purchased for $500. (Dr. Equipment and Cr. Cash)

2. *Increase an asset and increase a liability.*
   Example: $1,000 in cash is borrowed from the bank. (Dr. Cash and Cr. Notes payable)

3. *Increase an asset and increase an owners' equity account.*
   Example: The owner invests $1,000 in the business. (Dr. Cash and Cr. Owner, Capital)

4. *Increase one liability and decrease another liability.*
   Example: A note is made in exchange for an account payable. (Dr. Accounts payable and Cr. Notes payable)

5. *Decrease a liability and decrease an asset.*
   Example: A supplier is paid on account. (Dr. Accounts payable and Cr. Cash)

6. *Increase a liability and decrease an owners' equity account.*
   Example: Dividends are declared. (Dr. Retained earnings and Cr. Dividends payable)

7. *Decrease an asset and decrease an owners' equity account.*
   Example: Cash is withdrawn by the proprietor. (Dr. Owner, Capital and Cr. Cash)

8. *Decrease a liability and increase an owners' equity account.*
   Example: Long-term debt owed to the sole proprietor is converted to owners' equity. (Dr. Long-term debt and Cr. J. Doe, Capital)

9. *Increase an owners' equity account and decrease another owners' equity account.*
   Example: Preferred stock is converted to common stock. (Dr. Preferred stock and Cr. Common stock)

It is *not* possible to make entries that only

- Increase an asset and decrease a liability.
- Decrease an asset and increase a liability.
- Increase a liability and increase an owners' equity account.
- Decrease a liability and decrease an owners' equity account.
- Decrease an asset and increase an owners' equity account.
- Increase an asset and decrease an owners' equity account.

Determining Entries for a Transaction

There is a simple three-step procedure to determine entries in recording a business transaction:

1. Determine which *accounts* are affected.
2. Determine whether to *debit* or *credit* the accounts.
3. Determine the *amounts* to be recorded.

Assume Luis purchases a cash register for $3,000.

Step 1: (Affected accounts?) Equipment is obtained, and cash is disbursed.

Step 2: (Debit or credit?) Since the equipment account (an asset) increased, the account must be debited; cash is decreased so it must be credited.

Step 3: (Amount?) The accounts should be debited and credited for $3,000 each.

Account Balances

To determine an account balance, the debits and credits in the account must be totaled, and the lesser of the two is subtracted from the larger. An account has a debit balance if the sum of the debits for the account exceeds the sum of the credits for the same account. Conversely, an account has a credit balance if the sum of the credits for the account exceeds the sum of the debits for the same account.

In the following illustration for Luis's, the cash account has a debit balance of $1,755. The two debit entries total $5,015, and the three credit entries total $3,260. Since the debits exceed the credits, the balance of $1,755 is called a debit balance. The debit balance for the cash account is normal; that is, asset accounts generally have debit balances. The normal balance for the five major types of accounts is as follows:

Type of Account	*Normal Balance*
Asset	Debit
Liability	Credit
Proprietorship	Credit
Revenue	Credit
Expense	Debit

Trial Balance

A **trial balance** is a listing of all accounts with their debit and credit balances. A trial balance is prepared at the end of an accounting period and is the first step

LUIS'S RESTAURANT

Five transactions have been provided so far in our Luis's illustration. These five transactions will be used to illustrate debits and credits.

Transaction	Dr./Cr. Entry	Explanation
1. Investment of $5,000 by Luis in the restaurant	Dr. Cash 5,000 Cr. Luis Alvarez, Capital 5,000	Cash, an asset, is increased by $5,000, while Luis Alvarez, Capital, an owners' equity account, is increased by $5,000.
2. Payment of $2,250 for 3-months' prepaid rent	Dr. Prepaid Rent 2,250 Cr. Cash 2,250	Prepaid Rent, an asset, is increased by $2,250, while another asset account, cash, is decreased by $2,250.
3. Purchase of equipment costing $10,000 for cash of $1,000 and a note of $9,000	Dr. Equipment 10,000 Cr. Cash 1,000 Cr. Notes Payable 9,000	Equipment, an asset account, is increased by $10,000, while credits are to cash, an asset, and notes payable, a liability account, for a total of $10,000.
4. Dinner sold for $15	Dr. Cash 15 Cr. Luis Alvarez, Capital 15	Cash, an asset, is increased by $15, while Luis Alvarez, Capital, an owners' equity account, is credited for $15.
5. Food for the dinner sold cost $10.00.	Dr. Luis Alvarez, Capital 10 Cr. Cash 10	Luis Alvarez, Capital, an owners' equity account, is decreased by $10, while cash, an asset, is decreased by $10.

The preceding transactions are recorded in T accounts as follows:

Cash		Prepaid Rent		Equipment	
(1) 5,000	(2) 2,250	(2) 2,250		(3) 10,000	
(4) 15	(3) 1,000				
	(5) 10				
5,015	3,260	2,250		10,000	
−3,260					
1,755					

Notes Payable		Luis Alvarez, Capital		
	(3) 9,000	(5) 10	(1) 5,000	
			(4) 15	
	9,000	10	5,015	
			− 10	
			5,005	

LUIS'S RESTAURANT

The trial balance of Luis's accounts after five transactions is as follows:

Trial Balance
Luis's

Account	Debit Balance	Credit Balance
Cash	$ 1,755	
Prepaid Rent	2,250	
Equipment	10,000	
Notes Payable		$ 9,000
Luis Alvarez, Capital		5,005
Total	$14,005	$14,005

A trial balance, which is prepared after any transaction is recorded, should be in balance if all transactions are recorded with debits equaling credits.

in developing financial statements. The trial balance of accounts is "in balance" when the total of the debit balance accounts equals the total of the credit balance accounts. A trial balance provides proof that the debits equal the credits. (Still, problems may exist. For example, an amount may have been recorded in the wrong account, but the trial balance would still be in balance.)

TRIAL BALANCE A listing of all accounts with their debit and credit balances that is prepared at the end of an accounting period as a first step in the development of financial statements.

A trial balance is prepared in four steps:

Step 1: Determine the balance of each account.

Step 2: List all accounts, placing debit and credit balances in separate columns.

Step 3: Sum the debit and credit columns separately.

Step 4: Compare the total of the debit and credit columns.

MEASURING INCOME

To this point, revenue and expense concepts have only been mentioned briefly. However, the major purpose of a restaurant is to generate a profit (revenues should exceed expenses for an accounting period). When a profit is generated, owners' equity is increased, because revenue and expense accounts are "closed" into the owners' equity account (if the business is unincorporated) or into a retained earnings account (if business is incorporated). Therefore, revenue and expense accounts are really temporary owners' equity accounts.

Impact of Revenue and Expenses

The sale of goods and/or services to guests generally increases an asset (cash or accounts receivable) and also increases a sales account. Expenses are incurred by the restaurant to provide the goods and/or services. The cost of the expenses generally results in a decrease in assets and an increase in expenses. For example, if steaks are withdrawn from the refrigerator for preparation and sales, an asset account (inventory) is decreased and an expense account (food cost) is increased. Note: Sales and expense transactions do not need to involve cash directly. For example, food may be sold to a guest on account, and the food sold may be taken from inventory. A sale on account results in a debit to accounts receivable and a credit to food sales (both are increased). The food sold results in a debit to one account (cost of food sold) and a credit to an asset account (food inventory). When the guest pays the bill, the cash received will reduce the accounts receivable. The entry will be a debit to cash (to increase it) and a credit to accounts receivable (to decrease it). The food inventory was purchased either on account or for cash. If purchased for cash, then the entry debiting the food inventory (to increase its value) and crediting cash (to decrease its balance) was already recorded when the food was purchased. If the food inventory was purchased on account, then the entry at the time of purchase was a debit to the food inventory account (to increase it) and a credit to accounts payable (to increase it). In this case, when the accounts payable is paid, cash will be reduced. The entry would be to debit accounts payable (to decrease it) and credit cash (to decrease it).

Accruals and Adjustments to Income

In many restaurants, hundreds or even thousands of sales and expense transactions occur daily. However, even so, by the end of the accounting period, not all expenses will have been properly recorded. (In other words, sales that have been recorded less expenses that have been recorded will still not be an accurate measurement of income.) Accounting accruals and adjustments must be recorded to properly measure income according to Generally Accepted Accounting Principles (GAAPs). The major principle on which these adjustments are based is *matching*. (Expenses matched to revenues as discussed in chapter 1.) This GAAP states that expenses for the period must be *matched* to the revenue generated by incurring the expenses.

These accruals and adjustments can recognize, for example:

- Incurred rent expense when the rental payment was initially recorded as prepaid rent;
- cost of goods sold when food product purchases have been recorded in an inventory account and not expensed when sold;
- asset depreciation;
- accrued expenses such as payroll, interest, and utilities; and
- actual insurance expense when the initial payment for insurance was recorded as prepaid.

After the recognition of expenses based on accruals and adjustments, income for the period is determined.

At the end of an accounting period, several adjusting entries are necessary to match expenses with revenues for the period. The exact adjusting entries depend on the restaurant's accounting practices. Our discussion of adjustments will cover four representative types:

- inventory/cost of goods sold
- prepaids
- depreciation
- accruals

Inventory/Cost of Goods Sold. Food and beverages are purchased in large quantities so the restaurant can meet heavy demand, reduce the number of times that orders are placed, and sometimes, take advantage of discounts. The result is that a sizable inventory of food and beverage items will be on hand at the end of the period. These items must be physically counted and priced so inventory value can be costed. The result is an end-of-the-period inventory used

LUIS'S RESTAURANT

Luis's can illustrate how several sales and expense transactions affect revenue and expense accounts. Previously, two entries were provided that affected revenue and expense accounts:

4. Sale of food for $15.00.
5. Purchase of food for $10.00. (Note: The food was used when purchased.)

Additional entries are as follows:

6. Purchases of food on account—$15,000. (Recorded as food inventory.)
7. Payment of wages for the period—$10,000. (Payments are to several employees; to simplify, they are recorded as one entry.)
8. Purchase of supplies—$100. (Recorded as an expense and not inventoried.)
9. Payment of utility bill—$1,000.
10. Payment for newspaper advertising—$200.
11. Total of remaining sales for the period—$39,950. All sales were cash and, to simplify, are recorded as one entry.
12. Suppliers were paid $14,500 on account.

The T accounts are affected as follows:

Cash				Food Inventory		Prepaid Rent	
(1)	5,000	(2)	2,250	(6) 15,000		(2) 2,250	
(4)	15	(3)	1,000	15,000		2,250	
(11)	39,950	(5)	10				
		(7)	10,000				
		(8)	100				
		(9)	1,000				
		(10)	200				
		(14)	14,500				
	44,965		29,060				
	−29,060						
	15,905						

Equipment		Accounts Payable	
(3) 10,000		(12) 14,500	(6) 15,000
10,000			500

Notes Payable		Luis Alvarez, Capital		Food Sales	
	(3) 9,000		(1) 5,000		(4) 15
	9,000		5,000		(11) 39,950
					39,965

Cost of Food Sales		Wages Expense		Supplies Expense	
(5) 10		(7) 10,000		(8) 100	
10		10,000		100	

(Continued)

Utilities		Advertising	
(9) 1,000		(10) 200	
1,000		200	

A simplified income statement prior to adjustments follows:

Preliminary Income Statement
Luis's Restaurant
For One Accounting Period

Food Sales		$39,965
Less Expenses		
Cost of food sales	$ 10	
Wages expense	10,000	
Supplies expense	100	
Utilities	1,000	
Advertising	200	
Total Expenses		11,310
Net Income		$28,655

This income statement showing $28,655 of net income is incomplete for the following reasons:

- Cost of goods sold (food cost) have not been determined.
- Depreciation has not been calculated.
- Rent expense has not been determined.
- Interest expense has not been accrued.
- Unpaid bills on hand at the end of the period have not been recorded.

to determine the restaurant's cost of food sold for the period. In simplest terms, cost of goods sold is determined as follows:

Beginning inventory
+ Purchases
− Ending inventory
= Cost of goods sold

For example, assume a restaurant starts the month with $2,000 of food inventory, purchases $12,000 worth of food items, and ends the month with

$2,500 of food inventory. The cost of food sold would be $11,500, determined as follows:

Beginning food inventory	$ 2,000
+ Purchases	12,000
Total food available	$14,000
− Ending food inventory	2,500
= Cost of food sold	$11,500

Many restaurant managers record food purchased during the month as "purchases" or as "cost of food sold" in a method called **periodic inventory.** In

PERIODIC INVENTORY   A method of calculating food costs that reflects the differences in beginning and ending food inventory values (costs).

either case, an adjusting entry is required to accurately recognize the cost of food sold during the month. The adjustment reflects the difference between the value of ending inventory and the value of beginning inventory. If ending inventory exceeds beginning inventory, then the adjustment will reduce the cost of food sold and increase the food inventory. Using the above example (beginning inventory = $2,000; ending inventory = $2,500), the ending inventory is $500 larger than the beginning inventory, so the adjustment follows:

Food inventory	$500	
Cost of food sold		$500

If, on the other hand, the ending inventory were less than the beginning inventory, the reverse would be true; an adjustment would be made to increase cost of food sold and decrease the inventory account.

Prepaids.   Restaurants may purchase insurance coverage for an extended period or pay rent in advance and then debit a prepaid expense (asset account). Then, over the period of time benefited, the restaurant recognizes the expense by making periodic adjustments. For example, assume a restaurant manager bought a two-year fire insurance premium for $4,800 and recorded the entire amount as prepaid expense. At the end of each month thereafter during the two-year period an adjustment of $200 ($4,800 ÷ 24 months) is required as follows:

Insurance expense	$200	
Prepaid insurance		$200

This adjustment increases the insurance expense by $200 per month and reduces the prepaid insurance account by $200 per month. At the end of any month, the remaining prepaid insurance is easily calculated: the number of remaining months of insurance coverage (times) the monthly adjustment of $200.

Other expenditures that restaurant managers may record as prepaid and expense over time or with use include rent and office and cleaning supplies.

Depreciation. Fixed assets such as equipment are purchased by restaurant managers to produce the goods and services needed for guests. These assets will benefit the restaurant for several years, yet as the fixed assets are used, they are slowly consumed in a process called depreciation.

> **FIXED ASSETS Resources of the restaurant that are tangible, material in amount, used in operations to generate revenue, and will benefit the restaurant for more than one year into the future.**

There are several different methods of depreciation available that, when followed consistently, can provide a reasonable estimate of cost of a fixed asset used during a specific amount of time.

The best known depreciation method is called the straight-line method (SL). With this method, the same amount is depreciated each period. The formula for the SL method is:

$$\text{Annual depreciation} = \frac{\text{Cost} - \text{Salvage value}}{\text{Life (useful years)}}$$

The cost of the fixed asset refers to the original cost to the restaurant. Salvage value is the estimated value of what the fixed asset can be sold for at the end of its useful life. The useful life refers to the number of years the fixed asset should benefit the restaurant. The first element of the formula (the cost) is known; the second and third factors are based on estimates. However, an experienced manager working with experienced accountants can reasonably estimate the salvage value and expected useful life of the restaurant's fixed assets.

Assume that a dishwashing machine cost $5,500 and is estimated to have a five-year life and salvage value of $500. The annual depreciation would be $1,000, determined as follows:

$$\text{Annual depreciation} = \frac{\$5,500 - \$500}{5} = \$1,000$$

To record the depreciation adjustment, depreciation expense is debited, and accumulated depreciation is credited. An accumulated depreciation account

CONTRA-ASSET ACCOUNT
Asset accounts that normally
have credit balances and are
used to offset specific asset
accounts.

may be established for each group of fixed assets, such as equipment or buildings. The accumulated depreciation account is a **contra-asset account;** its normal balance is a credit.

Other common depreciation methods are sum-of-the-years digits and declining balance. Both of these methods result in greater amounts of depreciation in the early years of the life of the fixed asset. For this reason they are commonly referred to as **accelerated depreciation methods.**

ACCELERATED DEPRECIATION
METHOD A method of de-
preciation that results in
greater amounts of deprecia-
tion during the early years
of the life of a fixed asset
than would result using the
straight-line method.

Accruals.   Accrual transactions affect expense and liability accounts. Let's look at two examples.

Payroll accruals. Most restaurant managers pay employees on a weekly or biweekly (every two weeks) basis. As a result, at the end of an accounting period (such as a month), the employees may have worked a few days for which they have not been paid. The GAAP of matching requires that unpaid wages be calculated and recorded during the period in which the incurred expense resulted in revenue. The adjustment is a debit to wages expense and a credit to the liability account, "accrued payroll." Related payroll expenses such as FICA and unemployment taxes should also be accrued.

Here's an example: A manager paid employees on July 29 for work through July 27. The current pay period ends on August 10; therefore, the accrued payroll for four days (July 28–31) must be calculated and recorded for the present accounting period. Using payroll records for hourly workers and the appropriate wage rates, the accrued payroll is calculated at $1,520. This accrual is recorded as follows:

Wages expense	$1,520	
Accrued payroll		$1,520

Compensation paid to salaried employees would be recorded as "salaries" expense. For example, if $1,000 of salaries earned during July had not been paid at the end of the month, the transaction would be:

Salary expense	$1,000	
Accrued payroll		$1,000

Interest accruals. For a second example, consider the accrual of interest. Generally, notes signed by restaurant managers require periodic interest payments in addition to paying part or all of the principal (amount) of the note. However, at the end of an accounting period, the interest may not have been paid through the last day of the period. Therefore, the GAAP of matching requires that the interest be accrued. The formula for calculating interest is as follows:

$$\text{Interest} = \text{Principal} \times \text{Rate} \times \text{Time}$$

"Principal" is the amount of the unpaid loan. "Rate" refers to the interest rate expressed on an annual basis; "time" generally is shown as the number of days over which interest is to be calculated divided by the number of days in one year.

The adjustment to record accrued interest is a debit to interest expense and a credit to accrued interest (a liability account). Assume a restaurant owner borrowed $50,000 at 12% interest. The note indicates that interest is to be paid on March 15 and September 15 of each year. The interest that should be accrued for a 31-day month is $509.59:

$$\text{Interest expense} = \frac{\$50,000 \times 0.12 \times 31}{365} = \$509.59$$

If the restaurant had already paid $5,000 of principal, then the interest for a 31-day month would be $458.63:

$$\text{Interest expense} = \frac{(\$50,000 - \$5,000) \times 0.12 \times 31}{365} = \$458.63$$

The adjustment to record the interest expense is as follows:

Interest expense $458.63
Accrued interest $458.63

PREPARATION OF FINANCIAL STATEMENTS

After the adjusting entries are recorded, financial statements are prepared. The two major financial statements are the balance sheet (which shows the restaurant's assets and claims to its assets) and the income statement (which shows the

LUIS'S RESTAURANT

Luis's accountant must prepare adjustments to:

- assess the food inventory/cost of food sold;
- recognize depreciation expense;
- identify rent expense;
- determine interest expense; and
- record unpaid bills on hand.

Before making the food inventory adjustment, Luis's records show a food inventory of $15,000, which resulted from recording food purchases in the inventory account rather than recognizing the cost of food sales when the food was sold. A physical inventory on hand for Luis's at the end of the accounting period (one month) identified food worth $1,200.

To recognize the food inventory at the end of the period and to recognize the cost of food sold, the following adjustment (A1) is recorded.

Cost of food sold	$13,800	
Food inventory		$13,800

The credit of $13,800 to food inventory results in a reduction of the food inventory account to $1,200 (the amount of food inventory at the end of the accounting period).

Second, the equipment costing $10,000 must be depreciated. Assume the equipment has an estimated useful life of 5 years and a salvage value of $400. The monthly depreciation (depr.) based on the straight-line method would be $160:

$$\text{Annual depr.} = \frac{\text{Cost} - \text{Salvage Value}}{\text{Years}} = \frac{\$10,000 - \$400}{5} = \$1,920/\text{year}$$

$$\text{Monthly depr.} = \frac{\text{Annual depr.}}{12} = \frac{\$1,920}{12} = \$160/\text{month}$$

The depreciation adjustment (A2) is recorded as follows:

Depreciation expense	$160	
Accumulated depreciation		$160

Next, Luis's accountant must recognize rent expense for the month. Recall that Luis's second transaction was the payment of 3-months' rent of $2,250. Therefore, one-third of the $2,250 ($750) is the monthly rental expense. The adjustment (A3) is recognized as follows:

Rent expense	$750	
Prepaid rent		$750

(Continued)

Fourth, Luis must recognize interest expense on the $9,000 note made when the equipment was purchased. Assume the equipment was purchased on the first day of the month and that 29 additional days have passed by the end of the month. The interest rate is 15%. The interest calculation is as follows:

$$\text{Interest expense} = \frac{\$9,000 \times 0.15 \times 30}{365} = \$110.96$$

For illustrative purposes, interest expense is rounded up to $111 to simplify the example. The adjustment (A4) to recognize interest expense is:

Interest expense	$111	
Accrued interest		$111

Finally, Luis has not recognized any unpaid bills except those relating to food purchases. A review of unpaid invoices relating to goods and services received and used by the restaurant to generate sales during the month follows:

Laundry	$ 500
Kitchen fuel	$ 100
Supplies	$ 200
Radio advertising	$1,000
Administrative expenses	$2,000
Repairs and maintenance	$ 500
Total	$4,300

The matching principle dictates that these expenses be recorded with an adjustment (A5) as follows:

Laundry expense	$ 500	
Kitchen fuel	$ 100	
Supplies expense	$ 200	
Radio advertising	$1,000	
Administrative expenses	$2,000	
Repairs and maintenance	$ 500	
Accrued expenses payable		$4,300

(Continued)

These adjustments affect Luis's T accounts as follows:

Cash	
Bal. 15,905	
15,905	

Food Inventory	
Bal. 15,000	(A1) 13,800
15,000	13,800
−13,800	
1,200	

Prepaid Rent	
Bal. 2,250	(A3) 750
2,250	750
− 750	
1,500	

Equipment	
Bal. 10,000	
10,000	

Accumulated Depr.	
	(A2) 160
	160

Accounts Payable	
	Bal. 500
	500

Accrued Expenses Payable	
	(A5) 4,300
	4,300

Notes Payable	
	Bal. 9,000
	9,000

Accrued Interest	
	(A4) 111
	111

Luis Alvarez, Capital	
	Bal. 5,000
	5,000

Food Sales	
	Bal. 39,965
	39,965

Cost of Food Sales	
Bal. 10	
(A1) 13,800	
13,810	

Wages Expense	
Bal. 10,000	
10,000	

Supplies Expense	
Bal. 100	
(A5) 200	
300	

Utilities	
Bal. 1,000	
1,000	

Advertising	
Bal. 200	
200	

Depreciation Expense	
(A2) 160	
160	

Rent Expense	
(A3) 750	
750	

Radio Advertising	
(A5) 1,000	
1,000	

Administrative Expenses	
(A5) 2,000	
2,000	

Repairs and Maintenance	
(A5) 500	
500	

Interest Expense	
(A4) 111	
111	

Laundry Expense	
(A5) 500	
500	

Kitchen Fuel	
(A5) 100	
100	

(Continued)

Notice that the balance of each account was brought forward prior to recording the adjustments, reflected by (A1)–(A5) for the inventory adjustment through the unpaid bills adjustment, respectively.

An adjusted trial balance is prepared to prove that debits and credits are equal:

Adjusted Trial Balance
Luis's

	Debit Balance	Credit Balance
Cash	$15,905	
Food	1,200	
Prepaid Rent	1,500	
Equipment	10,000	
Accumulated Depreciation		$ 160
Accounts Payable		500
Accrued Expenses Payable		4,300
Notes Payable		9,000
Accrued Interest		111
Luis Alvarez, Capital		5,000
Food Sales		39,965
Cost of Food Sales	13,810	
Wages Expense	10,000	
Supplies Expense	300	
Utilities	1,000	
Advertising	200	
Depreciation Expense	160	
Rent Expense	750	
Interest Expense	111	
Laundry Expense	500	
Kitchen Fuel	100	
Radio Advertising	1,000	
Administrative Expenses	2,000	
Repairs and Maintenance	500	
Total	$59,036	$59,036

restaurant's revenues and expenses for the accounting period). Positive results of operations (net income) are added to the owners' equity account; negative results (net losses) are subtracted from the owners' equity prior to preparing the balance sheet.

The balance sheet and income statement will be covered in detail in later chapters. At this point, see Luis's financial data for an example of how adjusted trial balance information can be used to prepare financial statements.

LUIS'S RESTAURANT

In preparing the income statement for Luis's, only food revenue and expense information is used. A simple income statement follows:

Income Statement
Luis's Restaurant
For a Period of 1 Month

Food Revenue		$39,965
Expenses:		
Cost of food sales	$13,810	
Wages expense	10,000	
Supplies expense	300	
Utilities	1,000	
Advertising	200	
Depreciation expense	160	
Rent expense	750	
Interest expense	111	
Laundry expense	500	
Kitchen fuel	100	
Radio advertising	1,000	
Administrative expense	2,000	
Repairs and maintenance	500	30,431
Net Income		$ 9,534

The balance sheet is prepared using the asset, liability, and Luis Alvarez, Capital accounts. However, the Luis Alvarez, Capital, account is first adjusted for the net income for the month by increasing it by the net income of $9,534 shown in the Income Statement ($5,000 + $9,534 = $14,534). The simplified balance sheet follows:

Balance Sheet
Luis's Restaurant
For the Last Day of the Month

ASSETS	
Cash	$15,905
Food inventory	1,200
Prepaid rent	1,500
Equipment	10,000
Less: Accumulated depreciation	(160)
Total assets	**$28,445**
LIABILITIES AND OWNERS' EQUITY	
Accounts payable	$ 500
Accrued expenses payable	4,300
Notes payable	9,000
Accrued interest	111
Luis Alvarez, Capital	14,534
Total liabilities and owners' equity	**$28,445**

CLOSING ENTRIES

All sales and expenses are initially recorded in accounts called temporary owners' equity accounts. At the end of each accounting period, these accounts are "closed" to the owners' equity account. To **close** an account is to clear it to a zero balance. Since Luis owns the restaurant by himself (he is sole proprietor), the sales and expense accounts are closed to the "Luis Alvarez, Capital" account. (If the restaurant were a corporation the temporary accounts would be closed to the retained earnings account.)

> **CLOSE To clear a temporary owners' equity account to a zero balance.**

Sales accounts normally have a credit balance; therefore, for sales accounts to be closed, they must be debited. Since **closing entries,** like all accounting entries, must have equal debits and credits, the owners' equity account is credited by the amount debited to the sales account.

> **CLOSING ENTRY The debits and credits made to close a temporary owners' equity account.**

Expense accounts normally have a debit balance; therefore, for expense accounts to be closed, they must be credited by their balance, and the owners' equity account must be debited by the same amount. The result is that the sales and expense accounts are closed out.

The entries to close the sales and expense accounts follow:

To Close Sales Accounts

Sales accounts	XXX	
(Owner), Capital		XXX

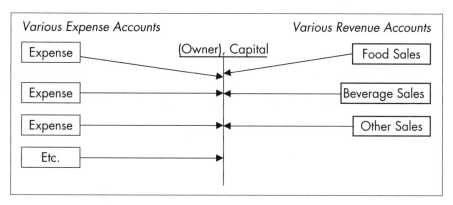

Figure 2.1 Process of Closing Revenue and Expense Accounts

LUIS'S RESTAURANT

All revenue and expense accounts are closed to the Luis Alvarez, Capital account with two entries as follows:

To Close The Food Sales Account		
Food sales	$39,965	
Luis Alvarez, Capital		$39,965
To Close The Expense Accounts		
Luis Alvarez, Capital	$30,431	
Cost of food sales		$13,810
Wages expense		$10,000
Supplies expense		$ 300
Utilities		$ 1,000
Advertising		$ 200
Depreciation expense		$ 160
Rent expense		$ 750
Interest expense		$ 111
Laundry expense		$ 500
Kitchen fuel		$ 100
Radio advertising		$ 1,000
Administrative expense		$ 2,000
Repairs and maintenance		$ 500

These entries result in all revenue and expense accounts being closed and the Luis Alvarez, Capital account being increased by the net income for the period of $9,534.

To Close Expense Accounts

(Owner), Capital	XXX	
Expense Accounts		XXX

The process of closing revenue and expense accounts is illustrated in Figure 2.1.

WITHDRAWALS AND DIVIDENDS

During an operating period, the owner of an unincorporated restaurant may withdraw funds for personal use. This action should be accounted for by debiting a temporary owners' equity account titled (Owner), Withdrawals. This is not an expense account and should not appear on the income statement. At the end of the accounting period, it is closed to the owners' equity account, (Owner), Capital.

The board of directors of a foodservice firm organized as a corporation may declare dividends. This declaration results in a legal liability of the firm and should be recorded by debiting "retained earnings" and crediting "dividends payable" (a liability account). When the dividends are paid, the dividends payable account is debited, and the cash account is credited.

THE ACCOUNTING CYCLE

So far this chapter has covered transactions, the recording of transactions, accounts, trial balances, financial statements, adjustments, and closing entries. Now, the cycle that encompasses all these accounting techniques will be discussed. The accounting cycle occurs every accounting period. A brief discussion of each of the steps in the accounting cycle follows.

Journalizing

Journalizing is the accounting procedure of recording transactions in a **journal.** In the journalizing process, the transaction is analyzed and classified. Analyzing determines what type of transaction is to be recorded and the amounts that are involved. Classifying involves determining which accounts are affected. Recording is simply writing, processing, or in some other way entering information in a journal (a book of original entry). The most simple and common journal is the general journal. All adjustments and closing entries are recorded in the general journal.

> **JOURNALIZING** The accounting procedure that involves recording financial transactions in a journal.

> **JOURNAL** A book for original entry of financial information into the accounting system.

Posting

Posting is the "recording" of debits and credits from journals to the proper accounts. A group of accounts is called a **ledger,** so often accountants will call an account a "ledger account." The most common and comprehensive ledger is the **general ledger.** The general

> **POSTING** The recording of debits and credits from journals to the proper account.

> **LEDGER** A group of related accounts.

Account: _____

Date		Explanation	Folio		Debit		Credit		Balance	

Figure 2.2   General Ledger Account

GENERAL LEDGER   A ledger housing all asset, liability, owners' equity, revenue, and expense accounts.

ledger consists of accounts for all assets, liabilities, owners' equity, revenues, and expenses. In most hand-written general ledgers, an account appears as in Figure 2.2.

The "explanation" column of the account is for notations that may be helpful to the bookkeeper later. The "folio" column indicates the source of the posting. This will generally be the initials and page number of a journal. For example, "GJ–18" stands for page 18 of the general journal.

For example, assume that on January 1, a restaurant receives cash of $100 from guests, which is recorded on page 1 of the cash receipts journal (CRJ). Assume the cash shown in the cash account prior to this transaction was $1,000. The transaction would be posted to the cash account as shown in Figure 2.3. The "balance" column is assumed to reflect normal balances for the account (in other words, assets have debit balances, etc.). If the balance for an asset account is a credit, then the credit balance is indicated by bracketing the total. For example, a negative cash balance of $100.00 would be shown as "(100.00)." Two alternative ways to indicate a balance opposite that normally expected would be to write the amount in red or circle the amount.

The account number for cash in Figure 2.3 is 1001. Restaurants generally assign ranges of account numbers to identify accounts. For example, a restaurant may assign account numbers 1001–1999 for asset accounts, 2000–2499 for liability accounts, etc. The major purpose is to simplify the posting process. When an amount is posted to an account, the account number rather than the account title is written in the journal. Each restaurant will use a different numbering system, depending on its needs.

Preparing a Trial Balance

Trial balances are prepared to prove that debit and credit balances are equal. This proof is usually conducted just prior to recording adjusting entries. If the debit

CASH   Acct. # 1001

Date		Explanation	Folio	Debit		Credit		Balance	
Jan	1	Balance beginning of period						1,000	00
	1	Received from customers	CRJ-1	100	00			1,100	00

Figure 2.3   General Ledger Transaction

and credit balance accounts are not equal, the reason must be determined, and the accounts in error must be corrected before making adjusting entries.

Adjustments

The fourth step in the accounting cycle involves determining and recording the appropriate adjustments (adjusting entries) at the end of the accounting period. Generally, adjusting entries are prepared for (a) inventory accounts, (b) prepaid expense accounts, (c) recording depreciation, and (d) recording accruals. Adjusting entries such as depreciation recorded at the end of every accounting period are often called standard journal entries. After the adjusting entries are recorded in the general journal, they must be posted to the general ledger accounts.

Preparing an Adjusted Trial Balance

As a check that adjusting entries have been properly posted, an adjusted trial balance is prepared. The process is the same as preparing a trial balance except that it follows the recording and posting of the adjusting entries.

Preparation of Financial Statements

The balance sheet and income statement may be prepared directly from either the adjusted trial balance or from the general ledger accounts. Other financial statements such as those involving cash flow and retained earnings may also be prepared at this time. (The information for these two statements does not come directly from account balances; it is taken from the details of both the accounts and specialized journals.)

Closing Temporary Proprietorship Accounts

This step in the accounting cycle includes recording and posting the closing entries. Revenue, expense, and withdrawal accounts (single owner) are closed with closing entries. The closing entries result clear these accounts so that operating results and withdrawals of the following period can be recorded.

Post-Closing Trial Balance

This final step, like the trial balances done earlier, tests the equality of debit and credit balance accounts. It consists only of asset, liability, and permanent owners' equity accounts, since all temporary owners' equity accounts have been closed at this point. If debit and credit balance accounts are equal, the accounting cycle is complete.

SPECIALIZED JOURNALS

To this point, only the general journal has been discussed. It is simple and will accommodate any transaction; however, every entry recorded in the general journal must be posted separately to general ledger accounts. To achieve efficiency in accounting, specialized journals are used. These journals have columns for frequently used accounts so that account titles are not written each time a routine transaction occurs. The column *total,* rather than each *entry,* is posted to the appropriate general ledger account. Specialized journals permit several bookkeepers to take part in the recording process—each handling a different journal. For example, a specialized journal for recording cash receipts will have a cash column. Rather than post each cash entry to the cash account, the total of all cash entries is posted.

The following discussion illustrates the use of specialized journals. Varied formats are used by restaurants in practice, and the specialized journals presented will not correspond with those of any particular business. However, the general functions discussed are performed in accounting systems of almost all restaurants.

Cash Receipts Journal

CASH RECEIPTS JOURNAL   A book used to initially record individual financial transactions involving cash receipts.

One common specialized journal records all transactions involving cash receipts (see Figure 2.4). One column is used for cash; other columns relate to common reasons for cash receipts. (Most commonly these are cash sales, collection of notes,

Date		Explanation	Cash. Debit		Accounts Receivable –Credit		Sales– Credit		Other– Credit		Folio	Account Title
Jan	1	Cash sales	1,000	00			1,000	00				
	1	Collection of notes and interest	550	00					500	00		Notes receivables
									50	00		Interest income
	1	Collection of M. Smith Acct.	100	00	100	00						

Figure 2.4 Cash Receipts Journal

and accounts receivable.) An account title must be supplied for each entry in the "other" column, and a folio column is provided for indicating that each amount in the "other" column has been posted to the proper general ledger account.

Note in each case cash is shown as received, and there is an equal amount of credits. At the end of the accounting period, the journal columns are totaled and cross-footed; that is, the totals of the credit columns must equal the total of the debit columns.

The totals of the cash, accounts receivable, and sales columns are posted to the proper general ledger accounts. Each entry in the "other" column is posted individually. In restaurants serving alcoholic beverages it is desirable to separate food and beverage sales by establishing separate columns for food sales and beverage sales. If sales tax is charged, a sales tax column should be included.

Sales Journal

Another specialized journal is the **sales journal.** Typically, it has columns for accounts receivable and sales, as shown in Figure 2.5 (on page 52). Restaurants that account for sales of food and beverages separately, need separate columns for each. If applicable, a sales tax column is also included. At the end of the ac-

> **SALES JOURNAL A book used to initially record individual financial transactions involving credit (accounts receivable) and cash sales.**

counting period, the columns are totaled, and the journal is cross-footed. After the proof that debits equal credits, the column totals are posted to the proper accounts. Some restaurants will combine the cash receipts and sales journals into a format similar to that illustrated in Figure 2.6 (page 52).

Date		Customer	Accounts Receivable–Debit	Sales–Credit
Jan	1	R. Rhoads	18 00	18 00
	1	J. Adams	22 00	22 00
	1	M. Gordon	34 00	34 00

Figure 2.5 Sales Journal

Cash Disbursements Journal

The **cash disbursements journal** is a specialized journal for recording all disbursements except for payroll (see Figure 2.7). This journal has separate columns for cash and accounts payable. In addition, there is a column titled "other" for accounts less frequently affected.

> **CASH DISBURSEMENTS JOURNAL A book used to initially record all non-payroll disbursements made with cash.**

Note in Figure 2.7 that the payee is listed as well as the check number. At the end of the accounting period, the columns are totaled and cross-footed. The totals of the accounts payable and cash columns are posted to the respective accounts. Each entry in the "other" column is posted separately. Most restaurants establish columns for frequently debited accounts.

			Debits			Credits				
Date		Explanation	Bank	Accounts Receivable	Sales	Accounts Receivable	Other	Folio	Account Title
Jan	1	Cash sales	1,000 00		1,000 00				
	1	Collection of notes and interest	550 00				500 00 50 00		Notes receivables Interest income
	1	Collection of M. Smith account	100 00			100 00			
	1	R. Rhoads		18 00	18 00				
	1	J. Adams		22 00	22 00				
	1	M. Gordon		34 00	34 00				

Figure 2.6 Cash Receipts and Sales Journal

Date	Payee	Check No.	Cash– Credit	Accounts Payable– Debit	Other– Debit	Folio	Account Title
Jan 1	J. Burns	6102	100 00		100 00		Advertising
1	Acme Food Services	6103	1,000 00	1,000 00			
1	Mark's	6104	500 00	500 00			

Figure 2.7 Cash Disbursements Journal

Purchases Journal

Another common specialized journal is called the **purchases journal** (see Figure 2.8). Only purchases on account are recorded here. Generally, individual columns are established for food purchases and accounts payable. Columns should be established for other accounts that are frequently charged. Also, an

> **PURCHASES JOURNAL A book used to initially record individual financial transactions involving purchases on account (accounts payable).**

"other" column is included for accounts that are infrequently charged.

Note that each entry in Figure 2.8 always results in an entry in the accounts payable column. At the end of the accounting period, the journal columns are totaled and cross-footed. The totals for the food inventory and accounts payable columns are posted to their respective accounts. The entries in the other column are posted to the individual accounts.

Payroll Journal

A final specialized journal is the **payroll journal,** used to record payroll checks (see Figure 2.9 on page 54). The columns in this journal include wages expense,

Date	Supplier	Accounts Payable– Credit	Food Inventory– Debit	Other– Debit	Folio	Account Title
Jan 1	Mid-Atlantic Meats	1,200 00	1,200 00			
1	Virginia Electric	640 00		640 00		Electricity
1	Rex Hardware	120 00		120 00		Repairs

Figure 2.8 Purchases Journal

| Employee | Debit | | | Credit | | | | | |
	Wages Expense	Salaries Expense	FICA	Federal Withholding	Health Ins. Payable	Union Dues	Net Pay	Check No.
R. Carson	200 00		13 40	25 00	15 00	5 00	141 60	2001
M. Davis	180 00		12 06	20 00	15 00	4 50	128 44	2002
G. Evans	300 00		20 10	50 00	15 00	0 00	214 90	2003

Figure 2.9 Payroll Journal

PAYROLL JOURNAL   A book used to initially record payroll check information applicable, on a by-employee basis, for wages/salaries and for credits including FICA, federal withholding, and deductions for other items.

federal withholding, FICA payable, and net pay (cash). There are generally several other columns, depending on additional tax withholdings and deductions for items including union dues, health insurance, etc. Note that there are also columns for the employee's name and the check number. As with the other specialized journals, at the end of the accounting period the columns are totaled, proved, and posted to the appropriate general ledger accounts.

WWW: Internet Assistant

Basic accounting courses are typically offered in college hospitality programs. To discover whether your area has a program offering such a course for practicing industry professionals, go to

http://www.hospitalitylawyer.com

then select "Hospitality schools" from the list of choices offered.

MANAGER'S 10 POINT EFFECTIVENESS CHECKLIST

Evaluate your need for and the status of each of the following financial management tactics. For tactics you judge to be important but not yet in place, develop an action plan including completion date to implement the tactic.

TACTIC	DON'T AGREE (DON'T NEED)	AGREE (DONE)	AGREE (NOT DONE)	IF NOT DONE	
				WHO IS RESPONSIBLE?	TARGET COMPLETION DATE
1. Manager has an up-to-date list of all business-related assets.	❑	❑	❑		
2. Manager has an up-to-date list of all business-related liabilities.	❑	❑	❑		
3. Manager thoroughly understands the difference between liabilities and owners' equity.	❑	❑	❑		
4. Revenue and expense accounts appropriate for the restaurant have been developed, have been reviewed by the restaurant's accountant, and are in use by the property.	❑	❑	❑		
5. Trial balances are prepared on all accounts on a monthly basis.	❑	❑	❑		
6. Where possible, expenses for a given time period are matched to revenue generated during that same time period.	❑	❑	❑		
7. Periodic food and beverage inventories are taken at the end of each accounting period (usually one month).	❑	❑	❑		
8. A balance sheet and income statement are produced by the restaurant at regular (monthly) intervals.	❑	❑	❑		
9. Management has designated one individual or entity to be in charge of each phase of the accounting cycle.	❑	❑	❑		
10. Specialized journals appropriate for the restaurant have been developed and are in use.	❑	❑	❑		

3

THE BALANCE SHEET

MANAGER'S BRIEF

In this chapter you will examine the balance sheet, which along with the income statement is one of the two most important financial statements produced for managers.

You will discover that the balance sheet provides a "point-in-time" picture of your restaurant. It will help you understand exactly where your restaurant stands financially at the time it is prepared. This is done by a careful and detailed listing of all the restaurant's assets, liabilities, and ownership claims.

The assets listed on the balance sheet include a variety of restaurant resources such as cash, money owed to the restaurant (accounts receivable), inventories, land, and equipment.

Liabilities detailed on the balance sheet will include amounts owed to vendors and in some cases employees, as well as any short- or long-term debts the restaurant has incurred.

Claims on ownership depend on the type of organizational entity chosen by the restaurant's owners. A sole proprietor (one person), a partnership, or a corporation may own restaurants, but all of these are interested in knowing their equity position in the restaurant. The balance sheet shows that equity position.

The chapter concludes with a sample of an actual balance sheet developed in accordance with the Uniform System of Accounts for Restaurants for your review.

The final outputs of the accounting cycle are financial statements. The balance sheet and the income statement are the best known and, to many users, the most useful of the financial statements. This chapter addresses the purposes and content of the balance sheet and presents a format recommended by the Uniform System of Accounts for Restaurants. General footnotes to financial statements are also discussed.

PURPOSES OF BALANCE SHEET

BALANCE SHEET Also known as the statement of financial position, this final output from the accounting cycle reports the assets, liabilities, and net worth of the restaurant at a single point in time (generally month-end).

The **balance sheet,** also known as the statement of financial position, reports the assets, liabilities, and net worth of the restaurant at a single point in time (generally month-end). It provides a static snapshot of the restaurant's financial position. If a second balance sheet were prepared for the operation even one day after the end of the accounting period, it would probably reflect a different "picture" of assets, liabilities, and net worth than did its counterpart prepared one day earlier.

Financial information from the balance sheet is used by different users for different reasons. It has several important purposes, including the following:

- It tells the amount of *cash on hand* at the end of an accounting period. All assets are eventually converted, either directly or indirectly, to cash. This process may result in a partial loss (such as uncollected accounts receivable). Alternatively, several months (or even years) may evolve before an asset such as a dishwasher is fully used. (It is converted to an expense through a depreciation process.) Cash on hand is cash available for alternative future uses such as paying bills and disbursing to owners.

- It explains *details about assets*. **Fixed assets** represent a fairly high percentage of the total assets of many restaurants. Several years are required to fully use these assets in the business.

> **FIXED ASSETS** Resources of the restaurant that are tangible, material in amount, used in the operation to generate revenue, and will benefit the restaurant for more than one year into the future.

- It reviews the *composition of debt and net worth* (if a proprietorship) or *stockholders' equity* (if a corporation). This reflects how the restaurant has been financed. The greater the amount of debt financing with equity, the greater the financial risk. A restaurant that has used debt to finance a large percentage of its fixed assets may have a difficult time securing financing for more debt. It shows the amount of the restaurant's *past earnings* that have been retained in the business. For a corporation, retained earnings is the sum of past earnings retained in the business. For a sole proprietorship, past earnings are part of the (name of proprietor), Capital. For example, the account for James Smith, the sole owner of a foodservice business, would simply be James Smith, Capital. Generally, the greater the retention of internally generated funds, the less borrowing will be required during an expansion period.

- The balance sheet provides insight into a restaurant's ability to pay bills; **liquidity** is important in the timing of cash flows.

> **LIQUIDITY** A measure of the restaurant's ability to convert assets to cash.

The past several years have seen a renewed interest in the balance sheet. Some firms that have consistently reported profits on their income statement have gone bankrupt (or are nearly bankrupt) a short time later because they were unable to pay their bills as they became due. The balance sheet reveals the amount of debt.

There are numerous ways to analyze a restaurant's balance sheet. This includes the use of ratios to relate balance sheet items to each other and to assess the relationship between operating (income statement) information and balance sheet items. (Note: Ratios will be discussed in chapter 5.)

CONTENT OF BALANCE SHEET

ASSET Something of value that is owned by the restaurant. Examples include cash, product inventories, equipment, land, and buildings.

LIABILITIES Obligations (money owed) to outside entities. Examples include amounts owed to suppliers, to lenders for long-term debt such as mortgages, and to employees (payroll that has been earned by but not paid to the restaurant's staff).

OWNERS' EQUITY The claims of owners (an individual, partnership, or corporation) to assets of the restaurant.

The balance sheet contains two major categories: **assets** and **liabilities.** Since assets equal liabilities, the name "balance sheet" is appropriate. Liabilities are further divided between the claims of creditors to assets (liabilities) and the claims of owners to assets (**owners' equity**). Owners' equity is referred to by several different titles, including the following:

Legal Organization	*Common Titles*
Sole proprietorship	Proprietorship, Net worth, Owner's equity
Partnership	Net worth, Owners' equity
Corporation	Stockholders' equity, Owners' equity

Assets

Assets are normally of four general categories: current assets, fixed assets, investments, and other assets. Each restaurant should develop a list of accounts, depending on its specific needs.

CURRENT ASSETS Cash, assets that can be readily converted to cash, and other assets expected to be used by the restaurant within one year.

Current Assets.   **Current assets** are the first type shown on the balance sheet. Current assets are cash, assets that can readily be converted to cash, and other assets expected to be used by the restaurant within one year. Current assets are normally listed in order of their liquidity; cash is listed first, followed by the next current asset that can be most quickly converted to cash. The major current asset accounts are:

- *Cash.* The cash account normally includes cash on hand in house funds, change banks, undeposited cash receipts, and cash on deposit with banks. It is common for different bank accounts to be shown separately on the balance sheet. For example, in addition to a general banking account, a restaurant may maintain a payroll account.

- *Accounts receivable.* The **accounts receivable** account includes money owed by guests, credit card companies, employees and officers, and by others such as concessionaires (for example, a business renting space from the restaurant). If the amount from employees and officers is significant, this should be shown separately. The value of accounts receivable should be that estimated to be collected; in other words, the total amount due is reduced by an allowance for doubtful accounts (the estimated amount of accounts receivable that is not likely to be collected).

> **ACCOUNTS RECEIVABLE**
> Money owed to the restaurant by guests, credit card companies, employees and officers, and by others such as concessionaires.

- *Notes receivable.* Promissory notes due to the restaurant are recorded here. Notes due beyond 12 months from the balance sheet date should be classified as a noncurrent investment. **Notes receivable,** like accounts receivable, should be reported on the balance sheet at their net realizable value. An allowance for doubtful notes should be established for notes (or portion of notes) not considered collectible.

> **NOTES RECEIVABLE**
> Promissory notes due to the restaurant within one year.

- *Inventory.* **Inventory** consists of the value of food, beverages, and other goods on hand at the end of the accounting period available for sale. This normally includes food in storerooms, freezers, pantries, kitchens, and storage warehouses, along with beverages in stock at the beverage outlets (bars) and in warehouses.

> **INVENTORY** The value of the food, beverages, and other goods on hand that are available for sale at the end of the accounting period.

Inventory values ideally should be reported at the lower of cost or market value. However, because of the rapid turnover of inventory, many restaurants value inventories at specific item cost, writing the purchase cost on the box, can, or bottle in which the item is packaged at time of receipt. Alternatively, it is common for restaurants to value the inventories at the latest (most recent) cost of each item. Regardless of the method used, the same procedure should be followed each accounting period.

- *Marketable securities.* This account identifies investments purchased to make temporary use of surplus funds that can be quickly converted

MARKETABLE SECURITIES
Investments purchased by
the restaurant to make temporary use of surplus funds;
marketable securities can be
quickly converted to cash.

to cash. At the end of the accounting period, **marketable securities** should be reported at their fair market value. Investments that are more permanent in nature should be recorded in the investments account.

■ *Prepaid expenses.* **Prepaid expenses** include unexpired insurance premiums and prepaid interest, taxes, licenses, and rent. The Generally Accepted Accounting Principle (GAAP) of matching dictates that disbursements for these items be shown as assets until the restaurant receives benefit; then the expense is recognized. Generally, prepaid items are amortized (spread over) on a straight-line basis. (For example, a 12-month insurance premium for $3,600 would be expensed at $300 per month; $3,600 ÷ 12 = $300.)

PREPAID EXPENSES Expenses
paid by the restaurant that
will benefit it within one year.

Fixed Assets.   Fixed assets are resources of the restaurant that are tangible, material in amount, will be used in operations to generate sales, and will benefit the restaurant for more than one year into the future. A writing tool such as an ink pen may be used by a clerical employee for more than a year. However, it would not be recognized as a fixed asset because its cost was insignificant. Instead, fixed assets include such items as land, buildings, furniture and fixtures, equipment, and leasehold improvements.

■ *Land.* This account is used for recording the purchase of **land** used immediately by the restaurant. Land purchased for future use or as an investment should be shown on the balance sheet as an investment. The land cost includes its purchase price and all costs related to the purchase, such as brokers' commissions and legal and title fees. As well, costs of clearing or otherwise *permanently* improving the land after purchase are part of this account. Cash receipts from materials salvaged in clearing the land, if any, should be subtracted from the cost of the land. When expenditures are made for land improvements with a limited life, such as paving the parking lot, these costs should be recorded in a separate account entitled "land improvements" and should be depreciated over the improvement's useful life.

LAND The cost of land used
by the restaurant, including
purchase cost, all costs
related to the purchase,
and costs incurred to permanently improve the land,
less any cash generated
from materials salvaged
from the land.

■ *Buildings.* Purchases of **buildings** used in the business should be recorded in these accounts with a separate account for each building. Renovation costs for a recently purchased building should be added to the building's cost.

> **BUILDING** The purchase cost including renovation (for a recently purchased building) and capitalized costs including materials, labor, and overhead (when a building is constructed).

When buildings are constructed, costs capitalized (to be depreciated over its useful life) include materials, labor, and overhead related to the construction as well as architects' fees, building permits, taxes during the construction period, and construction financing costs.

When land and buildings are acquired for a single amount, the purchase price must be divided. The purchase contract may provide a breakdown; if not, an appraisal may be required to allocate the purchase price between land and building(s).

Buildings wear out over time and therefore must be depreciated. Several methods can be used to depreciate fixed assets. For example, the straight-line method was discussed in chapter 2. We also noted that depreciation is recorded by debiting the "depreciation expense" account and by crediting an accumulated depreciation account that is maintained for each fixed asset being depreciated. (Accumulated depreciation accounts are called contra-asset accounts and normally have a credit balance. On the balance sheet, the amount recorded in the contra-account is subtracted from the fixed asset amount to yield a net book value.)

■ *Equipment.* **Equipment** accounts cover a wide range of items used by the restaurant. Ideally, separate records are maintained for each equipment item; however, on the balance sheet, these are generally combined. Equipment includes items such as kitchen and cleaning equipment, cash registers, delivery trucks, etc. The cost of equipment includes the purchase price, tax and duties on purchase, freight charges, insurance charges

> **EQUIPMENT** Items such as kitchen and cleaning equipment, cash registers, trucks, etc.; cost includes purchase price, tax, duties, freight/insurance charges, and installation. Items are recorded at cost and depreciated over their useful lives.

during shipping, and installation charges. As with buildings, equipment is depreciated over its useful life, and the net book value is shown on the balance sheet.

- *Furniture and fixtures.* **Furniture and fixtures** includes such items as desks, booths, tables, chairs, carpets, and drapes used by the restaurant. These items are recorded at cost, which includes the purchase price plus taxes, freight, insurance in transit, and installation costs. As with equipment and buildings, furniture and fixtures are depreciated over their useful lives. Some restaurants combine furniture and fixtures with equipment; furniture, fixtures, and equipment (abbreviated FF&E) is the account title.

> **FURNITURE AND FIXTURES**
> Items such as desks, booths, tables, and chairs used by the restaurant; items are recorded at cost and are depreciated over their useful lives.

- *Linens, china, glassware, silver, utensils, and uniforms.* **Linens, china, glassware, silver, utensils, and uniforms** are normally combined on the balance sheet and may be reported at cost less the depreciation allowance. If a reserve stock is maintained, restaurants often report this portion at cost. Alternatively, some restaurants capitalize and depreciate their original china, etc., and then expense future purchases of these items as a more practical approach.

> **LINENS, CHINA, GLASSWARE, SILVER, UTENSILS, AND UNIFORMS** These items may be recorded at cost less depreciation, or alternatively, original inventories may be depreciated and additional purchases expensed (charged against income at the time of purchase).

- *Leasehold improvements.* **Leasehold improvements** are capital expenditures made to property that is leased by a restaurant. For example, a building may be leased for 10 years and its interior may be remodeled. The cost of the remodeling is recorded as a leasehold improvement and should be amortized over either the life of the lease or the life of the leasehold improvement (whichever is shorter). Certain leases of buildings and equipment must be capitalized. They are recorded as fixed assets, and a liability is shown on the balance sheet.

> **LEASEHOLD IMPROVEMENTS**
> Renovations on or remodeling done to a leased building or space, the cost of which is amortized over the life of the lease or the life of the improvement (whichever is shorter).

Investments. **Investments** differ from other assets in that they cannot be readily liquidated (converted to cash), nor are they used for immediate business operations. In restaurant accounting, the use of surplus funds to buy common stock in a blue chip company would be called a current asset (marketable securities), rather than an investment. This asset may be quickly liquidated. By contrast, buying undeveloped land for a future building site would be called an investment.

> **INVESTMENTS** Invested surplus funds that are not expected to be converted to cash within one year.

Investments are generally reported on the balance sheet at cost.

Other Assets. Other assets are all of the restaurant's assets that are not included in the above three categories (current, fixed, or investments); they include intangible assets and deferred expenses. Examples follow.

> **OTHER ASSETS** Any restaurant asset that is not considered current, fixed, or an investment.

- *Rental deposit.* Some restaurant leases require a cash deposit to be applied to the last month's rent (referred to as the **rental deposit**). Since the cash in this deposit is not readily available, it should be shown as part of "other assets."

  > **RENTAL DEPOSIT** The amount, if any, of a cash deposit that is required according to the restaurant's lease to be applied to the last month's rent.

- *Organization costs.* The initial costs to organize the restaurant should be recorded as an asset and then amortized against revenue over a three- to five-year period. **Organization costs** include legal fees, promotional costs, stock certificate costs, and accounting and state incorporating fees.

  > **ORGANIZATION COSTS** The initial costs to organize a restaurant, which are initially recorded as an asset and then amortized against revenue over a three- to five-year period.

- *Preopening costs.* The costs associated with opening a new restaurant, such as payroll prior to opening, training, and promotional costs, should be recorded in this account. **Preopening costs** are generally amortized against revenue over a one- to three-year period.

  > **PREOPENING COSTS** The costs associated with opening a new restaurant, including preopening payroll, training, and promotional costs. These are generally amortized against revenue over a one- to three-year period.

- *Franchise fees.* Franchise costs normally include an initial **franchise fee** and continuing royalties based on revenue. The initial fee is an "other asset." In addition to the franchise fee, the franchisee should also use this account for legal fees and other costs incurred to obtain the franchise. These costs should be amortized over the life of the franchise agreement.

■ *Bond discount and issue costs.* The cost of issuing bonds includes legal and accountants' fees and other costs, such as those of certificates and state registration. **Bond discount and issue costs** should be amortized over the life of the bond issue. Discounted bonds are issued at less than their face amount, and the amount of discount is recorded in this account and then amortized over the life of the bond issue.

■ *Cost of improvements in progress.* The cost of improvements to buildings that are incomplete are recorded in this account. When completed, these **costs of improvements in progress** should be transferred to the building account. (Alternatively, some restaurants carry these costs as fixed assets and show them on the balance sheet as an item under fixed assets.)

■ *Goodwill.* **Goodwill** is the sum of all special advantages not otherwise identified that relate to a restaurant. Goodwill can include excellent reputation, well-trained staff, highly motivated management, and favorable location. Goodwill is not recognized on the restaurant's books unless it has been purchased. (Purchased goodwill results when the cost of an acquired business exceeds the amount assigned to individual assets.) Goodwill should be reported on the balance sheet at cost less the amount written off based on impairment (loss of value of the goodwill due to factors such as greater competition, change in location, bad recognition, etc.).

■ *Costs of bar (or other) license.* The **costs of bar (or other) license** should be recorded in this account. The cost should be amortized over a reasonable number of years.

Liabilities

Liabilities may be considered either current or long-term. The distinction is important, since **current liabilities** are considered in the calculation of **working capital** and in the measurement of the restaurant's liquidity. The following list of liability accounts is not exhaustive; each restaurant may have different accounts depending upon its needs.

> **CURRENT LIABILITIES** The total of all obligations due to be paid within 12 months of the balance sheet date.

> **WORKING CAPITAL** The current assets less current liabilities.

Current Liabilities.   A liability is current if it must be satisfied with current assets within one year.

- *Accounts payable—trade.* The **accounts payable—trade** account is used to record the cost of goods and services purchased on account by the restaurant. Technically, accounts payable should be recorded when "legal title" is transferred to the buyer. Practically speaking, this occurs when the goods or services are received. If a cash discount is available and used, the cost should be recorded net of the cash discount.

> **ACCOUNTS PAYABLE—TRADE** The cost of goods and services (net of discount) purchased on account by the restaurant.

- *Accounts payable—others.* **Accounts payable—others** is for amounts owed to concessionaires for collections from guests or large open accounts, such as purchases of equipment, etc., and should be shown separately on the balance sheet.

> **ACCOUNTS PAYABLE—OTHERS** Amounts due to vendors for purchases of equipment that the restaurant desires to report separately from accounts payable—trade.

- *Notes payable.* **Notes payable** includes notes to be paid within one year that are issued to suppliers, to banks for loans, and to the restaurant's officers/stockholders. Notes should be recorded at their net present value (the amount needed to retire the note at the balance sheet date). The net present value is the amount of the note if its interest rate is reasonable. If a note has no stated interest rate or if it is an unreasonable rate, the note should be discounted using the prevailing interest rate. Notes due to different

> **NOTES PAYABLE** The portion of loans from suppliers, banks, and others that must be paid within one year.

sources of funds (bankers, trade creditors, and officers, for example) should be shown separately.

- *Salaries and wages payable.* **Salaries and wages payable** represents unpaid compensation that has been earned by and is owed to restaurant employees. These costs are recorded by an adjusting entry at the end of the accounting period. There is no need to identify the portions relating to tax withholdings and deductions. The amounts related to bonuses and commissions should also be recognized in this account.

> **SALARIES AND WAGES PAYABLE**
> Salaries and wages earned by and owed to restaurant employees that are unpaid at the end of the accounting period.

- *Payroll and withholding taxes.* Separate accounts should be established for each **payroll and withholding tax.** These normally include FICA (federal retirement taxes), federal and state unemployment taxes, federal income tax withheld, and where applicable, state and city income taxes. Note: In addition to withholding FICA from employees' pay, the restaurant must pay a comparable amount for most employees. Amounts withheld from employees' wages and the unemployment taxes generally paid by employers are a function of tax rates and other factors that change periodically. Tax authorities should be consulted for current information.

> **PAYROLL AND WITHHOLDING TAXES** The amounts withheld from employee salaries/wages and any amounts contributed by the restaurant for FICA (social security and medicare), federal/state unemployment taxes, federal income tax, and, as applicable, city and state income taxes.

- *Sales tax payable.* A tax must be charged by the restaurant on most food and beverage sales. This **sales tax payable,** in amounts established by individual states, should be recorded when the sale is recorded and must be periodically remitted to the proper sales taxing authority.

> **SALES TAX PAYABLE** Taxes on products/services sales that have been collected by the restaurant and that are owed to the taxing authority.

- *Deposits on banquets.* The **deposits on banquets** account records cash received from guests for the future sale of products and services. (When the event occurs, this account is debited, and a revenue account is credited.)

> **DEPOSITS ON BANQUETS** Cash received from guests for the future sale of products and services.

- *Income taxes payable.* The **income taxes payable** account is for taxes relating to the restaurant's taxable income. Each month income taxes should be estimated and accrued with an adjusting entry. (The estimated

INCOME TAXES PAYABLE The estimated amount of income taxes to be paid based on the restaurant's taxable income.

  amount is eventually adjusted based on the actual taxes due as calculated on the tax returns.)

- *Accrued expenses.* Expenses incurred for the period but not payable until after the balance sheet date. **Accrued expenses** include rent, franchise royalties, interest, and utilities. For balance sheet purposes, these may be combined; however, it is desirable to show any significant amounts separately.

ACCRUED EXPENSES Expenses incurred for the period that are not payable until after the balance sheet date.

- *Dividends payable.* **Dividends payable** (those unpaid at the balance sheet date) are shown as a current liability. Declared dividends become a liability at the date of declaration; stockhold-

DIVIDENDS PAYABLE Cash dividends unpaid at the balance sheet date.

  ers become unsecured creditors for them. Stock dividends are satisfied by distributing shares of stock and are never considered liabilities.

- *Gift certificates outstanding.* Restaurants may sell gift certificates. When sold, the amount received should be credited to the **gift certificates outstanding account.** As gift certificates are redeemed, this account is debited, and the appropriate sales account is credited. (Note: It is common for a certain percentage of certificates not to be redeemed. This should be considered at the balance sheet date; the account balance should reflect the value of those gift certificates expected to be redeemed.)

GIFT CERTIFICATES OUSTANDING The value of gift certificates that have been sold but are yet to be redeemed.

- *Current portion of long-term debt.* The **current portion of long-term debt** (the amount of long-term debt due within one year of the balance sheet date) should normally be reclassified from long-term to current debt.

CURRENT PORTION OF LONG-TERM DEBT The amount of long-term debt due within one year of the balance sheet date.

LONG-TERM DEBT The category of liabilities relating to that portion of debt that will not be paid within 12 months of the balance sheet date. Long-term debt is also referred to as "noncurrent liabilities."

MORTGAGE PAYABLE The amount of the restaurant's mortgage that will *not* be paid within 12 months of the balance sheet date.

BONDS PAYABLE The amount of bonds issued by the restaurant that are not due to be paid within 12 months of the balance sheet date.

DUE TO OFFICERS AND STOCKHOLDERS Loans and other amounts due to officers and stockholders that are not part of stockholders' equity or net worth and are not due within one year.

DUE TO AFFILIATED OR ASSOCIATED COMPANIES Amounts due to affiliated or associated companies that are not part of stockholders' equity or net worth and are not due within one year.

Long-Term Debt. The second major category of liabilities is **long-term debt** (also called noncurrent liabilities).

- *Mortgage payable.* The **mortgage payable** account records long-term debt when a creditor has a secured prior claim against fixed assets of the restaurant. (Note: The portion due within one year of the balance sheet date should be reclassified as a current liability.)

- *Bonds payable.* Bonds can be issued by restaurants to raise capital needed for expansion, renovation of facilities, etc. Generally, bonds have maturity dates of five years or more. When bonds are sold, certificates are issued, and the debt should be recorded in the **bonds payable** account.

- *Due to officers and stockholders.* Loans and other amounts **due to officers and stockholders** that are not part of stockholders' equity (if a corporation) or net worth (if a proprietorship or partnership) and that are not due within one year are shown in this account.

- *Due to affiliated or associated companies.* Amounts **due to affiliated or associated companies** that are not part of stockholders' equity (if a corporation) or net worth (if a proprietorship or partnership) and are not due within one year are shown in this account.

- *Deferred income taxes.* When restaurants account for certain items differently for tax purposes than for reporting purposes, differences in income result. For example, a restaurant may use the straight-line method for depreciating fixed assets for reporting purposes but an accelerated method of depreciation for depreciating fixed assets for tax purposes. In this case, in the first half of the life of the fixed asset, depreciation for tax purposes is greater than for reporting purposes; in the second half of the life of the fixed asset, the reverse is true. The tax effect (basically the tax rate times the difference between the two methods on a yearly basis) is reported in the balance sheet as **deferred income taxes.**

> **DEFERRED INCOME TAXES**
> **Represents the tax effects of temporary differences between the basis of noncurrent assets and noncurrent liabilities for financial and income tax reporting differences.**

- *Owners' equity.* The final section of the balance sheet relates to **owners' equity.** Accounts differ depending upon the restaurant's organization.

> **OWNERS' EQUITY The residual claims that owners have on assets. (Assets − Liabilities = Owners' Equity)**

Corporations

Corporations are legal entities that have an existence separate from their owners. Corporations are authorized by the state in which they are incorporated to issue stock to raise capital. Generally, stock may be freely

> **CORPORATION A legal entity that exists separately from its owners.**

traded by its owners without the permission of the corporation. For large food-service organizations stock price is established by the market system. For accounting purposes, the organization is not involved in the selling/buying of stock between stockholders. Different classes of stock may be issued and should be accounted for separately.

- *Common stock account.* When only one class of capital stock is issued, it is normally called common stock. The **common stock account** records the par or stated value of common stock.

> **COMMON STOCK ACCOUNT The par or stated value of capital stock that is issued when there is only one type of stock.**

- *Preferred stock account.* The par or stated value of capital stock issued by a corporation that has preference over common stock is carried in the **preferred stock account.** Generally, dividends are paid first to preferred stock holders and if sufficient cash is available, dividends can be paid to common stockholders.

> **PREFERRED STOCK ACCOUNT The par or stated value of capital stock that has preference over common stock.**

PAID-IN CAPITAL IN EXCESS OF PAR ACCOUNT The amounts paid by stockholders in excess of the par value of stock.

- *Paid-in capital in excess of par account.* Amounts paid by stockholders in excess of the par value are recorded in the **paid-in capital in excess of par account.**

RETAINED EARNINGS ACCOUNT An account used to record the undistributed earnings of a restaurant corporation.

- *Retained earnings account.* Earnings retained by corporate restaurants are reported as retained earnings. The major changes to retained earnings occur from the declaration of dividends and operating results. Profitable operations increase this account, and unprofitable operations decrease the **retained earnings account.**

Some restaurants report the change in retained earnings on the balance sheet as follows:

Retained earnings (beginning of period)	$ XXX
Plus:	
Net income	XXX
or	
Less:	
Net loss	(XXX)
Dividends declared	(XXX)
Retained earnings (end of period)	$ XXX

- *Treasury stock.* Common or preferred capital stock repurchased by the restaurant for possible future reissue is called **treasury stock.** Stock

TREASURY STOCK Common or preferred capital stock repurchased by the restaurant for possible future reissue.

may be repurchased (a) to obtain shares for later issuance to executives; (b) to invest excess cash temporarily; (c) to support the stock's market price; or (d) to improve earnings per share by reducing the number of shares outstanding. Treasury stock is normally recorded at cost and is reported in the balance sheet as a deduction in the stockholders' equity section.

Unincorporated Restaurants

SOLE PROPRIETORSHIP An unincorporated restaurant that has one owner.

Unincorporated restaurants are organized as either **sole proprietorships** (one owner) or **partnerships** (two or more owners). If the restaurant is a sole proprietorship, the equity section of the balance sheet consists of a single line called "(Owner), Capital." This account includes the initial and later capital contributions by the owner, less owner withdrawals, plus the results of operations (profits or losses). If the restau-

PARTNERSHIP An unincorporated restaurant that has two or more owners.

rant is a partnership, the net worth of each partner is shown as follows:

Net worth	
Partner A	$ XXX
Partner B	XXX
Partner C, etc.	XXX
Total net worth	$ XXX

BALANCE SHEET FORMAT

The details of the balance sheet used by restaurants vary based on business size and complexity, the related businesses of the restaurant owners, and the type of organization (sole proprietorship, partnership, or corporation).

Related balance sheet items are normally combined to keep information concise. For example, all cash accounts may be combined and reported as "Cash"; all inventory accounts may be combined and reported as "Inventory." The amount of consolidation depends on, first, the similarity of items (only similar items should be combined), and second, the complexity of items (consolidation should make the balance sheet more understandable). Users' needs, then, should be a major consideration in the preparation of the balance sheet.

When important details about balance sheet items are left off the statement itself, they may be included in supporting schedules. For example, all long-term notes may be shown as one item on the balance sheet if there is a supplementary schedule that lists the notes along with their interest rates and maturity dates.

Another way to enhance the balance sheet presentation is to use notations. For example, the inventory value may be shown as follows:

Inventory for resale (FIFO) $22,300

This disclosure informs the reader about the basis of inventory valuation. The term "FIFO" — first in, first out — means that the inventory value is based upon the latest (most recent) purchase price, because items first purchased are

Restaurant Name: _____   Date: _____

Retained earnings at (date—beginning of period)		$XXX
Additions: Net Income	$XXX	
Other	XXX	XXX
Deductions: Dividends Declared	(XXX)	
Other	(XXX)	(XXX)
Retained earnings at (date—end of period)		$XXX

Figure 3.1   Statement of Retained Earnings

first used. This technique is useful for other items such as marketable securities, accounts receivable, fixed assets, long-term debt and capital stock.

Generally, restaurants provide balance sheets for two periods. This comparative form enables readers to compare two sets of financial information so that trends can be assessed.

Statement of Retained Earnings

Some restaurants provide a separate statement depicting changes in retained earnings rather than including this detail on the balance sheet. This approach results in a more concise balance sheet but does require another statement. The recommended form for this approach is as shown in Figure 3.1.

Footnotes to the Balance Sheet

Footnotes to balance sheets help to explain their content. Footnotes are meant to clarify, not to replace, content. They can relate to methods of valuation, the existence of contingencies, details of long-term debt, significant accounting policies, and other matters that require explanation to make them more understandable.

Balance Sheet: Uniform System of Accounts

The Uniform System of Accounts for Restaurants (USAR)[2] contains a recommended balance sheet format and provides a dictionary of financial terms for the various balance sheet accounts. Much of the discussion above has been based upon the NRA's Uniform System. Figure 3.2 shows the USAR balance sheet format.

[2]*Uniform System of Accounts for Restaurants,* Seventh Edition, National Restaurant Association (Washington, D.C., 1996).

Balance Sheet Format

Name of Restaurant Company as of (Insert Date)

Current Assets

Cash on Hand	$ 15,000	$ 40,000
Cash in Banks	25,000	
Accounts Receivable:		
Trade	6,000	
Employees	2,000	
Other		
Total Receivables		
Deduct Allowance for Doubtful	2,000	9,500
Accounts	10,000	
Inventories:	(500)	
Food		
Beverages		
Gift and Sundry Shop	9,500	11,650
Supplies	1,050	6,500
Prepaid Expenses		**67,650**
Total Current Assets	100	
	1,000	
Due from officers, stockholders, partners and employees		1,000
Due from affiliated or associated companies		500
Cash held by trustee—restricted		400

FIXED ASSETS:

Land	60,000	
Buildings	150,000	
Cost of Improvements in Progress	5,000	
Leasehold and Leasehold Improvements	40,000	169,000
Furniture, Fixtures and Equipment	12,000	
Uniforms, Linens, China, Glass, Silver, Utensils	3,000	
Deduct Accumulated Depreciation and Amortization	(101,000)	
Net Book Value of Fixed Assets		

DEFERRED EXPENSES:

Organization and Pre-opening Expenses	4,000	
Bond Discount and Loan Initiation Fees	6,000	
		10,000

OTHER ASSETS:

Amount Paid for Goodwill	5,000	
Cost of Bar License	20,000	
Rental Deposits	8,000	
Cash Surrender Value of Life Insurance	5,000	
Deposit on Franchise or Royalty Contract	25,000	
		63,000
TOTAL ASSETS		$ 311,550

Figure 3.2 Uniform Systems of Accounts for Restaurants (USAR)

Liabilities and Shareholders' Equity

Current Liabilities

Accounts Payable:		
Trade	$ 145,000	
Others	4,000	$ 149,550
Notes Payable—Banks		15,000
Taxes Collected		4,000
Accrued Expenses:		
Salaries and Wages	5,000	
Payroll Taxes	3,000	
Real Estate and Personal Property Taxes	4,000	
Rent	5,000	
Interest	2,000	
Utilities	1,000	
Other	2,000	22,000
Employees' Deposits		500
Deposits on Banquets		500
Income Taxes—State and Federal		7,000
Current Portion of Long-Term Debt		9,000
Dividends Declared and Payable		5,000
Total Current Liabilities		**212,500**
Due to officers, stockholders, partners		1,000
Due to affiliated or associated companies		2,000
Long-term debt, net of current portion		30,000
Deferred income taxes		9,000
Other noncurrent liabilities		7,000
TOTAL LIABILITIES		**261,550**

SHAREHOLDER'S EQUITY (if a Corporation):		
Capital Stock	5,000	
Description of Each Type of Stock,		
Shares Authorized and Issued,		
Stated Value per Share		
Paid-in Capital	30,000	
Retained Earnings	15,000	
Total Shareholders' Equity		**50,000**

NET WORTH (if an Individual Proprietor or Partnership):		
Proprietor's Account	50,000	
Partner A	25,000	
Partner B	25,000	
Total Net Worth	50,000	
TOTAL LIABILITIES AND CAPITAL		**$ 311,500**

Figure 3.2 *(Continued)*

MANAGER'S 10 POINT EFFECTIVENESS CHECKLIST

Evaluate your need for and the status of each of the following financial management tactics. For tactics you judge to be important but not yet in place, develop an action plan including completion date to implement the tactic.

TACTIC	DON'T AGREE (DON'T NEED)	AGREE (DONE)	AGREE (NOT DONE)	IF NOT DONE	
				WHO IS RESPONSIBLE?	TARGET COMPLETION DATE
1. The restaurant's accountant prepares a balance sheet at the end of each accounting period that meets the standards of the Uniform System of Accounts for Restaurants (National Restaurant Association).	❑	❑	❑		
2. The manager receives and studies a balance sheet at the end of each accounting period.	❑	❑	❑		
3. Cash banks are balanced on a daily basis.	❑	❑	❑		
4. Listings of current assets (excluding cash) are accurate and easy to identify.	❑	❑	❑		
5. An accurate accounts receivable list is maintained with effective collection efforts in place.	❑	❑	❑		
6. Physical inventories are taken at the end of each accounting period.	❑	❑	❑		
7. An accurate and up-to-date equipment inventory is in place.	❑	❑	❑		
8. An accurate and up-to-date accounts payable list is maintained.	❑	❑	❑		
9. Deposits for banquets are recorded as revenues (sales) when the event is held, *not* when payment is received.	❑	❑	❑		
10. The restaurant manager has discussed any areas of the balance sheet that do not conform to the USAR with the restaurant's accountant.	❑	❑	❑		

4

THE INCOME STATEMENT

MANAGER'S BRIEF

In this chapter you will examine the income statement. Also known as the profit and loss statement, or "P&L," this document details the revenue, expenses, and profit (or loss) generated by a restaurant during a fixed period of time. Like the balance sheet reviewed in the last chapter, the income statement is useful to managers, creditors, stockholders, and others because it focuses on the efficiency and profitability of a restaurant.

The income statement is prepared at the end of the accounting period (usually monthly). Following a format established by the Uniform System of Accounts for Restaurants (USAR), it first lists all of the restaurant's revenues. Next, all expenses incurred by the restaurant to generate its revenues are listed. The costs of sales (the cost of the food and beverage products sold by the restaurant) are listed and then costs related to labor are reported. These costs are followed by other direct and indirect costs, including marketing, utilities, repairs, and taxes.

Finally, the income statement identifies the amount of net income or loss. Since most restaurants operate as "for profit" entities, the income statement is a critical indicator of the manager's ability to meet identified profit objectives.

> **INCOME STATEMENT** Also known as a "profit and loss statement," this final output from the accounting cycle reports on the restaurant's profitability, including details regarding revenues earned and expenses incurred during a given period of time.

The **income statement** (also called "statement of operations," "income and expense statement," "profit and loss statement," and "earnings statement") reports the financial results of operating the restaurant. It is a flow statement, in contrast to the balance sheet (which relates only to the last day of the accounting period). As a flow statement, the income statement reflects the revenues and expenses of the entire accounting period.

USERS OF THE INCOME STATEMENT

The income statement is used by the same parties who use the balance sheet. Some consider it to be the most useful financial report. (In fact, no single statement yields sufficient information to serve as the sole basis for complex decisions. All statements, including footnotes, must be carefully studied and analyzed. For example, a restaurant could have had a very profitable year according to the income statement, yet have insufficient cash to make interest and principal payments during the next week; the result may yield to bankruptcy!)

How does income statement information meet the needs of external users (suppliers, bankers, investors, etc.) who are primarily interested in cash flows? Although the income statement does not directly reveal cash flows, it does show the restaurant's profitability. (Note: Profitability does not necessarily yield positive cash flows; however, profitable operations for several years generally suggest positive cash flows. Therefore, the income statement provides some indication of future cash flows.) Everything else being equal, the greater a restaurant's profitability, the more lenders will lend, the more credit suppliers will provide, and the higher the market value of the stock (if the business is a publicly traded corporation).

Taxing authorities are interested in the restaurant's operating results. Even though there are some differences between "taxable income" and "book income," the restaurant's tax returns contain much information found in the income statement. Corporate restaurant organizations whose stock is traded publicly are required to provide detailed financial information, including income statements, to the Securities and Exchange Commission annually.

The primary users of the income statement and its supplementary schedules are the restaurant's management. Years ago, most managers believed that they had an intuitive "feel" for the financial health of their business. Today, managers rely heavily on financial information to make decisions. This change is due, in part, to the increasing complexity of operations in restaurant chains, in which top managers are often geographically removed from their properties.

The income statement indicates revenues and expenses for a specific accounting period, which should then be compared to budget goals. The income statement and its supplementary schedules answer such questions as:

- What were revenues for the period?

- What were the food and beverage cost percentages?

- How much money was spent on advertising?

- What was the tax expense for the period?

- Were payroll costs kept within the budget?

Large restaurants may operate businesses using the concept of **responsibility accounting:** Revenues and expenses are reported separately for separate areas of responsibility. For example, a restaurant chain with five units and a different manager for each would generate separate statements for each unit. These reports would most likely contain revenues and expenses for the current and previous period in addition to the budget figures for the period. This concept can also be applied to a single unit. For example, revenues and costs can be separated (allocated), and the applicable managers can be held responsible for the food, beverage, and catering (banquet) operations.

RESPONSIBILITY ACCOUNTING The organization of accounting information on an income statement that focuses attention on results specific to one restaurant property (in the example of a restaurant chain) or one department (such as the food, beverage, or catering department) within a specific restaurant.

NATURE OF INCOME

The primary purpose of a restaurant is to increase the wealth of its owners. The operation of a successful restaurant over time results in net income. Does the amount of net income necessarily equal the increase in wealth of the owners? This depends on how wealth and net income are measured.

Wealth and Net Income

Net income, as reflected in the restaurant's income statement, occurs when revenues exceed expenses, both of which are based on recorded transactions. The owners' wealth, on the other hand, may increase because of increases in the value of the restaurant building(s) and land. This increase is not reflected on the income statement until the building(s) and land are sold. In this example, wealth is based upon market value: The market value of the net assets at the end of the period less the market value of the net assets at the beginning of the period, after allowing for owner contributions and withdrawals, equals the increase in wealth. By contrast, net income as reported in the income statement results primarily from the "transaction approach" to measuring revenues and expenses occurring during operations. The concept of income in this chapter is net income based on the transaction approach.

Revenues

Revenues result from the sale of food and beverage products and from the provision of other services, if any, that are central to the restaurant's operation. Increases in cash (assets) from business loans or from the sale of capital stock do not qualify as revenues. As well, increases in cash or other assets from a promise to perform, such as a cash receipt for a future banquet recorded as "deposit on banquets," do not qualify as revenues until the revenue has been earned (the banquet has occurred). For example, $100 is received for a banquet to be held two months in the future. Assets (cash) have increased but so have liabilities since the restaurant has the responsibility for future performance. In this case, no revenue is recognized when the cash is received. Instead, revenue

> **REVENUE** Inflows of assets (cash, check, credit card, or a promise to pay—a receivable) that result from the products and services sold to guests.

should be recognized when two conditions are satisfied:

- The earnings process is completed.

- An exchange has taken place.

The earnings process is completed when the food and beverage products have been produced and served to meet the guests' expectations. An exchange takes place as the products or services are provided to the guests, and either cash (or check or credit card) or a promise to pay in the future (a receivable) is received. In other words, revenue is recognized at the point of sale.

Expenses

Expenses occur as assets are used and/or as liabilities are incurred in the process of generating revenues as part of the restaurant's central operation. For example, the purchase of a fixed asset involves using cash (an asset), but since it does not occur in the process of delivering or producing goods, etc., this use is not recognized as an expense. (Recall

> **EXPENSES** Costs incurred by the restaurant to provide food and beverage products and services to guests.

that the amount of the fixed asset that is used each accounting period is recorded as a depreciation—which is an expense.) When a restaurant pays for labor to produce and serve food, this is clearly an expense.

Expenses are often categorized as direct or indirect. **Direct expenses** are closely related to the products and/or services provided to guests. For example, the cost of the food sold and the cost of labor to prepare and serve the food relates directly to the food sold. However, what about depreciation or the maintenance of the freezer in which the food was stored? These are commonly called **indirect expenses.** Recognizing direct expenses generally causes no problem; assessing indirect expenses is more difficult.

> **DIRECT EXPENSES** Expenses that are closely related to the products or services provided to guests. Examples include product costs, payroll, and related expenses.

Indirect costs are divided into two categories: (a) those recognized as expenses based upon a systematic and rational allocation and (b) those expensed immediately. An example of a systematic and rational allocation is depreciation expense. The cost of most fixed assets is systematically spread against revenue using an acceptable (rational) method of depreciation. Costs

> **INDIRECT EXPENSES** Costs include depreciation, interest expense, property taxes, and rent expense. Indirect costs can be recognized as an expense based upon a systematic and rational allocation method or can be expensed immediately.

with which no future revenues can be associated are expensed immediately; an example of this is the cost to settle a lawsuit.

Gains

Gains are increases in equity (net assets) that do not result from revenues or investments by owners.

A restaurant is not in business to invest in other businesses; however, it may buy shares in another business to invest idle cash. When the sale of this

GAINS Increases in equity (net assets) that do *not* result from revenues or investments by owners.

stock results in a greater amount than originally paid for the stock, the difference is classified as a gain. It is recorded in an account titled "gains on sale of marketable securities." Restaurants do invest in various fixed assets to provide guests with products and services. If, for example, a fixed asset such as a painting or specialized equipment is

| Income Statement |
| XYZ Restaurant |
| For the Year Ended December 31, 20XX |

Food sales
Cost of food sales
Gross profit
Operating expenses:
     Labor expenses
     Advertising
     Utilities
     Other operating expenses
     Rent
     Interest
     Depreciation
Income before gains and losses
     Gain on sale of equipment
     Loss due to flood
Income before income taxes
Income taxes
Net income

Note that the restaurant is reporting a gain from the sale of equipment, and, on the same invoice statement, a loss due to a flood.

Figure 4.1   Sample Income Statement Showing a Gain and a Loss

sold, a gain may be realized; the amount received may exceed the net book value. Since the sale was incidental to the purpose of the operation of the restaurant (to sell food/beverage products) this net asset increase is properly classified as a gain on the sale of fixed assets rather than as revenue.

Losses

Losses are decreases in equity (net assets) that do not result from expenses or distributions to owners.

In the example above, where a painting or specialized production equipment is sold, if the book value exceeds the proceeds, a loss is incurred. Other losses can result from natural catastrophes such as floods, earthquakes, and tornadoes. When the decrease

> **LOSSES Losses are decreases in equity (net assets) that do not result from expenses/distributions to owners.**

in an asset's book value (generally either a fixed asset or inventory) from a natural catastrophe is greater than the recovery from the insurance company, a loss results.

Gains and losses are normally reported in the income statement after results of operations are presented. Footnotes describing the gains and/or losses may provide clarification. A sample simplified income statement reporting a gain and a loss is shown in Figure 4.1. (Note: The income statement suggested by the Uniform System of Accounts for Restaurants [see next section] does not provide for the reporting of gains/losses.)

WWW: Internet Assistant

If you are interested in following trends in income statements, a good place to start is with a subscription to *Nation's Restaurant News* (NRN), which is the foodservice industry's weekly newspaper. To subscribe, go to

www.NRN.com

and select "Subscribe to NRN."

NRN, along with other trade magazines/resources, periodically compiles and publishes income statement operating ratios for a variety of foodservice industry segments.

CONTENT OF INCOME STATEMENT

The income statement should reflect the restaurant's revenues and expenses in the degree of detail that best meets users' needs. Generally, an income statement provided to outsiders (suppliers, bankers, investors, etc.) is less detailed than an income statement with supporting schedules provided to managers and owners.

The remainder of this chapter addresses income statement recommendations for management as suggested by the **Uniform System of Accounts** for Restaurants (USAR).[3] The USAR is highly recommended for internal users for several reasons:

- It is a time-tested system developed by the best accounting experts in the restaurant industry.

- It is revised as necessary to keep it current with changes in the industry.

- To make a reasonable comparison of a restaurant's operating results with published industry averages, it is necessary for financial statements to be prepared according to industry standard definitions, which are based on the USAR.

(Note: Industry statistics are issued annually by the NRA in conjunction with Deloitte & Touche, LLP.[4] Readers should be aware that averages are simply that: averages. Restaurants responding to the annual survey are located from Maine to California, are small to large, are independent to chain-affiliated, and offer fine dining to fast food. There is no single restaurant like the industry average; users of industry averages must use the information carefully.)

A final compelling reason for restaurateurs to adopt the USAR is that it provides an almost "turn-key" accounting system. Managers can rely on a time-tested system. The restaurant industry differs substantially from other industries, and these differences are reflected in the USAR. The USAR presented in this chapter should not be viewed as a system to be strictly followed; rather it is a flexible guideline to be adapted as desired by each user.

---

[3]*Uniform System of Accounts for Restaurants,* Seventh Edition, National Restaurant Association (Washington, D.C., 1996).

[4]*Restaurant Industry Operations Report,* National Restaurant Association (Washington, D.C. New issues are published yearly.)

Format of Statement

Figure 4.2 shows the USAR's Summary Statement of Income. Note that operating results are presented with details provided in 14 supplemental exhibits (schedules).

Sales

Sales are divided between food and beverage.

Cost of Sales

Food and beverage cost of sales are subtracted from food and beverage sales to determine gross profit from food and beverage sales.

> **UNIFORM SYSTEM OF ACCOUNTS** An accounting system including financial statement formats and dictionaries of financial terms developed specifically for the restaurant industry, which, with minimal modification if necessary, can be used to drive the accounting system for a specific restaurant.

The reporting of food sales and the related cost of food sales separately from beverage sales is useful for analyzing the restaurant's operation. Without this separation, an ineffective food operation could be covered up by a highly profitable beverage operation (or the reverse could occur).

Operating Expenses

The next major category on the USAR income statement is **operating expenses.** Note that all 11 line items under operating expenses have a supplementary schedule, which allows extensive detail for this major division of expenses. Operating expenses are those that are generally the direct responsibility of the restaurant's managers; in other words, they are influenced by the managers' operating policies and efficiencies. (Note: Two operating expenses [occupancy costs and depreciation] are not likely to be freely, if at all, within control of the manager.) [Generally, operating expenses should be charged to one of the major categories that comprise operating expenses.] Other income is subtracted from the operating expenses to determine "total operating expenses."

> **OPERATING EXPENSES** Expenses that are generally the direct responsibility of the restaurant's managers. The USAR provides detailed supplementary schedules for all operating expenses cited on the income statement.

All salaries and wages should be combined into one figure and shown as "salaries and wages." In a supplementary schedule, these can be separated by department, by position, etc. Separate categories should be shown for related labor expenses (employee benefits) as follows:

- payroll taxes
- insurance

Name of Restaurant Company

Description of Period Covered by Statement

	Exhibit	Amounts	Percentages
SALES:			
Food	D	$	%
Beverage	E		
Total Sales			
COST OF SALES:			
Food			
Beverage			
Total Cost of Sales			
Gross Profit			
OPERATING EXPENSES:			
Salaries and Wages	F		
Employee Benefits	G		
Direct Operating Expenses	H		
Music and Entertainment	I		
Marketing	J		
Utility Services	K		
General and Administrative Expenses	L		
Repairs and Maintenance	M		
Occupancy Costs	N		
Depreciation	N		
Other Income	O		
Total Operating Expenses			
Operating Income			
Interest	P		
Income Before Income Taxes			
Income Taxes			
NET INCOME		$	%

Figure 4.2   Summary Statement of Income

- employee meals
- other expenses

Expenses for uniforms, laundry, supplies, menus, kitchen fuel, etc., which are incidental to service in the dining areas and support in the kitchen and storage areas, are reported as "direct operating expenses."

Music and entertainment costs, if significant, should be shown separately. (Many restaurants offer little or no music or entertainment. If this expense is small, it may be recorded as "miscellaneous" within the direct operating expense category.)

The "marketing" category includes newspaper, magazine, and radio/television advertising and other expenses for outdoor signs, direct mailings, donations, and entertainment that promote the business.

"Utility services" include the cost of all utilities (except for kitchen fuel, which is treated as a direct operating expense). When facilities are rented and the restaurant pays the utilities, these should be recorded as "utilities" rather than rent.

The "general and administrative" category includes expenses generally classified as operating overhead. These are expenses that are considered necessary for the operation of the restaurant as opposed to being directly connected with serving guests. This category includes costs of office stationery, postage, telephone, data processing, general insurance, professional fees, protective services, etc.

"Repairs and maintenance" expenses include painting and decorating, maintenance contracts for elevators and machines, and repairs to the restaurant's various equipment and mechanical systems. Any expenditures for equipment should be capitalized. (See the discussion in chapter 12 for guidelines for recording expenditures as equipment.)

"Occupancy costs" include the costs of renting building(s) and land, property taxes, and insurance on fixed assets. These expenses will vary considerably between restaurants.

"Depreciation expense" is the result of depreciating buildings and furniture, fixtures, and equipment (FF&E). In addition, this expense should include the amortization of leaseholds and leasehold improvements. Note: As suggested earlier, owners/board members usually decide these expenses.

Gift and sundry shop sales, commissions from vending machines, telephone, etc., rentals of banquet rooms, and other miscellaneous sales are recorded as "other income."

Interest and Income Taxes

"Interest expense" is the cost of borrowing money and should be recorded in this account even if the interest incurred has not been paid. Unpaid interest must be accrued at the end of the applicable accounting period.

"Income before income taxes" is operating income minus interest.

Finally, "income taxes" are shown immediately before the bottom line for restaurants organized as corporations. This includes income taxes paid to all levels of government (federal, state, and city). Generally, restaurants organized as sole proprietorships or partnerships will not show income taxes, since these are the responsibility of the owners as individuals rather than the restaurant itself.

Reporting Gains and Losses

Even though the USAR does not include lines for reporting gains and losses, these must be shown as they occur. When a gain and/or loss occurs, a line "income before gain/loss" should be inserted prior to "income before income taxes." Then the gain/loss should be included followed by income before income taxes.

For example, assume a restaurant had operating income of $150,000, interest of $40,000, and a gain in sale of equipment of $20,000. The income statement would then show the following:

Operating income	$150,000
Interest	40,000
Income before gain on sale of equipment	110,000
Gain on sale of equipment	20,000
Income before income taxes	130,000

SUPPLEMENTARY SCHEDULES

The USAR's Summary Statement of Income (Figure 4.2) refers to supplementary schedules D through P. The content of these schedules is discussed in the remainder of this chapter. The actual schedules are not included in this text: Readers interested in greater detail are encouraged to obtain the Uniform System of Accounts for Restaurants from the National Restaurant Association.

- **Food sales.** Schedule D, for food sales, is designed to tell the number of meals served and dollar amounts by meal period, and then by dining area. Food sales should include sales of coffee, tea, milk, fruit juices, bottled water, and soft drinks if there is no service of liquor, wine, and beer. (If alcoholic beverages are sold, soft drinks are normally reported on the beverage sales schedule.)

  Another approach to reporting food sales is by menu item or food groups on the menu. This approach, though less common, is helpful in determining the best-selling menu items, and it lends itself to "menu engineering, a process in which menu items are classified by their profitability and popularity that enables managers to make menu planning and design decisions."[5]

  Bakery, takeout, and outside catering sales are also included in the food sales on this schedule.

- **Beverage sales.** The recommended schedule (Exhibit E) for beverage sales reports beverage sales by type of beverage (mixed drinks/cocktails, beer/ale, and wine) and by location (main bar/ service bar). In addition, if desirable, beverage sales may also be summarized by meal periods.

- **Salaries and wages.** The suggested salaries and wages schedule (Exhibit F) includes all payroll broken down for service, beverage, preparation, sanitation, purchasing/storing, administrative, and other. Under each section, the position is listed. For example, under sanitation, "warewashers," "porters," and "cleaners" are listed. For each position, the schedule reports the number of employees, the regular payroll, and any extra wages.

  When restaurants are organized as sole proprietorships or partnerships, the owners' payment(s) for their management efforts is not reflected as payroll, but rather as withdrawals from the business. Alternatively, the administrative payroll for incorporated restaurants generally includes officers' salaries. (In some cases, these salaries are disproportionately high, and this factor should be considered when comparing restaurants.)

---

[5]Michael L. Kasavana and Donald Smith, *Menu Engineering: A Practical Guide to Menu Analysis* (Okemos, Mich., 1990).

- *Employee benefits.* Employee benefits are detailed in Exhibit G with four major categories: payroll taxes, insurance, employees' meals, and other expenses. For example, details for the payroll taxes section are:

Federal retirement tax (FICA)	$XXX
Federal unemployment tax	XXX
State unemployment tax	XXX
State health insurance tax	XXX
Other payroll taxes	XXX
Total payroll taxes	$XXX

As with other supplementary schedules, Exhibit G must be adapted to the specific restaurant. For example, some restaurants are not subject to a state health insurance tax. Therefore, this line would not be used but would be replaced as necessary with other relevant expense items.

- *Direct operating expenses.* Direct operating expenses (DOE) are expenses directly involved in serving guests excluding product costs and direct labor. The USAR supplementary schedule for DOE (Exhibit H) includes the following expense categories: uniforms, laundry and dry cleaning, linen rental, tableware and linen, kitchen utensils, kitchen fuel, supplies, etc.

- *Music and entertainment.* The USAR recommends reporting the details of the music and entertainment expenses in Exhibit I using the following categories:

  ❏ Orchestras and musicians

  ❏ Professional entertainers

  ❏ Mechanical music

  ❏ Contractual wire services

  ❏ Piano rental and tuning

  ❏ Films, records, sheet music

  ❏ Programs

  ❏ Booking agent's fees

  ❏ Meals served to musicians and entertainers

Most restaurants do not incur all these expenses, so as with other schedules, Exhibit I must be revised as necessary.

- *Marketing.* The next supplementary schedule (Exhibit J) is for marketing. This includes diverse general areas such as selling/promotion expenses, advertising, public relations/publicity, fees/commissions, and research. Selling and promotion includes all in-house promotional efforts and direct mailings. Advertising relates primarily to outside marketing efforts such as newspaper advertising, radio and television advertising, outdoor signs, etc. Public relations and publicity encompasses community projects, donations, and goodwill-type expenditures. Fees/commissions expenses for advertising agencies and royalties and for fees paid to franchisors are included. Finally, the research segment relates to costs to develop new products and themes and includes payments to outside research agencies, travel costs relating to research, and product testing costs.

- *Utility services.* The utility services supplementary schedule (Exhibit K) shows the utilities expense for the restaurant, including amounts for electricity, electric bulbs, fuel, water, ice and refrigeration supplies, waste removal, and engineers' supplies. Restaurants that allocate or sell "utilities" to tenants, subtenants, or concessionaires should credit these accounts with the sales rather than reporting them as "other income." In addition, any waste or other items recycled for cash should be treated as a reduction in utility services.

- *General and administrative services.* Operating overhead expenses are reported on the supplementary schedule (Exhibit L) as general and administrative expenses. In general, these costs are related to operating the business rather than directly providing services to guests. This schedule lists items such as office stationery, postage, telephone and telegraph, data processing costs, dues and subscriptions, management fees, traveling expenses, insurance (general), collection and professional fees, protective services, sales taxes, etc.

  Several items listed above need clarification. Telephone and telegraph includes the rental of equipment and the cost of all calls with the exception of those relating to advertising and sales promotion. Traveling expenses in connection with the business are charged as an administrative and general expense except when the traveling is for business promotion. (Then it is charged to "selling and promotion.") The insurance (general) account should be charged with all insurance costs other than those relating directly to employees (which are charged to "employee benefits"). Insurance costs for fire and extended coverage on property and equipment are properly charged to "occupancy costs." Insurance included in this account includes fidelity bonds, public liability, burglary, robbery, etc. The sales tax account is charged when the restaurant pays the sales tax and has not collected it from guests.

- **Repairs and maintenance.** This schedule (Exhibit M) is used to report all repairs and maintenance expenses of the restaurant including detailed expenses for painting/decorating, maintenance contracts, plastering, upholstering, repairs to dining room furniture, repairs to kitchen equipment, etc. Expenditures to "repair" property and equipment that result in either extending the assets beyond original expectations or substantially increasing the restaurant's earning power should be capitalized rather than expensed. For example, a van that was estimated to have a three-year useful life is completely overhauled at a substantial cost at the end of year three of its life. The result is that the vehicle is expected to be useful for two additional years. This expenditure should be recorded as a fixed asset and then be depreciated over its new useful life rather than being expensed during the period in which the costs were incurred. Most repairs, however, are of a maintenance nature and should be expensed. Categories for classifying repairs in addition to those listed above are provided in this supplementary schedule and should be adapted as required by the restaurant.

- **Occupancy costs.** The next two supplementary schedules recommended by the USAR (Exhibit N) show occupancy costs including depreciation and amortization expenses. These include rent, real estate taxes, personal property taxes, insurance on building and contents, and other related accounts.

- **Other income.** "Other income" (Exhibit O) includes all foodservice operating income other than food and beverage sales. Other income includes net service charges, net gift and sundry shop sales, vending machine commissions, and similar revenues. Income resulting from sales

of tangible items (for example, gift and sundry shop) is the net difference between sales and cost of sales. Generally, the sales and cost of
sales should be shown on this schedule.

- **Interest expense.** The final schedule (Exhibit P) addresses interest expense. This supplemental schedule should detail interest by type of
  obligation such as bank loans, loans from owners, etc.

OTHER EXPENSES

Cost of Goods Sold

The cost of goods sold expense that follows the reporting of sales on the income
statement includes product costs of food and beverages sold. The cost of food
sold should be its actual cost after considering inventory on hand at the beginning and end of the accounting period, employee meals, and other factors. For
many retail businesses, the cost of goods sold is determined as: Beginning inventory + Purchases − Ending inventory. This model is not acceptable to many
restaurants because employee and complimentary meals are part of the cost of
food sold. A better model to calculate cost of food sold for restaurants is:

Beginning inventory (food)	$ _____	
Add:		
Food purchases including freight and		
delivery charges	_____	
Food available for sale		_____
Less:		
Ending inventory (food)	_____	
Cost of food consumed		_____
Less:		
Employee meals	_____	
Transfers to beverage	_____	
Add:		
Transfers from beverage		_____
Cost of food sold		_____

An example will illustrate the calculation of cost of food sold. A restaurant had $5,000 worth of food inventory at the beginning of the accounting period and $6,000 worth at the end of the period. During the period, $25,000 worth of food was purchased including delivery charges. Complimentary meals and employee meals totaled $500. The cost of food sold is determined as follows:

Beginning inventory	$ 5,000	
Add:		
Purchases of food	25,000	
Food available for sale		30,000
Less:		
Ending inventory	6,000	
Cost of food consumed		24,000
Less:		
Complimentary meals, etc.	500	
Cost of food sold		$23,500

The calculation of cost of beverages sold is similar to the calculation of the cost of food sold:

Beginning inventory		$ _____
Add:		
Purchases (including delivery charges)		_____
Transfers of beverages		_____
Total available		_____
Less:		
Ending inventory		_____
Cost of beverages sold		$ _____

Additional information about the calculation of food and beverage costs is reported in chapter 10.

Gross Profit

GROSS PROFIT   Total food and beverage sales minus total food and beverage cost of sales.

Gross profit results from subtracting the total cost of sales (Food cost + Beverage cost) from the total revenue generated from the sale of food and beverage products:

Sales
  Food   _____
  Beverage   _____
Total Sales   _____
Less Cost of Sales
  Food   _____
  Beverage   _____
Total Cost of Sales   (_____)
Gross Profit   =========

The separate listing of food sales/cost of sales and beverage sales/cost of sales enables the restaurant manager to easily calculate food/beverage percentages (cost of sales: food ÷ food sales; cost of sales: beverage ÷ beverage sales), which are integral to product control procedures. (This topic will be discussed fully in chapter 10.)

Service Charges

Some restaurants add a service charge representing a specified percentage to guests' checks in place of voluntary tipping. This amount (for service charges) is then distributed in whole or in part to employees. The USAR recommends that the service charges billed to guests be credited to a revenue account titled "service charges" that is part of the "other income" category on the summary statement of income. This approach, rather than recording service charges as sales, allows for better comparisons to other restaurants that do not add a service charge. When service charges are distributed to employees, the USAR recommends that they be charged to another "service charges" account. This yields the net amount of service charges, if any, retained by the restaurant.

Employee Meal Costs

Many restaurants give employees a complimentary meal after a specified number of hours worked. Failure to properly account for this cost can result in an overstatement of cost of food sold and an understatement of the cost of labor. Employee meal costs should be subtracted from the cost of food consumed when determining cost of food sold and should then be charged to a separate account titled "employee meals."

The process for calculating the cost of employee meals differs among restaurants. In theory, one could determine the actual food, labor, and overhead costs of preparing each employee meal. Few, if any, restaurant managers are willing to make this calculation, since the time and cost involved exceeds the value of the information received. In practice, only the cost of food is considered when determining employee meal cost; no labor or overhead are considered. Three practical approaches to determining the cost of employee meals follow:

- *Actual cost.* This approach involves determining the cost of each item served to employees by tracking food items served. For example, if the cost of a hamburger is $.60 and if 10 hamburgers are provided to employees, a $6.00 charge would be made to the employee meals account. All other food items provided to employees would be costed and charged to the employee meals account in the same manner.

- *Use of actual food cost percentage.* This model uses the restaurant's food cost percentage and sales value (potential selling price) of employee meals. The food cost percentage is multiplied by the sales value of total employee meals to determine the cost of employee meals. For example, assume the food cost percentage for a restaurant is 40% and that, during a seven-day period, the sales value of employee meals based on menu prices totaled $500. Then $200 ($500 × 40%) would be charged to the employee meals account.

- *Government allowable amount.* This model uses the amount allowed by the federal or state government. [For example, the federal government allows a specified amount per hour to be used in meeting its minimum wage requirement.] Assume $0.10 per hour is allowed. If all employees in a restaurant worked 820 hours in one week, the amount recorded as cost of employee meals would be $82 (820 hours × $0.10 per hour).

Depreciation

Fixed assets are purchased by the restaurant to produce the products and services sold to guests. They will benefit the property for several years; however, as the asset is used, it is slowly consumed through a process called **depreciation.**

DEPRECIATION The reduction in the value of a fixed asset.

Depreciation is an expense related to fixed assets. It can only be estimated over a short time period; it cannot be accurately measured. There are several alternative methods of depreciation available; some of those most widely used by restaurants will be discussed in chapter 12.

Income Taxes

Income taxes must be paid on a restaurant's profits to the federal and state governments and to some municipalities. Income taxes are shown on the summary statement of income just above net income.

Income taxes are a function of taxable income as defined by tax codes. "Taxable income" on the restaurant's tax return and "income before taxes" on the income statement are generally not the same. The differences between these two amounts are called timing and permanent differences. A **permanent tax difference** results when either a revenue or expense item recognized for book purposes is not recognized for tax purposes (or vice versa). A **timing difference** results from an expense or revenue item being included in one year for book purposes and in a different year for tax purposes. One expense that may cause a timing difference is depreciation. Assume a restaurant uses the straight-line depreciation method for book purposes and an accelerated depreciation method for tax purposes. Further, assume the amount of depreciation is $5,000 and $8,000 for book and tax purposes, respectively. The difference in taxable income and income before income taxes created by the different methods is $3,000. Everything else being equal, if the income before income taxes is $10,000, then taxable income is $7,000 ($10,000 − $3,000 = $7,000). Assuming a tax rate of 20% for book purposes, the income tax expense is $2,000, while only $1,400 is shown on the tax return. The journal entry to record the income taxes is as follows:

> **PERMANENT TAX DIFFERENCE** A difference between "taxable income" on the restaurant's tax return and "income before taxes" on the income statement, which results when either a revenue or an expense item recognized for book purposes is not recognized for tax purposes (or vice versa).

> **TIMING DIFFERENCE** The difference between "taxable income" on the restaurant's tax return and "income before taxes" on the income statement when an expense or revenue item is included in one year for book purposes and in a different year for tax purposes.

Income tax expense	2,000	
Income tax payable		1,400
Deferred income taxes		600

In the above example, the restaurant temporarily saved $600 in cash by using an accelerated method for income tax purposes even though it used the straight-line method to calculate depreciation for book purposes. This cash savings may be invested and generate increased earnings for the restaurant.

MANAGER'S 10 POINT EFFECTIVENESS CHECKLIST

Evaluate your need for and the status of each of the following financial management tactics. For tactics you judge to be important but not yet in place, develop an action plan including completion date to implement the tactic.

TACTIC	DON'T AGREE (DON'T NEED)	AGREE (DONE)	AGREE (NOT DONE)	IF NOT DONE	
				WHO IS RESPONSIBLE?	TARGET COMPLETION DATE
1. An income statement is available to the manager within several days of the end of each accounting period.	❑	❑	❑		
2. Responsibility accounting has been implemented where appropriate to hold department heads accountable for specified revenue and/or expense goals.	❑	❑	❑		
3. An accrual accounting system is in place; revenue is recorded only when the earnings process is complete and an exchange has taken place.	❑	❑	❑		
4. The income statement format follows that suggested by the NRA Uniform System of Accounts for Restaurants.	❑	❑	❑		
5. Food and beverage sales are reported separately if alcoholic beverages are sold.	❑	❑	❑		
6. The cost of employee salaries and wages is reported separately from the cost of employee benefits.	❑	❑	❑		
7. Appropriate supplementary schedules for the income statement are prepared and shared with the proper managers.	❑	❑	❑		
8. The cost of employee meals is recorded as a labor-related (not food) cost.	❑	❑	❑		
9. Using recommendations of the Uniform System of Accounts for Restaurants, all service charges, when collected, are recorded as "other income" rather than as revenue.	❑	❑	❑		
10. The manager and other affected personnel clearly understand the difference between "taxable income" on the restaurant's tax return and "income before taxes" on the income statement.	❑	❑	❑		

ANALYSIS AND INTERPRETATION OF
FINANCIAL STATEMENTS

MANAGER'S BRIEF

In this chapter you will learn about procedures managers can use to analyze and interpret their financial statements. Compiling financial information is useful only if the data is reviewed and understood by the managers so they can learn where the operation is doing well and, just as important, where improvements can be made.

You will discover the ways to differentiate between significant and insignificant variations in your analysis of operating results so time can efficiently be spent investigating only those variations that are unusual or unexplained.

Techniques used to compare one financial statement to another are presented in this chapter, as is ratio analysis: the process of comparing related information (most of which is presented in financial statements). Some important ratios such as that relating to cost of sales are presented and fully explained. Nonfinancial ratios can also help you understand your business, and these are presented as well.

A thorough understanding of techniques for reading and interpreting your financial statements is a critical managerial attribute and is one this chapter helps you to attain.

Much financial information can be produced for the restaurant each accounting period. Most is almost meaningless until it is analyzed and interpreted. For example, assume a restaurant's cost of food sales for a month is $34,348. By itself, this statistic is not useful. However, it may be compared to the prior month's figure of $32,942 to shed some meaning. It could also be related to food sales of $102,000 for the period, and the resulting ratio (food cost percentage) of 33.67% provides fuller meaning. Still another comparison would be to the budgeted cost of food sales of $35,000 and to the budgeted food cost percentage of 34%. These comparisons provide managers with considerable insight into the meaning of the $34,348 cost of food sales.

COMPARATIVE FINANCIAL STATEMENTS Balance sheets and/or income statements that show both the current year's (and month's) financial information and similar data for the previous year (month).

This chapter deals with the analysis and interpretation of financial statements. First, **comparative financial statements** and common-size statements are discussed. Then ratio analysis techniques for understanding financial statements are explained and applied to a hypothetical restaurant.

COMPARATIVE FINANCIAL STATEMENTS

Many restaurant managers compare the current year's (and month's) financial information to the prior year's (and month's) financial information to determine the absolute and relative differences between the financial information for the two periods.

Absolute and Relative Changes

ABSOLUTE CHANGES Changes in dollars for items between two accounting periods shown on a comparative financial statement.

Absolute changes show the change in dollars between the two periods. For example, in year 20X1, total sales were $500,000, while in year 20X2, total sales were $550,000. The absolute change is $50,000 ($550,000 − $500,000).

Relative changes show the percentage change from one period to the next. Using the above example, the relative change is 10% (absolute change [$50,000] ÷ 20X1 sales [$500,000]). Sometimes an absolute change may seem large (such as an increase in sales of $10,000,000);

> **RELATIVE CHANGES**
> Percentage change for items between two accounting periods shown on a comparative financial statement.

however, when compared to a sales base of $1,000,000,000, it represents only a 1% change and may be insignificant. Similarly, a relative change such as 100% may seem significant; however, if it is due, for example, to an absolute change in miscellaneous expense to $50 from $25 for the prior period (a 100% increase), it may not be worth management's study. Readers of comparative financial statements must, then, study both absolute and relative changes when analyzing figures.

Comparative Balance Sheets

Restaurants may provide both comparative balance sheets and comparative income statements. Figure 5.1 is a comparative balance sheet for the Smithville Restaurant on December 31, 20X1 and 20X2. Both absolute changes (amounts) and relative changes (percentages) are shown.

Changes of at least $10,000 and 10% are noted as follows:

- accounts receivable (net) increased by $48,000 (80.0%);

- current assets increased by $50,000 (50.0%); and

- accounts payable increased by $43,000 (100.0%).

All other balance sheet changes were less than $10,000 or 10%. Some of the changes exceeded $10,000 but were less than 10%; for example, the change in mortgage payable decreased $20,000 (6.7%). Other changes exceeded 10% but were less than $10,000; for example, the payroll payable increased 20.0% ($1,000).

The manager should be concerned about the major increase in accounts receivable. Failure to collect receivables may have resulted in a buildup in accounts payable. This concern should cause managers to review accounts receivable and payable. Some questions to be answered are:

- What caused the significant increase in accounts receivable?

- Are these accounts collectible?

- What is the age of the accounts receivable?

- What is the breakdown of the accounts payable?

Smithville Restaurant
December 31, 20X1 and 20X2

	20X1	20X2	Change from 20X1 to 20X2 Amount	Percentage
ASSETS				
Current Assets:				
Cash	$ 13,000	$ 15,000	$ 2,000	15.4%
Accounts receivable (net)	60,000	108,000	48,000	80.0%
Inventory	14,000	15,000	1,000	7.1%
Prepaid expenses	13,000	12,000	(1,000)	(7.7%)
Total	100,000	150,000	50,000	50.0%
Fixed Assets:				
Land	60,000	60,000	-----------	--------
Buildings	500,000	500,000	-----------	--------
Furniture and equipment	240,000	250,000	10,000	4.2%
Less: Accumulated depreciation	(230,000)	(245,000)	(15,000)	(6.5%)
Total	570,000	565,000	(5,000)	(0.9%)
Other Assets	80,000	75,000	(5,000)	(6.3%)
Total Assets	$750,000	$790,000	$40,000	5.3%
LIABILITIES				
Current Liabilities:				
Accounts payable	43,000	86,000	$43,000	100.0%
Payroll payable	5,000	6,000	1,000	20.0%
Income taxes payable	7,000	8,000	1,000	14.3%
Current portion of long-term debt	20,000	20,000	-----------	--------
Total	75,000	120,000	45,000	60.0%
Long-Term Debt:				
Notes payable	50,000	50,000	-----------	--------
Mortgage payable	300,000	280,000	(20,000)	(6.7%)
Less: Current portion due	(20,000)	(20,000)	-----------	--------
Total	330,000	310,000	(20,000)	(6.1%)
Total Liabilities	405,000	430,000	25,000	6.2%
STOCKHOLDERS' EQUITY				
Common stock	50,000	50,000	-----------	--------
Paid-in capital in excess of par	10,000	10,000	-----------	--------
Retained earnings	285,000	300,000	15,000	5.3%
Total	345,000	360,000	15,000	4.3%
Total liabilities and stockholders' equity	$750,000	$790,000	$40,000	5.3%

Figure 5.1   Smithville Restaurant Balance Sheets, December 31, 20X1 and 20X2

- Are suppliers being paid regularly?
- Have supplier relationships been damaged by the increase in accounts payable (which suggests slow payments to suppliers)?

Managers should concentrate on significant changes. In our example, the balance sheet items that were considered significant were those represented by changes of $10,000 and 10%. In practice, significance factors must be established by management and must be consistently applied.

Significance may differ by item. For example, significance factors for income statement items may be broader for revenues than for expenses and broader for variable expenses than for fixed expenses. Generally, the more control exercised over an income statement item, the smaller the significance factors.

Comparative Income Statements

Figure 5.2 shows the comparative income statements for the Smithville Restaurant for the two years ending December 31, 20X1 and 20X2. Note that the actual amounts are provided for years 20X1 and 20X2 along with absolute changes (amounts) and relative changes (percentages). The absolute and relative changes for each item have been determined in the same way as were changes for the comparative balance sheet.

> **SIGNIFICANCE FACTOR** The amount in dollars and percentage by which an item on a comparative financial statement must differ (present period to previous period) before management analysis and corrective action, if any, must be taken.

Assume **significance factors** are established as follows:

Item	Factors
Sales	$10,000 and 10%
Expenses:	
Cost of sales	$5,000 and 5%
Operating expenses	$5,000 and 5%

Based on the above factors the following items are of special concern:

- cost of food sales increased by $25,000 (11.1%) and
- cost of beverage sales increased by $5,000 (7.9%).

Smithville Restaurant
For the Years Ended December 31, 20X1 and 20X2

Change from 20X1 to 20X2

	20X1	20X2	Amount	Percentage
Sales:				
Food	$600,000	$630,000	$30,000	5.0%
Beverage	258,000	281,000	23,000	8.9%
Total	858,000	911,000	53,000	6.2%
Cost of Sales:				
Food	225,000	250,000	25,000	11.1%
Beverage	63,000	68,000	5,000	7.9%
Total	288,000	318,000	30,000	10.4%
Gross Profit:				
Food	375,000	380,000	5,000	1.3%
Beverage	195,000	213,000	18,000	9.2%
Total	570,000	593,000	23,000	4.0%
Operating Expenses:				
Payroll	234,000	245,000	11,000	4.7%
Employee benefits	38,000	40,000	2,000	5.3%
Direct operating expenses	42,000	45,000	3,000	7.1%
Music and entertainment	2,000	2,000	----------	--------
Marketing	19,000	20,000	1,000	5.3%
Utilities	26,000	28,000	2,000	7.7%
General and administrative services expenses	27,000	29,000	2,000	7.4%
Repairs and maintenance	13,000	13,000	----------	--------
Occupational costs	38,000	40,000	2,000	5.3%
Depreciation	24,000	25,000	1,000	4.2%
Total Operating Expenses	463,000	487,000	24,000	5.2%
Operating Income	107,000	106,000	(1,000)	1.0%
Interest	30,000	30,000	0	0%
Net Profit Before Income Tax	77,000	76,000	(1,000)	1.3%
Income Tax	23,000	23,000	----------	--------
Net Profit	$ 54,000	$ 53,000	$ (1,000)	(1.9%)

Figure 5.2   Smithville Restaurant Comparative Income Statements for the Years Ended December 31, 20X1 and 20X2

After determining the causes and resolving problems, if any, managers may elect to review other changes that came close to the significance factor, such as payroll (which increased by $11,000 [4.7%]).

Common-Size Financial Statements

The analysis process for comparative financial statements discussed above is called **horizontal analysis;** the reference point is to the earliest year, and each category of accounts is compared independently of the rest. By contrast, analysis of financial statements from top to bottom is called **vertical analysis.** Statements analyzed in this way are called **common-size financial statements.** This is an accurate description, because the dollar figures are reduced to percentages of the total shown on the statement. For example, a common-size balance sheet would show assets equal to 100%, and all asset categories would be expressed as a percentage of total assets.

> **HORIZONTAL ANALYSIS An analysis of comparative financial statements in which figures in each category of accounts are compared to each other, independently of other account categories.**

Sometimes it is more meaningful to compare an expense item with revenue than to compare the expense to a similar expense of the prior period. For example, comparing cost of food sold in a period with food sales of the same period is more meaningful than comparing cost of food sold for the current period with the prior period. This and similar comparisons will be discussed later in this chapter in the section on ratio analysis.

> **VERTICAL ANALYSIS The top to bottom analysis of common-size financial statements. For example, balance sheets allowing for vertical analysis would express total assets at 100%; individual asset categories would be stated as percentages of the total; income statements would express sales at 100% and each category of expense as a percentage of that total.**

Common-Size Balance Sheet

A common-size balance sheet reports dollar amounts of items for two periods and then compares the amounts relative to the total category of accounts for

> **COMMON-SIZE FINANCIAL STATEMENT A balance sheet or income statement reduced to percentages allowing for comparisons between accounting periods.**

each period. For example, assume cash and total assets are $10,000 and $200,000, respectively, at the end of year 20X1, and $12,000 and $180,000, respectively, at the end of year 20X2. The common-size balance sheet would show cash of $10,000 and $12,000 for the two years, and it would also show cash as a percentage of total assets (for example, 5% for 20X1 and 6.67% for 20X2).

There are two frequent instances when a common-size balance sheet can be helpful:

- When comparative statements reveal a potential problem
- When the manager wishes to compare financial statements from two or more different properties that are significantly different in size

Suppose, for example, the following data is reported on a comparative balance sheet:

	Year 1	Year 2	Change from Year 1 to Year 2	
			Dollar	**Percentage**
Cash	$ 100,000.00	$ 200,000.00	$ 100,000.00	100%
Total Assets	$1,000,000.00	$2,000,000.00	$1,000,000.00	100%

A common-size balance sheet would show the following:

	Year 1	Year 2	Common-Size	
			Year 1	**Year 2**
Cash	$ 100,000.00	$ 200,000.00	10%	10%
Total Assets	$1,000,000.00	$2,000,000.00	100%	100%

Review of the comparative balance sheet above may suggest an excess of cash; review of the common-size statement, however, reveals that, as a percentage of total assets, the amount of cash in Year 2 is in line with the amount of cash in Year 1.

Figure 5.3 shows the common-size balance sheets for the Smithville Restaurant for the years of 20X1 and 20X2.

Examination of Smithville Restaurant's common-size balance sheets suggests some important changes in the following areas:

- accounts receivable (net)—this increased from 8% of total assets (20X1) to 13.7% of total assets (20X2)
- accounts payable—this increased from 5.7% of total liabilities and stockholders' equity (20X1) to 10.9% of total liabilities and stockholders' equity(20X2)
- mortgage payable—this decreased from 40% (20X1) to 35.4% (20X2)

Smithville Restaurant
December 31, 20X1 and 20X2

	20X1	20X2	Common-Size 20X1	Common-Size 20X2
ASSETS				
Current Assets:				
Cash	$ 13,000	$ 15,000	1.7%	1.9%
Accounts receivable (net)	60,000	108,000	8.0%	13.7%
Inventory	14,000	15,000	1.9%	1.9%
Prepaid expenses	13,000	12,000	1.7%	1.5%
Total	100,000	150,000	13.3%	19.0%
Fixed Assets:				
Land	60,000	60,000	8.0%	7.6%
Buildings	500,000	500,000	66.7%	63.3%
Furniture and equipment	240,000	250,000	32.0%	31.6%
Less: Accumulated depreciation	(230,000)	(245,000)	(30.7)%	(31.0)%
Total	570,000	565,000	76.0%	71.5%
Other Assets	80,000	75,000	10.7%	9.5%
Total Assets	$750,000	$790,000	100.0%	100.0%
LIABILITIES				
Current Liabilities:				
Accounts payable	43,000	86,000	5.7%	10.9%
Payroll payable	5,000	6,000	0.7%	0.8%
Income taxes payable	7,000	8,000	0.9%	1.0%
Current portion of long-term debt	20,000	20,000	2.7%	2.5%
Total	75,000	120,000	10.0%	15.2%
Long-Term Debt:				
Notes payable	50,000	50,000	6.7%	6.3%
Mortgage payable	300,000	280,000	40.0%	35.4%
Less: Current portion due	(20,000)	(20,000)	(2.7)%	2.5%
Total	330,000	310,000	44.0%	39.2%
Total Liabilities	405,000	430,000	54.0%	54.4%
STOCKHOLDERS' EQUITY				
Common stock	50,000	50,000	6.7%	6.3%
Paid-in capital in excess of par	10,000	10,000	1.3%	1.3%
Retained earnings	285,000	300,000	38.0%	38.0%
Total	345,000	360,000	46.0%	45.6%
Total liabilities and stockholders' equity	$750,000	$790,000	100.0%	100.0%

Figure 5.3   Smithville Restaurant Common-Size Balance Sheets, December 31, 20X1 and 20X2

The buildup in accounts receivable and accounts payable was addressed previously. The reduction of 4.6% in mortgage payable should be studied. The decreased percentage is due to two factors. First, mortgage payable has declined by $20,000 (the amount reclassified as a current liability). Second, total liabilities and stockholders' equity have increased by $40,000 from 20X1 to 20X2.

Common-Size Income Statement

Figure 5.4 shows the common-size income statements for 20X1 and 20X2 for Smithville Restaurant. The dollar figures are shown just as they were on the comparative income statements (Figure 5.2). In addition, percentages are shown for each income statement classification for both years. Total sales equals 100%. Cost of food sales percentage is computed based on food sales as follows:

$$\textbf{20X2} \qquad\qquad \textbf{20X1}$$

$$\frac{\text{Cost of food sales}}{\text{Food sales}} \quad \frac{\$250{,}000}{\$630{,}000} = 39.7\% \qquad \frac{\$225{,}000}{\$600{,}000} = 37.5\%$$

Cost of beverage sales percentage is computed based on sales as follows:

$$\textbf{20X2} \qquad\qquad \textbf{20X1}$$

$$\frac{\text{Cost of beverage sales}}{\text{Beverage sales}} \quad \frac{\$68{,}000}{\$281{,}000} = 24.2\% \qquad \frac{\$63{,}000}{\$258{,}000} = 24.4\%$$

Total cost of sales percentage is based on total sales:

$$\textbf{20X2} \qquad\qquad \textbf{20X1}$$

$$\frac{\text{Total cost of sales}}{\text{Total Sales}} \quad \frac{\$318{,}000}{\$911{,}000} = 34.9\% \qquad \frac{\$288{,}000}{\$858{,}000} = 33.6\%$$

Gross profit percentage is based upon the differences between the sales for each product and its respective cost, expressed as a percentage:

Gross Profit Percentage: Food

$$\textbf{20X2} \qquad\qquad \textbf{20X1}$$

$$\frac{\text{Gross profit (food)}}{\text{Sales (food)}} \quad \frac{\$380{,}000}{\$630{,}000} = 60.3\% \qquad \frac{\$375{,}000}{\$600{,}000} = 62.5\%$$

Smithville Restaurant
For the Years Ended December 31, 20X1 and 20X2

	20X1	20X2	Common Size 20X1	Common Size 20X2
Sales:				
Food	$600,000	$630,000	69.9%	69.2%
Beverage	258,000	281,000	30.1%	30.8%
Total	858,000	911,000	100.0%	100.0%
Cost of Sales:				
Food	225,000	250,000	37.5%	39.7%
Beverage	63,000	68,000	24.4%	24.2%
Total	288,000	318,000	33.6%	34.9%
Gross Profit:				
Food	375,000	380,000	62.5%	60.3%
Beverage	195,000	213,000	75.6%	75.8%
Total	570,000	593,000	66.4%	65.1%
Operating Expenses:				
Payroll	234,000	245,000	27.3%	26.9%
Employee benefits	38,000	40,000	4.4%	4.4%
Direct operating expenses	42,000	45,000	4.9%	4.9%
Music and entertainment	2,000	2,000	0.2%	0.2%
Marketing	19,000	20,000	2.2%	2.2%
Utilities	26,000	28,000	3.0%	3.1%
General and administrative services expenses	27,000	29,000	3.1%	3.2%
Repairs and maintenance	13,000	13,000	1.5%	1.4%
Occupational costs	38,000	40,000	4.4%	4.4%
Depreciation	24,000	25,000	2.8%	2.7%
Total Operating Expenses	463,000	487,000	54.0%	53.5%
Operating Income	107,000	106,000	12.4%	11.6%
Interest	30,000	30,000	3.5%	3.3%
Net Profit Before Income Tax	77,000	76,000	8.9%	8.3%
Income Tax	23,000	23,000	2.7%	2.5%
Net Profit	$ 54,000	$ 53,000	6.2%	5.8%

Figure 5.4   Smithville Restaurant Common-Size Income Statement for the Years Ended December 31, 20X1 and 20X2.

Gross Profit Percentage: Beverage

20X2   **20X1**

$$\frac{\text{Gross profit (beverage)}}{\text{Sales (beverage)}} \quad \frac{\$213,000}{\$281,000} = 75.8\% \qquad \frac{\$195,000}{\$258,000} = 75.6\%$$

All other percentages in the income statement are computed based on total sales. For example, the depreciation percentage for 20X2 of 2.7% is the result of dividing $25,000 by $911,000.

Common-size income statements for a restaurant should be reviewed to determine significant changes over the prior period. As mentioned previously, managers must define what is significant. Once noted, managers should investigate to determine the cause of undesirable changes and take appropriate action to remedy the problem.

In Smithville Restaurant's common-size income statement the most significant change that requires investigation is the cost of food sales. The cost of food sales percentage increased from 37.5% to 39.7%. A number of factors may have caused this:

- Food costs increased faster than menu prices changed.

- The mix of food sales changed from the prior year with more relatively high-cost menu items being sold.

- The physical inventory of food at year-end is understated, resulting in higher food costs than actually occurred.

- The bookkeeper improperly recorded other expenditures as food purchases.

An investigation should determine the reason for the increase and, if unjustified, corrective action should be taken.

Other Comparisons

In addition to comparing the operating results to the prior year on a dollar and percentage basis, managers should also compare their operating results to their operating budgets. The comparison of actual data to the budget is preferred if only a single comparison is undertaken, because the budget not only considers prior year results but also expected internal/external changes for the current period.

Some restaurants also compare their operating results to foodservice industry averages. These averages are published jointly by the National Restaurant Association and Deloitte & Touche, LLP on an annual basis.[6] In the authors' judgment, industry averages are interesting but must be used with care. The preferred benchmark is budgeted figures for the specific restaurant; however, for the manager not using budgets, the industry averages can be of some help.

RATIO ANALYSIS

Discussion to this point has focused on data within a single financial statement. It is also helpful to compare figures on the balance sheet with the income statement and vice versa. For example, cost of food used may be compared to food inventory as a measure of the use of the food inventory. This process is commonly referred to as **ratio analysis.**

> **RATIO ANALYSIS** The comparison of related information, most of which is found on financial statements.

A **ratio** is the comparison of two figures and may be expressed in several ways: percentages (cost of food sold of 36%), times (the fixed asset turnover of 1.2 times), or dollars (earnings per share of $2.10). To be useful, there must be a meaningful relationship between the two numbers. For example, the cost of food sold compared to food sales yields a useful cost of food sold percentage. By contrast, bad debts expense compared to fixed assets yields a ratio that lacks usefulness.

> **RATIO** A ratio expresses the relationship between two numbers and is computed by dividing one number by the other number.

Many users of financial statements find ratios helpful. Different users have different interests: A food supplier is concerned about the restaurant's ability to pay an invoice; a bank that has made a long-term loan is concerned about the short- and long-run profit prospects of the restaurant. Department heads focus attention on revenue and expense information applicable to their departments. All the ratios presented in this section will be of interest to some, but not necessarily to all, users of financial information.

---

[6]*Restaurant Industry Operations Report,* National Restaurant Association (Washington, D.C. New issues are published yearly.)

Ratios are commonly divided into five classifications:

- liquidity
- solvency
- activity
- profitability
- operating

Selected dollar amounts from the Smithville Restaurant's comparative financial statements will be used to discuss ratios in this section. In addition, the following summations of accounts at the beginning of 20X1 will be used:

Working capital	$ 23,000
Accounts receivable	$ 54,000
Total inventory of food and beverages	$ 13,000[7]
Fixed assets	$550,000
Total assets	$740,000
Stockholders' equity	$325,000

Detailed operating amounts not shown in the financial statements earlier in the chapter for the two years are as follows:

	20X1	20X2
Charge sales	$600,000	$650,000
Rent expense	$ 10,000	$ 8,000
Cost of employee meals	$ 5,300	$ 5,400

Liquidity Ratios

LIQUIDITY RATIOS The category of ratios that indicates the restaurant's ability to pay its current obligations.

Ratios that reveal a restaurant's ability to pay current obligations are called **liquidity ratios.** A restaurant may be profitable but lack the cash to pay its bills on time; this can result in financial difficulties and, possibly, bankruptcy.

Liquidity ratios to be discussed are (1) current ratio, (2) accounts receivable to charge sales ratio, and (3) accounts receivable turnover ratio.

---

[7]Inventory consists of 60% food and 40% beverages.

Current Ratio. The best known liquidity ratio is

$$\text{Current ratio} = \frac{\text{Current assets}}{\text{Current liabilities}}$$

This ratio indicates the restaurant's ability to pay its current obligations in a reasonable period of time. Included in current assets are cash, accounts receivable, notes receivable, marketable securities, inventory, and prepaid items. It may take a few months to liquidate a restaurant's noncash current assets, and in the process, the conversion to cash may be short of the amount of stated assets; therefore, a current ratio of greater than 1 to 1 is preferred.

The Smithville Restaurant's current ratios for 20X1 and 20X2 are determined as follows (see Figure 5.1):

	20X1		20X2	
$\dfrac{\text{Current assets}}{\text{Current liabilities}}$	$\dfrac{\$100,000}{\$75,000}$	$= 1.33 \text{ to } 1$	$\dfrac{\$150,000}{\$120,000}$	$= 1.25 \text{ to } 1$

The **current ratio** is greater than 1 to 1 for both years. The two-year trend, however, is downward. Users must not only determine the ratio but evaluate it against related ratios. Also, trends for several periods should be assessed.

Term loans from financial institutions often require the borrower to maintain a specified current ratio. Failure to maintain the required current ratio can then be considered a violation of the loan agreement and may result in the lender calling the loan. Managers of restaurants with this type of requirement must carefully assess the current ratio at or near year-end to ensure compliance.

> **CURRENT RATIO** This liquidity ratio is a comparison of current assets to current liabilities and indicates the restaurant's ability to pay its current obligations in a reasonable time period.

> **ACCOUNTS RECEIVABLE TURNOVER RATIO** This liquidity ratio indicates the number of times during the period the average accounts receivable are converted to cash.

Accounts Receivable Turnover Ratio. The accounts receivable turnover ratio is determined as follows:

$$\text{Accounts receivable turnover} = \frac{\text{Charge sales}}{\text{Average accounts receivable}}$$

(Total sales are substituted for charge sales when charge sales are not known.) The accounts receivable turnover indicates the number of times during the period that average accounts receivable are converted to cash. Everything else being the same, the preference is for this ratio to be as high as possible.

For the Smithville Restaurant, the accounts receivable turnover ratios for 20X1 and 20X2 are as follows.

	20X1		20X2	
$\dfrac{\text{Charge sales}}{\text{Average accounts receivable}}$	$\dfrac{\$600,000}{\$57,000}$	$= 10.5$ times	$\dfrac{\$650,000}{\$84,000}$	$= 7.7$ times

The accounts receivable turnover for 20X1and 20X2 for Smithville Restaurant has decreased, suggesting the restaurant had more difficulty in collecting its accounts in 20X2 than in 20X1. (On the other hand, this may be due to a less restrictive credit policy resulting in an increase in charge sales of $50,000 [$650,000 − $600,000] from 20X1 to 20X2.)

The number of days in the accounting period under study (for example, one year = 365 days) can be divided by the accounts receivable turnover ratio to determine the average collection period:

$$\frac{365 \text{ days}}{7.7} = 47.4 \text{ days}$$

The result (47.4 days in the case of the Smithville Restaurant) should be compared to the terms of the property's sales; if payment is expected within 30 days, there is a problem. New accounts receivable collection tactics are in order. By contrast, if terms of sale are 60 days, no problem with the collection of accounts receivable appears to exist.

Solvency Ratios

> **SOLVENCY** The ability of a restaurant to meet its long-term financial obligations as they become due.

Solvency refers to the ability of a restaurant to meet its financial obligations as they become due. Solvency ratios include (1) the solvency ratio, (2) the debt-equity ratio, and (3) the number of times interest earned ratio.

A restaurant is solvent when its assets exceed its liabilities. Assets in the form of cash are received from stockholders, from successful operations (although the relationship between profits and cash is indirect), and finally, by borrowing from lenders. The risk of insolvency is increased when a restaurant relies more heavily on debt financing than financing provided by stockholders and internally generated financing.

The first two solvency ratios we will discuss approach risk from a balance sheet perspective (each is looking at debt compared to other elements of the balance sheet). The final ratio (number of times interest earned ratio) addresses risk from an income statement perspective. (It looks at the coverage of interest by operations.)

Solvency Ratio. The **solvency ratio** is a measure of total assets against total liabilities:

> **SOLVENCY RATIO A ratio that measures total assets against total liabilities.**

$$\text{Solvency ratio} = \frac{\text{Total assets}}{\text{Total liabilities}}$$

This ratio measures the restaurant's ability to pay debts with its assets and assumes the assets can be liquidated at net book value. To the extent that this ratio exceeds 1.0, a cushion is provided for liquidating the assets for less than the value they carry on the books.

The solvency ratios for the Smithville Restaurant for 20X1 and 20X2 follow:

	20X1		**20X2**	
$\dfrac{\text{Total assets}}{\text{Total liabilities}}$	$\dfrac{\$750,000}{\$405,000}$	$= 1.85$	$\dfrac{\$790,000}{\$430,000}$	$= 1.84$

The above suggests a slight decrease in the safety of the lenders' debt from 20X1 to 20X2; the restaurant's ability to obtain additional debt financing has decreased slightly.

> **DEBT-EQUITY RATIO This ratio compares equity to total liabilities; in other words, it contrasts the amount of money that creditors have loaned the restaurant to the number of dollars owners have invested in the restaurant.**

Debt-Equity Ratio. The **debt-equity ratio** is a second example of a solvency ratio. It looks at debt, but compares it to stockholders' equity:

$$\text{Debt-equity ratio} = \frac{\text{Total liabilities}}{\text{Total equity}}$$

For Smithville Restaurant the debt-equity ratios for 20X1 and 20X2 follow:

$$\underline{\text{20X1}} \qquad\qquad\qquad \underline{\text{20X2}}$$

$$\frac{\text{Total liabilities}}{\text{Total equity}} \quad \frac{\$405,000}{\$345,000} = 117.4\% \qquad \frac{\$430,000}{\$360,000} = 119.4\%$$

The restaurant's creditors have loaned it $1.17 and $1.19 for 20X1 and 20X2, respectively, for each dollar the owners have invested. This ratio also suggests the creditworthiness has decreased slightly from 20X1 to 20X2.

FINANCIAL LEVERAGING Debt financing used to improve operating results to increase the return on the owners' investment.

As long as the restaurant can generate earnings from borrowing that exceed the cost of debt, additional borrowing is wise. This process of increasing earnings by borrowing is called **financial leveraging** and is done by many restaurants.

Number of Times Interest Earned Ratio. The **number of times interest earned ratio** correlates figures from the income statement:

$$\text{Number of times interest earned} = \frac{\text{Operating income}}{\text{Interest expense}}$$

NUMBER OF TIMES INTEREST EARNED RATIO This ratio generally indicates how many times the interest expense could be paid given the restaurant's operating income and interest expense for the period.

This ratio basically indicates how many times the interest expense could be paid given the operating income and interest expense for the period. Note: Recall that interest is paid with cash *not* profits. (To obtain operating income, income taxes are added back to net income, since interest expense is deductible in calculating income taxes.)

For Smithville Restaurant, the number of times interest earned ratio follows:

$$\underline{\text{20X1}} \qquad\qquad\qquad \underline{\text{20X2}}$$

$$\frac{\text{Operating income}}{\text{Interest expense}} \quad \frac{\$107,000}{\$30,000} = 3.57 \text{ times} \qquad \frac{\$106,000}{\$30,000} = 3.53 \text{ times}$$

The results reveal a very minor decrease in this ratio and, therefore, a slight increase in the risk of lending to Smithville Restaurant. Further, profits could decline significantly and the restaurant would still be able to make its interest payments.

Activity Ratios

Activity ratios show how effectively a restaurant uses its resources. The major activity ratios, based on amounts from the financial records, include (1) inventory turnover, (2) fixed asset turnover, and (3) asset turnover. An important nonfinancial activity ratio relates to (4) seat turnover.

> **ACTIVITY RATIOS** These ratios indicate how effectively the restaurant uses its resources.

Managers are given resources to produce quality goods and services to guests and a profit for owners. These ratios measure the manager's performance, and are also useful to the manager for planning purposes.

Inventory Turnover Ratio. The formula for the inventory turnover ratio is:

> **INVENTORY TURNOVER RATIO** This activity ratio, calculated separately for food and beverage products, assesses the manager's efficiency in using product inventory and is determined by dividing the cost of goods used by average inventory.

$$\text{Inventory turnover} = \frac{\text{Cost of goods used}}{\text{Average inventory}}$$

This ratio should be calculated separately for food and beverages. The results are a function of a manager's efficiency in using inventory. The ratio generally relates directly to the type of restaurant: a fast food operation usually has a much higher (faster) food inventory turnover than does a full-menu restaurant.

Cost of goods *used* is recommended for the numerator of this ratio, although some writers suggest using cost of goods *sold*. (A restaurant often produces a product provided to its employees as part of its remuneration package: employee meals. These and other uses of goods should be added to cost of goods *sold* to equal cost of goods *used*.) The average inventory is the average of the sums of the monthly beginning and ending inventories of food or beverage products.

The food inventory turnovers for the Smithville Restaurant for 20X1 and 20X2 are calculated as follows:

	20X1		20X2	
$\dfrac{\text{Cost of food used}}{\text{Average food inventory}}$	$\dfrac{\$230,300^8}{\$8,100^9}$	= 28.4 times	$\dfrac{\$255,500}{\$8,700}$	= 29.4 times

[8]Cost of food sold plus cost of employee meals. For 20X1, the cost of food sold was $225,000; cost of employee meals was $5,300 to equal $230,300.

[9]The average food inventory is the result of dividing the sum of the beginning and ending food inventories by two. For 20X1, beginning food inventory was $7,800 (13,000 × 60%) while the ending food inventory was $8,400 (14,000 × 60%). Then ($7,800 + $8,400) ÷ 2 = $8,100.

These results indicate that the Smithville Restaurant is turning over its food inventory faster in 20X2 than 20X1. A food inventory turnover of 29.4 times per year is equivalent to approximately every 12.5 days (365/29.4). Restaurants may have food delivered at least weekly, so the manager should strive to increase the food inventory turnover to reflect greater efficiency. Some foodservice industry segments, including fast food restaurants, turn their food inventory over several times weekly. As long as there is an adequate food inventory to generate required sales with few stockouts, higher food inventory turnover ratios are better.

FIXED ASSET TURNOVER RATIO **This activity ratio measures the relationship between the revenues generated by fixed assets and the net book value of the fixed assets.**

Fixed Asset Turnover Ratio. A second activity ratio, **fixed asset turnover,** measures the relationship between the revenues generated by fixed assets and the net book value of the fixed assets. (Fixed assets constitute the majority of many restaurants' assets.)

This ratio is computed as follows:

$$\text{Fixed asset turnover} = \frac{\text{Total revenue}}{\text{Average fixed assets}}$$

Generally total revenue, including income related to investments, constitutes the denominator of this ratio and is used in computing Smithville Restaurant's fixed asset turnover for 20X1 and 20X2 as follows:

20X1	20X2
$\dfrac{\text{Total revenue}}{\text{Average fixed assets}}$ $\dfrac{\$858,000}{\$560,000} = 1.5 \text{ times}$	$\dfrac{\$911,000}{\$567,500} = 1.6 \text{ times}$

These results suggest that the Smithville Restaurant made better use of its fixed assets in 20X2 than in 20X1. However, further evaluation is required, since the major change is the increase of revenues by $53,000. The manager should determine how much of the revenue increase is due to inflation (price increases) rather than to more food and beverage items sold.

ASSET TURNOVER RATIO **This activity ratio suggests the change, if any, in the use of total assets.**

Asset Turnover Ratio. The **asset turnover ratio** also considers total revenue and fixed assets.

The asset turnover ratio is calculated as follows:

$$\text{Asset turnover ratio} = \frac{\text{Total revenue}}{\text{Average total assets}}$$

Smithville Restaurant's asset turnover ratios for the two years are calculated as follows:

	20X1		**20X2**	
$\dfrac{\text{Total revenue}}{\text{Average total assets}}$	$\dfrac{\$858,000}{\$745,000}$	$= 1.15$ times	$\dfrac{\$911,000}{\$770,000}$	$= 1.18$ times

The results suggest little change in the use of total assets by Smithville Restaurant for 20X2 as compared to 20X1.

Seat Turnover Ratio. The **seat turnover ratio** is nonfinancial and is determined by dividing the number of guests served by the number of the seats in the restaurant. It is desirable for planning purposes to calculate the turnover by meal period, by day of the week, and by season. For example, a restaurant may experience a seat turnover of 1.5 at lunch on Monday through Friday but have a significantly lower seat

> **SEAT TURNOVER RATIO** This nonfinancial activity ratio is calculated by dividing the number of guests by the number of seats in the restaurant or lounge/bar. This ratio measures the rate at which guests are served.

turnover on the weekends. Further, the restaurant may experience seasonal differences such as significantly smaller sales during summers, as experienced by some restaurants in college towns.

The seat turnover ratio should also be calculated for each profit center of the business, i.e., for the restaurant separate from the bar/lounge.

The Smithville Restaurant has 120 seats; its lounge has 40 seats. During 20X1 and 20X2, 90,000 and 91,000 guests, respectively, were served in the restaurant. The daily seat turnovers for the restaurant for the two years are calculated as follows:

	20X1		**20X2**	
$\dfrac{\text{Guests served}}{\text{Days open} \times \text{Available seats}}$	$\dfrac{90,000}{120 \times 365}$	$= 2.05$	$\dfrac{91,000}{120 \times 365}$	$= 2.08$

The results show that on the average, the restaurant seats were turned over 2.05 times in 20X1 and 2.08 times in 20X2. This ratio is a good measure of activity, since economics (inflation) is excluded from both elements of the formula.

The seat turnover will vary greatly by type of restaurant: fast food operations generally have the highest seat turnover; full menu, table service restaurants have lower seat turnover.

Profitability Ratios

Profitability ratios relate the bottom line (net income) or the income before income taxes to various measures of capacity.

Profitability ratios include (1) return on owners' equity, (2) return on assets, (3) profit margin, (4) operating efficiency, and (5) earnings per share.

Return on Owners' Equity Ratio. The **return on owners' equity ratio** is computed as follows:

$$\text{Return on owners' equity ratio} = \frac{\text{Net income}}{\text{Average owners' equity}}$$

This ratio indicates the percentage of average owners' equity earned during the period. The Smithville Restaurant's return on owners' equity ratios for 20X1 and 20X2 follow:

	20X1		**20X2**	
$\dfrac{\text{Net income}}{\text{Average owners' equity}}$	$\dfrac{\$54,000}{\$335,000}$	$= \underline{\underline{16.1\%}}$	$\dfrac{\$53,000}{\$352,500}$	$= \underline{\underline{15\%}}$

Profitability relative to the average owners' equity has declined from 20X1 to 20X2. This is an effect of decreased net income and increased average owners' equity in 20X2 over 20X1.

When evaluating this ratio, the user needs to consider whether the average owners' equity is reflective of the market value of the restaurant. If the average owners' equity according to the financial statements is a reasonable representation of market value, then the owner should compare this return to the alternative investment opportunities.

Return on Assets Ratio. The **return on assets ratio** compares the restaurant's earnings for the period to the average total assets. It tells how well managers have used assets to generate profits. The ratio follows:

$$\text{Return on assets ratio} = \frac{\text{Net income}}{\text{Average total assets}}$$

Smithville Restaurant's return on assets ratios for 20X1and 20X2 are computed as follows:

	20X1		**20X2**	
$\dfrac{\text{Net income}}{\text{Average total assets}}$	$\dfrac{\$ 54,000}{\$745,000}$	$= 7.3\%$	$\dfrac{\$53,000}{\$770,000}$	$= 6.9\%$

Consistent with other profitability ratios discussed to this point, this ratio shows a decline in profitability for Smithville Restaurant from 20X2 compared to 20X1.

Profit Margin Ratio. The **profit margin ratio** reflects the net income for the restaurant to its total revenues:

$$\text{Profit margin} = \frac{\text{Net income}}{\text{Total revenue}}$$

This ratio is also part of a common-size income statement and is considered an operating ratio. As an indicator of overall operating and financial efficiency, managers, owners, and lenders consider the profit margin ratio to be important.

Smithville Restaurant's profit margins for 20X1 and 20X2 follow:

	20X1		**20X2**	
$\dfrac{\text{Net income}}{\text{Total revenue}}$	$\dfrac{\$54,000}{\$858,000}$	$= 6.3\%$	$\dfrac{\$53,000}{\$911,000}$	$= 5.8\%$

This ratio, as does other profitability ratios, reflects a less profitable year in 20X2 than in 20X1. However, the profits generated in 20X2 may be adequate. In this case, even if profits had been as high as $57,300 for 20X2, the profit margin for 20X2 would have been less than the previous year.

Managerial Operating Efficiency Ratio. This ratio is useful in measuring profitability from management's perspective. When reviewing an income statement for a restaurant, the manager is generally held accountable for revenues, cost of sales, and controllable expenses. For the income statement prepared according to the Uniform System of Accounts for Restaurants (NRA, 1996)[10], the manager is responsible for operations down to the level of "operating income." Note, however, that two expenses (occupational costs and depreciation) are *not* generally within the manager's control. A more realistic definition of managerial operating efficiency might be:

> **MANAGERIAL OPERATING EFFICIENCY RATIO This profitability ratio measures the manager's performance by comparing those cost categories most in his/her control with total revenue (which is also within the manager's control).**

$$\text{Total operating expenses} - (\text{Occupancy costs} + \text{Depreciation})$$

Expenses below this line generally relate to decisions by the owner. The operating efficiency ratio is calculated as follows:

Managerial operating
   efficiency ratio

$$= \frac{\text{Operating income} + \text{Depreciation} + \text{Occupancy expenses}}{\text{Total income}}$$

The **managerial operating efficiency ratios** for Smithville Restaurant follow:

	20X1	20X2
$\dfrac{\text{Operating income} + \text{Depreciation} + \text{Occupancy expenses}}{\text{Total revenue}}$	$\dfrac{\$169,000}{\$858,000} = 19.7\%$	$\dfrac{\$171,000}{\$911,000} = 18.8\%$

[10]*Uniform System of Accounts for Restaurants,* Seventh Edition, National Restaurant Association (Washington, D.C., 1996).

The restaurant's operating income adjusted by depreciation and occupancy expense increased from 20X1 to 20X2 but by a lesser percentage than did the increase in total revenue. This resulted in a decline in the operating efficiency ratio from 19.7% to 18.8%.

Earnings Per Share (EPS) Ratio.   The **earnings per share ratio** is calculated for corporations that issue stock to stockholders. Corporations whose stock is not publicly traded have little or no interest in this ratio.

> **EARNINGS PER SHARE (EPS) RATIO** This profitability ratio indicates the average amount of net income generated per outstanding share of common stock issued.

For those restaurants interested in earnings per share (EPS), the calculation is dependent upon its capital structure. Assume the restaurant has a single class of stock: common stock. Earnings per share is determined as follows:

$$EPS = \frac{\text{Net income}}{\text{Average number of shares outstanding}}$$

However, if the restaurant has a second class of stock (such as preferred stock) then the calculation of EPS is:

$$EPS = \frac{\text{Net income} - \text{Preferred dividends}}{\text{Average number of common shares outstanding}}$$

This calculation becomes more complex when a corporation has preferred stock or debt that is convertible to common stock. These more complex situations are beyond the scope of this text.

Smithville Restaurant had 10,000 shares outstanding throughout 20X1 and 20X2. Therefore, the EPS for 20X1 and 20X2 are $5.40 and $5.30, respectively:

	20X1		20X2	
$\dfrac{\text{Net income}}{\text{Avg. no. common shares outstanding}}$	$\dfrac{\$54,000}{10,000}$	$= \$5.40$	$\dfrac{\$53,000}{10,000}$	$= \$5.30$

Operating Ratios

Numerous ratios can be used to analyze a restaurant's operation. The preparation of common-size income statements (for example, relating expenses to

OPERATING RATIOS These ratios help managers to analyze their restaurant operation. They relate revenue/expense accounts summarized in a common-size income statement.

sales) provides examples of many **operating ratios.** Therefore, major operating ratios indicated in a common-size income statement are covered only briefly. Other operating ratios will also be presented.

Food/Beverage Sales Ratio. Common ratios in analyzing sales include the mix of food and beverage sales. **Food/beverage sales ratios** are determined by dividing the food or beverage sales by the total sales: Food sales ÷ Total sales = Food sales percentage; Beverage sales ÷ Total sales = Beverage sales percentage.

FOOD/BEVERAGE SALES RATIOS These operating ratios indicate the percentage of total sales generated by the food and beverage operations.

The Smithville Restaurant's food and beverage sales percentages for the two years are calculated as follows:

	20X1		20X2	
$\dfrac{\text{Food sales}}{\text{Total sales}}$	$\dfrac{\$600,000}{\$858,000}$	$= 69.9\%$	$\dfrac{\$630,000}{\$911,000}$	$= 69.2\%$
$\dfrac{\text{Beverage sales}}{\text{Total sales}}$	$\dfrac{\$258,000}{\$858,000}$	$= 30.1\%$	$\dfrac{\$281,000}{\$911,000}$	$= 30.8\%$

FOOD AND BEVERAGE SALES PER SEAT RATIOS These operating ratios indicate the dollars of food sales generated by each restaurant seat (food sales per seat) and the number of beverage sales represented by each seat in the lounge, bar, or other beverage-service area (beverage sales per seat).

The trend of increasing beverage sales relative to food sales from 20X1 and 20X2 suggests greater profits for 20X2 over 20X1 for the Smithville Restaurant, since there is generally a higher contribution margin (revenue − product cost) from beverage sales.

Sales Per Seat Ratio. A restaurant has a limited number of seats; the greater the sales per seat, the higher the potential profits. For Smithville Restaurant, the **food and beverage sales per seat ratios** are calculated as follows:

	20X1		20X2	
$\dfrac{\text{Food sales}}{\text{Restaurant seats}}$	$\dfrac{\$600,000}{120}$	$= \$5,000$	$\dfrac{\$630,000}{120}$	$= \$5,250$

$$\frac{\text{Beverage sales}}{\text{Beverage dept. seats}} \quad \frac{\$258,000}{40} = \$6,450 \qquad \frac{\$281,000}{40} = \$7,025$$

Note: This analysis assumes all food sales are in the restaurant and all beverage sales are in the lounge. In practice, beverage sales are also generated in the restaurant, and food sales are made in the lounge.

The above results show greater sales per seat for beverages than for food and also indicate that the sales per seat in both operations increased in 20X2 over the previous year.

Cost of Sales Ratio. Cost of sales ratios are determined by dividing cost of sales by sales for each type of sale. For example, the cost of food sold percentage results from dividing cost of food sold by food sales. The restaurant should not incorporate cost of food *used* in this ratio. Employee meals and food used to garnish beverages, for example, actually reduce the cost of food used to generate food sales. One, employee meals, is actually a labor cost. The other, beverage garnishes, is a beverage cost since it generates beverage revenue. In part, the cost of food sold is a function of portion sizes, quality of food purchased, amount of spoilage and other waste, theft, etc. For Smithville Restaurant, the cost of sales percentages for food and beverages are determined as follows:

> **COST OF SALES RATIOS These operating ratios indicate the percentage of product (food or beverage) sales needed to purchase the product (food or beverage) required to generate the sale.**

	20X1		**20X2**	
$\dfrac{\text{Cost of food sold}}{\text{Food sales}}$	$\dfrac{\$225,000}{\$600,000}$	$= 37.5\%$	$\dfrac{\$250,000}{\$630,000}$	$= 39.7\%$
$\dfrac{\text{Cost of beverages sold}}{\text{Beverage sales}}$	$\dfrac{\$63,000}{\$258,000}$	$= 24.4\%$	$\dfrac{\$68,000}{\$281,000}$	$= 24.2\%$

The increase in cost of food sales percentage in 20X2 over the previous year is a management concern. The cost of beverages sold percentage has changed very little between the two years being analyzed.

Labor Cost Ratio. For many restaurants, the second largest expense after product cost is labor. Labor costs include both the payroll and employee benefits shown on the income statement. The **labor cost ratio** is determined as follows:

$$\text{Labor cost ratio} = \frac{\text{Labor costs}}{\text{Total sales}}$$

In addition to this general labor cost percentage calculation, labor costs incurred by revenue-producing departments may be compared to their respective sales. For example, identifiable labor costs of the restaurant (food operation), can be divided by food sales to yield a food department labor cost percentage. Further, the major labor categories may be calculated as a percentage of the total payroll costs. A possible format follows:

Labor category	Payroll costs	Percentage[11]
Food Service	$	%
Beverages		
Preparation		
Sanitation		
Purchasing/Storing		
Administrative		
Other		
Total		

Other commonly used labor ratios include:

- total sales per full-time equivalent employee (FTE)
- food sales per FTE
- beverage sales per FTE
- average hourly wage per employee

Each ratio can be used by management to control labor costs. The best evaluation of labor cost is the result of computing several labor ratios rather than using only one or two.

---

[11]Percentage of total labor costs.

The cost of labor percentage for Smithville Restaurant for the two years follows:

	20X1		20X2	
$\dfrac{\text{Labor costs}}{\text{Total sales}}$	$\dfrac{\$272,000}{\$858,000}$	$= 31.7\%$	$\dfrac{\$295,000}{\$911,000}$	$= 32.4\%$

The results show a two-year trend increase, which, although not significant, should be closely monitored since labor is a major controllable expense.

Operating Expense Ratios.   Other controllable expenses, including direct operating expenses, repairs and maintenance, and related costs, should be analyzed by comparison to total revenue. For example, utilities expense divided by total revenue yields the utilities expense percentage. For Smithville Restaurant, the utilities expense percentage for 20X1 and 20X2 follows:

	20X1		20X2	
$\dfrac{\text{Utilities expense}}{\text{Total revenue}}$	$\dfrac{\$26,000}{\$858,000}$	$= 3.0\%$	$\dfrac{\$28,000}{\$911,000}$	$= 3.1\%$

The results reveal a slight increase in 20X2 over 20X1. The manager must carefully analyze operating expenses by comparing them to revenue. Certain expenses consist of both fixed and variable elements; i.e., part of the expense is fixed while the remaining varies directly with revenue. Therefore, as the total sales increase, everything else being equal, the expense percentage based on total revenue should decline. Note: The concept of costs will be discussed in detail in chapter 7. **Operating expense ratios** should be calculated for all categories of controllable expenses.

> **OPERATING EXPENSE RATIOS**
> These ratios represent the amount of total sales utilized for various categories of operating expenses such as direct operating expenses, repairs and maintenance, and related costs.

Bases for Comparison

Ratios by themselves are nearly meaningless. However, when compared to a relevant financial base, they may be extremely valuable analysis tools. There are four major bases for comparison of ratios:

- budget (plan)
- prior period information

- industry averages
- specific competition

Comparison to the budget (plan) is preferred, because an effective budget should consider the past, the competition, and expectations for the future. Comparisons to prior periods are common but should not be considered too seriously since most restaurants operate in a dynamic environment.

Industry averages are simply that—averages. Surveys made to determine the averages consider restaurants over vast geographical areas, using different approaches to marketing, producing, and serving products and with different organizational structures. There may be no single firm that is like the average. A new operation may find averages useful but should be extremely cautious in making comparisons to them.

Specific competitors' ratios may be useful when the firms are similar. Generally, however, the competition is different, and detailed information is unavailable so comparisons between one's restaurant and the competition will not be accurate.

Limitations of Ratio Analysis

Ratio analysis has several limitations. Generally, the process uses information based on historical costs, not current market value. For example, the calculation of return on fixed assets is the result of dividing net income by average fixed assets. However, the average fixed assets on the books may not closely reflect their actual value. The result is a ratio that, by itself, suggests a reasonable return but that is much too high because the value of fixed assets is overstated.

Different restaurants use different accounting procedures. This limits the usefulness of comparisons between restaurants. The National Restaurant Association's Uniform System of Accounts[12] contributes to greater consistency within the foodservice industry; however, different restaurants still use different depreciation methods, inventory costing methods, etc.

Ratios at best only alert managers to potential problems. They do not suggest causes or the solutions. For example, a cost of food sold percentage of 40%

---

[12]*Uniform System of Accounts for Restaurants,* Seventh Edition, National Restaurant Association (Washington, D.C., 1996).

when the budget is 38% suggests a problem and nothing more. The difference may be due to a sales mix difference yielding more dollars than expected but a higher cost of food sold percentage.

When used cautiously and in comparison to a reasonable standard such as the budget plan, however, ratios can help signal a restaurant's problems and strengths.

MANAGER'S 10 POINT EFFECTIVENESS CHECKLIST

Evaluate your need for and the status of each of the following financial management tactics. For tactics you judge to be important but not yet in place, develop an action plan including completion date to implement the tactic.

TACTIC	DON'T AGREE (DON'T NEED)	AGREE (DONE)	AGREE (NOT DONE)	IF NOT DONE	
				WHO IS RESPONSIBLE?	TARGET COMPLETION DATE
1. Financial statements include comparisons to previous operating periods.	❑	❑	❑		
2. Current financial statements are analyzed for both absolute and relative changes from previous statements.	❑	❑	❑		
3. Significance factors (the amounts by which an item on a comparative statement must differ before analysis is required) have been defined by management.	❑	❑	❑		
4. Both comparative and common-size statements are developed to enable, respectively, horizontal and vertical analyses.	❑	❑	❑		
5. Financial statement results are reviewed in both numerical and common-size formats.	❑	❑	❑		
6. The most important ratios for evaluating the restaurant's liquidity and solvency have been identified and are analyzed monthly.	❑	❑	❑		
7. Activity, profitability, and operating ratios are studied for restaurant improvement possibilities.	❑	❑	❑		
8. Inventory turnover and cost of food (beverage) sold ratios are computed and reviewed each accounting period.	❑	❑	❑		
9. At least one profitability ratio is computed and analyzed each accounting period.	❑	❑	❑		
10. Ratio analysis is used to identify potential problem areas and to take corrective action.	❑	❑	❑		

6

CASH FLOW

MANAGER'S BRIEF

Cash! In this chapter you will learn about the critical role it plays in the operation of your restaurant. Cash refers to all the restaurant's receipts that a bank will accept at face value. The special circumstances affecting increases and decreases in the amount of cash available to you must be understood. This chapter presents these as well as suggestions for the best ways to manage your cash.

Also in this chapter, the important distinction between income flow and cash flow is discussed. These two concepts are important and must be understood by an effective restaurateur so bills can be paid when they are due.

The actual flow of cash into and out of a restaurant is documented in the statement of cash flows (SCF), a tool that is critical to budgeting for your restaurant's cash needs. The ability to create a cash budget that utilizes cash flows effectively is an important one, and in this chapter you will learn how to create a cash budget. We conclude with an example you can use as a model when building your own cash budget.

The proper management of **cash** as it flows through the restaurant operation is absolutely critical. The term "cash" can be defined as "any medium of exchange that a bank will accept at face value." Cash can be easily transferred and, therefore, is the one restaurant asset that is most likely to be improperly used (stolen) by staff members. Additionally, many transactions affect the receipt of and/or payment of cash, either directly or indirectly.

CASH Any medium of exchange that a bank will accept at face value.

CASH INCREASES AND DECREASES

The amount of cash available to the restaurant normally increases as:

- accounts receivable decrease (monies owed to the restaurant are collected)
- inventories decrease (cash is saved because products are being withdrawn from inventory rather than purchased)
- borrowing increases (cash is received from financial institutions)
- accounts payable and accrued expenses increase (purchases are made with short-term debt obligations rather than with cash)

By contrast, available cash normally decreases as:

- accounts receivable increase (money that is owed to the restaurant is not being paid)
- inventory increases (products are purchased and placed in inventory)
- borrowing from financial institutions decreases (cash is used to pay interest and debt)
- accounts payable and accrued expenses decrease (cash is used to pay short-term debt)

Effective restaurant managers consistently utilize tactics to control the flow of cash into and out of restaurant operations.

MANAGEMENT OF CASH

Restaurant managers must control the property's cash balances (currency on hand and demand deposits in the bank), cash flow (cash receipts and disbursements), and short-term investments in securities. This process of **cash management** is critical to restaurants of all sizes. Insufficient cash can lead to bankruptcy; excess cash not properly invested is a resource being wasted.

CASH MANAGEMENT The process used to effectively control the restaurant's cash balances (currency on hand and demand deposits in the bank), cash flow (cash receipts and disbursements), and short-term investments in securities.

Types of Cash Available

Restaurants generally have several types of cash available: petty cash funds, cash on hand for operating uses such as house banks, undeposited cash receipts, and cash in the bank, including demand deposits. Some managers also consider time deposits and certificates of deposit to be cash.

Petty cash funds are used to make small purchases and are usually maintained on an **imprest system:** they are replenished as necessary so that a preestablished balance is always maintained.

IMPREST SYSTEM   A method of maintaining the petty cash fund in which funds are always replenished by the amount of disbursements. An imprest system always has the same balance in cash and/or receipts for cash that has been disbursed.

House banks are needed to facilitate cash transactions with guests. Each cash bank should contain only the amount of money normally needed to transact business during a specific shift/business day.

Ideally, the restaurant's cash balance in a demand deposit bank account (checking account) should be zero. (Daily deposits should equal daily disbursements.) However, the amounts of cash received and disbursed do not normally equal each other on the same day. Therefore, the restaurant must maintain a minimum checking account balance to cover checks drawn.

Checking Account Balances

Banks sometimes demand that depositors maintain specified amounts in their accounts to cover bank services and to compensate for bank loans. For example,

EFFECTIVE COST   The interest on a loan compared to the usable loan amount.

if a restaurant borrows $100,000, a bank may require the restaurant to maintain a 10% compensating balance in its checking account. Since no interest is earned on this balance, the **effective cost** of the loan to the restaurant is higher than its stated interest rate.

The effective loan cost is determined as follows:

$$\text{Effective Interest Rate} = \frac{\text{Annual Interest on Loan}}{\text{Loan-Compensating Balance Requirement}}$$

Assume that a restaurant receives a one-year loan of $100,000 at 10% interest and is required to maintain a compensating balance of $10,000. The effective interest rate is really 11.1%:

$$\text{Interest} = \text{Principal} \times \text{Rate} \times \text{Time}$$
$$= \$100,000 \times 10\% \times 1 \text{ year}$$
$$= \$10,000$$

$$\text{Effective Interest Rate} = \frac{\$10,000}{\$100,000 - \$10,000} = 11.1\%$$

Cash Balances

Managers should try to keep cash balances as low as possible while considering in-house cash needs and banking requirements. The cost of maintaining higher amounts of in-house cash or checking accounts is an **opportunity cost:** the value of the earnings that could be made if the cash were invested. For example, if a restaurant has an average annual checking account balance of $10,000 when the bank requires only $5,000, the opportunity cost equals the interest that could be earned on $5,000. At an interest rate of 10%, the opportunity cost is $500 per year ($10,000 − $5,000 × 0.10).

> **OPPORTUNITY COST The value of the best foregone alternative. In cash management, it is the cost of maintaining higher than necessary amounts of in-house cash or checking accounts; the cost is equal to the earnings that would be available if the cash were invested.**

If the restaurant is a corporation, investors will be concerned about the restaurant's cash position because it can affect them in two ways: (a) they will receive cash dividends, and (b) their wealth increases as the stock prices increase. Corporations can pay cash dividends only if cash is available. Investors review financial statements, especially the statement of cash flows, to assess whether there is sufficient cash to pay dividends currently and if it appears that dividend payments will be possible in the future. As excess cash is invested by corporations, additional net income is realized; therefore, the market price of the stock (all other things being equal) should increase.

INCOME AND CASH FLOWS DIFFER

Income flows occur when the restaurant generates revenues and when it incurs expenses from daily operations. They are shown on the income statement and reflect the results of operations. **Cash flows** occur when cash is received and disbursed. A restaurant can generate profits (income flow) but have a negative cash flow (cash disbursements exceed cash receipts).

> **INCOME FLOWS The movement of income into the restaurant (when it generates revenues) and out of the restaurant (when it incurs expenses) from daily operations. Income flows are shown on the income statement and reflect operating results.**

Figure 6.1 illustrates the difference between income and cash flows. The Anytown Restaurant realized a net income flow of $15,000; however, cash disbursements exceeded cash receipts by $40,000.

The differences in income and cash flow for the Anytown Restaurant were:

Income Flows	**Cash Flows**

Income Flows

1. Cash received from the bank loan does not impact income flows.
2. Depreciation $50,000.

3. Interest expense $25,000.

4. The purchase of equipment has no direct effect on income flows. The write-off (depreciation) will affect income flows over several years.
5. Dividends do not affect income flows as they are not an expense.

Cash Flows

1. Loan from bank for $50,000.

2. Depreciation has no effect on cash flows.
3. Interest expense is part of the mortgage payment of $50,000. The $25,000 difference between the mortgage payment ($50,000) and the interest expense ($25,000) represents the principal reduction on the mortgage payable.

4. There was a payment of $50,000 for equipment purchased during the last month of the year.

5. Dividends of $30,000 were paid.

CASH FLOWS Movement of cash that occurs when receipts are received by the restaurant and when cash is disbursed by the restaurant.

A restaurant can withstand negative cash flows for short periods of time if its cash reserves are adequate to cover the deficits. However, over long periods, negative cash flows will probably cause restaurant failure even if income flows are positive.

Restaurants often have peaks and valleys in their operations. Generally, more cash is required during peak periods because cash is tied up in inventories and accounts receivable. Cash planning is important to ensure sufficient cash is available at all times. This is achieved by preparing cash budgets for several months in the future. (Cash budgets will be discussed later in this chapter.)

Condensed Income Statement and Cash Flow Statement
Anytown Restaurant
For the Year Ended December 31, 20X1

Income Statement		Cash Flow Statement	
Sales	$800,000	Cash Receipts:	
Cost of Food Sold	300,000	Cash Sales	$500,000
Payroll Cost	300,000	Collection of Accounts Receivable	300,000
		Loan from Bank	50,000
Other Operating Expenses	100,000	Total Cash Receipts	850,000
Depreciation	50,000	Cash Disbursements:	
Interest	25,000	Food Purchases	300,000
Income Taxes	10,000	Payroll	300,000
Net Income	$ 15,000	Other Operating Costs	100,000
		Income Taxes	10,000
		Equipment Purchase	100,000
		Mortgage Payment	50,000
		Dividends Paid	30,000
		Total Cash Disbursements	890,000
		Excess Cash Disbursements Over Cash Receipts (net cash outflow)	$ (40,000)

Figure 6.1   Income and Cash Flow for Anytown Restaurant

STATEMENT OF CASH FLOWS

The **statement of cash flows** (SCF) shows the impact of (change in) cash on a restaurant's operating, investing, and financing activities for the accounting period. This statement is historical; that is, it reflects what has happened in the past accounting period. The cash budget (to be discussed later) shows expectations for the future period. If cash decreases by $3,000 from January 1, 20XI (when the accounting period begins), to December 31, 20XI (when the accounting period ends), the SCF will detail the decrease in cash from the restaurant's various activities.

> **STATEMENT OF CASH FLOWS (SCF) This document shows the impact of (change in) cash on a restaurant's operating, investing, and financing activities for the accounting period.**

Note: The SCF considers cash to include both cash and cash equivalents (short-term, highly liquid investments such as U.S. Treasury bills and money-market accounts used to invest funds that are temporarily not needed for operating purposes). Since cash and cash equivalents are considered the same, transfers between them are not considered cash receipts or disbursements for SCF purposes.

Benefits of Statements of Cash Flows

The SCF provides information about the cash receipts and disbursements to help managers (internal) and investors and creditors (external) to assess:

- the restaurant's ability to generate positive future net cash flows. Users are generally less interested in the past than in the future. However, external users must frequently rely on historical financial information to gauge the restaurant's future abilities. Therefore, an investor interested in future cash dividends will review the SCF to determine past sources and uses of cash in an effort to evaluate the restaurant's ability to pay future dividends.

- the restaurant's ability to meet its obligations. Financial statement users want to determine the restaurant's ability to pay bills as they come due. If the restaurant cannot, suppliers will probably be less interested in selling goods and services (or, at least, cash on delivery [COD] will be necessary).

- the difference between the restaurant's net income and cash receipts and disbursements. The SCF allows one to quickly assess the major net sources of cash and to determine how much cash inflow relates directly to operations. Investors, creditors, and other users prefer restaurants to generate cash from operations rather than solely from financing and investing activities that are incidental to the restaurant's primary purpose.

- the effect of cash and noncash investing/ financing during the accounting period. **Investing activities** include acquiring and disposing of primarily noncurrent assets such as property and equipment. **Financing activities** include the borrowing and payment of long-term debt and the sale and purchase of capital stock. **Noncash activities**

> **INVESTING ACTIVITIES**
> Activities of the restaurant that relate to acquiring and disposing of primarily non-current assets such as property and equipment.

include such transactions as the acquisition of a restaurant in exchange for stock or long-term debt.

Managers may use the SCF to assess the restaurant's liquidity and its financial flexibility to determine its dividend policies and to plan investing and financing needs. Investors and creditors normally use the SCF to assess the restaurant's ability to pay its bills when due, to pay dividends when desired, and to ob-

tain additional financing (including borrowing funds and selling capital stock).

The relationship of the SCF to other financial statements is shown in Figure 6.2 on page 142. Restaurant corporations use the statement of retained earnings to reflect operating results and dividends declared; it reconciles the retained earnings accounts of two successive balance sheets. Net Income (from the income statement) is transferred to the retained earnings account when the temporary accounts (revenues and expenses) are closed at the end of the accounting period. Unincorporated restaurants utilize equity—not retained earnings—accounts, but the relationship between equity accounts and other financial statements is similar. The SCF shows the change in cash from the beginning of the accounting period to the end of the period. Finally, the SCF indirectly reconciles most noncash accounts on the balance sheet by showing the sources and uses of cash.

Types of Cash Flow Activities

The SCF classifies three types of cash receipt and disbursement activities: operating, investing, and financing. Cash inflows and outflows are included within each type. Figure 6.3 (page 143) shows cash flows under the three types of activities:

- *Operating Activities.* These include cash transactions related to revenues and expenses. Revenues (cash inflows) include sales of food, beverages, and other goods and services to restaurant guests as well as interest and dividend income. Expenses (cash outflows) result from cash expenditures for operations including payments for food/beverage products, salaries/wages, taxes, supplies, interest expense, etc.

- *Investing Activities.* These relate to cash flows from buying and selling the restaurant's noncurrent assets, including property, equipment, investments,

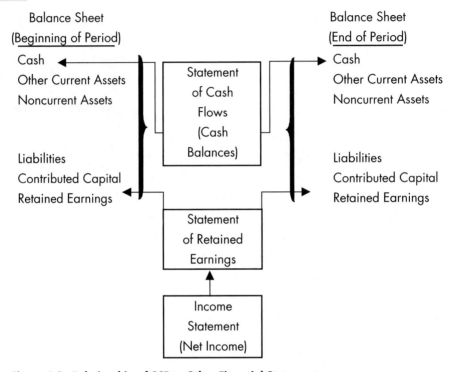

Figure 6.2 Relationship of SCF to Other Financial Statements

and other assets. Cash flows from purchase and disposal of short-term investments (not considered a cash equivalent) are another example.

- *Financing Activities.* These relate to cash flows from issuing and retiring debt and issuing and repurchasing capital stock. Inflows include cash received from issues of stock (corporate organizations) and from short- and long-term borrowing. Outflows include repayments of loans (the interest expense portion of debt is an operating activity) and payments to owners for dividends and stock repurchases (in a corporate restaurant).

Sample Statement of Cash Flows

Figure 6.4 shows an SCF for the Anytown Restaurant. The three activities show the following cash flows:

- Operating activities (provided cash) $116,000
- Investing activities (used cash) $ (30,000)
- Financing activities (used cash) $ (56,000)

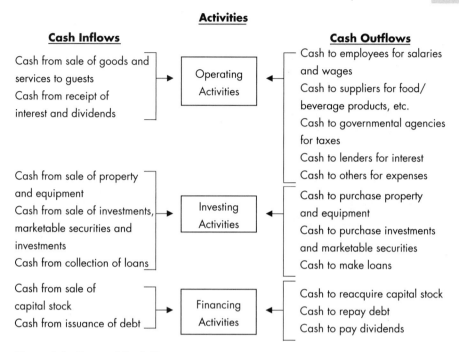

Figure 6.3 Types of Cash Flows

The Anytown's Restaurant SCF tells us:

- While net income was $74,000, cash flows from operations increased by $116,000. The major differences are the depreciation expense ($50,000) and the gain on sale of investments ($10,000).

- Cash flows from operations were sufficient to allow the restaurant to (1) pay off long-term debt ($26,000); (2) pay dividends to stockholders ($30,000); (3) invest $15,000; and (4) purchase $20,000 of new equipment with cash.

CASH BUDGETS

The SCF shows cash flows in and out of the restaurant in the past. A **cash budget** considers future cash flow by estimating cash receipts and cash disbursements.

Anytown Restaurant
Statement of Cash Flows
For the Year Ended December 31, 20XX

Net Cash Flow From Operating Activities:		
Net income		$ 74,000
Adjustments to reconcile net income to net cash flows		
from operating activities:		
Depreciation	$ 50,000	
Gain on sale of investments	(10,000)	
Decrease in accounts receivable	4,000	
Increase in inventory	(2,000)	
Increase in accounts payroll	500	
Increase in accrued payroll	500	
Decrease in income taxes payable	(1,000)	42,000
Net cash flow from operating activities		116,000
Investing Activities:		
Sale of investments	$ 5,000	
Purchase of investments	(15,000)	
Purchase of equipment	(20,000)	
Net cash flow used in investing activities		(30,000)
Financing Activities:		
Payment of long-term debt	$(26,000)	
Dividends paid to stockholders	(30,000)	
Net cash flow used in financing activities		(56,000)
Net increase in cash during 20XX		30,000
Cash at the beginning of 20XX		20,000
Cash at the end of 20XX		$50,000
Supplementary Disclosure of Cash Flow Information		
Cash paid during the year for:		
Interest		$ 34,000
Income taxes		$ 28,000

Figure 6.4   Statement of Cash Flows for the Anytown Restaurant

Purpose of Cash Budget

CASH BUDGET An estimate of future cash receipts and disbursements that helps managers prepare for expected deficits or excesses.

Cash may be in short supply; a cash deficit may be projected. If the estimated cash receipts and beginning cash balances will not cover projected cash disbursements, managers must take action. Even if the estimated available cash is more than projected cash disbursements, the projected cash balance must be reviewed to assess whether there is a sufficient buffer for cash shortfalls and/or unplanned cash disbursements. If the estimated cash balance is insufficient, a manager must find ways to increase cash receipts and/or to decrease cash disbursements. Actions to address temporary deficits include obtaining short-term loans from banks.

Investing Excess Cash

If the estimated cash balance at the end of the period is more than required, excess cash should be temporarily invested. Factors to be considered when investing excess cash include:

- *Risk*—the probability of losing the investment. Owners/managers should generally take a minimum risk when investing in short-term funds. (Investments in government securities such as Treasury bills, for example, are considered risk-free.)
- *Return*—the rate of return received on the funds. Generally, the greater the risk and the longer the investment period, the greater the return.
- *Liquidity*—the ability to convert the investment to cash. Cash invested temporarily should generally be invested in fairly liquid investments so it can be quickly converted to cash as required.
- *Cost*—the fees charged for the investment.
- *Size*—the amount of funds available for investing. Generally, the more money available, the higher the return.
- *Time*—the amount of time excess funds are invested. Generally, the longer the investment time, the higher the return.

Format for Cash Budget

It is helpful to estimate cash receipts and disbursements for periods of up to six months (projections beyond six months are less reliable) to show (a) the direct sources of cash receipts such as cash sales, collection of accounts receivable, bank loans, sale of capital stock, etc., and (b) direct uses of cash such as food/beverage purchases, payroll, mortgage payments, and dividend payments.

Figure 6.5 shows the format for a cash budget. It consists of two major sections: estimated cash receipts and estimated cash disbursements. Estimated cash receipts are added to the estimated cash (beginning of period) to estimate cash available for the period. Estimated cash disbursements are subtracted from the

Cash Budget
January–June, 20XX

	January	February	March	April	May	June
Estimated Cash (Beginning of Period)	$	$	$	$	$	$
Estimated Cash Receipts:						
Cash Sales						
Collection of Accounts Receivable						
Proceeds from Bank Loans						
Proceeds from Sale of Fixed Assets						
Proceeds from Sale of Capital Stock						
Other	___	___	___	___	___	___
Total	___	___	___	___	___	___
Estimated Cash Available						
Estimated Cash Disbursements:						
Inventory						
Payroll						
Operating Expenses						
Taxes						
Insurance						
Mortgage Payments						
Rent						
Other	___	___	___	___	___	___
Total	___	___	___	___	___	___
Estimated Cash (End of Period)	___	___	___	___	___	___
Minimum Cash Required	___	___	___	___	___	___
Cash Excess (shortage)	$___	$___	$___	$___	$___	$___

Figure 6.5 Format for Cash Budget

total estimated cash available to project ending cash available. This difference is then compared to the minimum amount of cash required to identify any shortage or excess. (The process of estimating cash receipts and cash disbursements is discussed later in this chapter.)

Developing the Cash Budget

The operating budget provides most information needed for preparing a cash budget. For example, total budgeted sales provide the basis for estimated cash collections, and the budget is also used to estimate expenses and when they are to be paid.

Some additional information is also necessary for preparing a cash budget:

- Estimated percentages of cash and credit revenues to total revenues.

- Estimated collection experience for credit sales. Most restaurants have few, if any, credit sales other than from bank or travel/entertainment credit cards, which can basically be treated as cash. When other kinds of credit are extended, however, the collection experience becomes important. For example, a restaurant's collection experience may be 30% during the month of sale, 60% in the following month, and 10% during the second month after sale. Some credit sales may never be collected; this must eventually be charged off to a "bad debts" expense account.

- Estimated other cash receipts such as bank loans, sale of capital stock, and proceeds from the sale of fixed assets and investments.

- Estimated payments for inventory items. For example, 10% of purchases may be paid during the month of purchase and 90% paid in the following month.

- Estimated payroll payments. If the restaurant has monthly payroll (all employees are paid on the last day of the month for that month) payroll expense estimates from the operations budget can be used. Payroll distributed in any other way requires more calculations.

- Payment schedules for other operating periods. Some operating expenses such as utilities are generally paid the month after they are expensed. Operating supplies are often paid for before the expense is incurred. (They are then carried as "supplies − inventory.") Each expense must be reviewed to assess when the related cash expenditure is made.

- Expenses related to the capacity (equipment, buildings, and land), such as property taxes and insurance, are paid only once or twice per year. The payment date, not when the expense is charged in the operating budget based on accrued accounting, must then be considered.

- A schedule of debt payments that is not part of the operating budget is required to determine total debt payments. Interest expense, which is part of the debt payment, is shown in the operations budget, while the portion of the debt payment related to debt reduction is not.

- Additional information, including forecasted dividend payments and fixed asset and investment purchases, may be needed.

Illustration: Forest Acres Restaurant

The Forest Acres Restaurant will be used to illustrate the process of developing a three-month cash budget for April–June, 20XX. Figure 6.6 shows its operating budget for March–July, 20XX. (This budget, then, estimates revenues and expenses for one month before and one month after the April–June time period for the cash budget.)

Cash receipts and sales relationships follow:

- Cash sales are 80% of each month's sales. Therefore, the restaurant's estimated cash receipts from cash sales in April is $48,000 ($60,000 × 0.8).

- Charge sales represent the remaining 20%. Twenty percent of the charge sales are collected in the month of sale, while the remaining 80% are collected in the following month. Estimated cash receipts from April charge sales for the Forest Acres Restaurant total $2,400 ($60,000 × 0.2 × 0.2). In addition, March charge sales collected in April yield $10,080 of cash receipts ($63,000 × 0.2 × 0.8).

- The Forest Acres Restaurant receives cash each month for the projected interest income as shown in Figure 6.6. Its cash receipts from interest income total $2,000 for April.

The restaurant's cash disbursement and expense relationships follow:

- Food purchases (cost of sales) are paid during the current month as follows:

Operating Budget
Forest Acres Restaurant
March–July, 20XX

	March	April	May	June	July
SALES	$ 63,000	$ 60,000	$ 65,000	$ 70,000	$ 75,000
COST OF SALES	18,900	18,000	19,500	21,000	22,500
Total Gross Profit	**44,100**	**42,000**	**45,500**	**49,000**	**52,500**
OPERATING EXPENSES:					
Salaries and Wages	17,000	16,000	18,000	19,000	20,000
Employee Benefits	3,000	2,500	3,000	3,000	3,500
Direct Operating Expenses	3,000	2,500	2,500	2,500	3,000
Marketing Expenses	4,000	4,200	4,000	4,500	5,000
Utility Costs	3,000	2,500	2,000	2,000	2,200
Repairs and Maintenance	2,000	2,000	2,000	2,000	2,000
Occupancy Expenses	3,000	3,000	3,000	3,000	3,000
Depreciation	1,700	1,700	1,700	1,700	1,700
General and Administrative	2,000	1,800	1,700	1,800	2,000
Other Income (Interest)	(2,000)	(2,000)	(2,000)	(2,000)	(2,000)
Total Operating Expenses	**36,700**	**34,200**	**35,900**	**37,500**	**40,400**
Operating Income	**7,400**	**7,800**	**9,600**	**11,500**	**12,100**
Interest Expense	1,000	1,000	1,000	1,000	1,000
Income Before Income Taxes	**$ 6,400**	**$ 6,800**	**$ 8,600**	**$10,500**	**$11,100**

Figure 6.6 Operating Budget for Forest Acres Restaurant

30% of cost of sales of previous month
70% of cost of sales of current month

Its cash disbursements for food during April total $18,270:

March cost of sales × 0.3 = $18,900 × 0.3 = $ 5,670
April cost of sales × 0.7 = $18,000 × 0.7 = $12,600
$18,270

- Salaries, wages, and benefits are paid in the month they are expensed. The April cash disbursement totals $18,500.

- With the exception of marketing, one-half of all remaining controllable expenses are paid in the month expensed. The remaining 50% are paid in the following month. The Forest Acres cash disbursements of $12,400 for these expenses are shown in Figure 6.7.

- Marketing expense is paid for as follows: In January, $24,000 was paid to an advertising agency for $2,000 of advertising for each month during 20XX. The remaining marketing expense (from the operating budget) is paid during the month it is expensed. The Forest Acres Restaurant has, then, an actual cash disbursement in April of $2,200 ($4,200 − $2,000) for marketing expense.

- Interest expense of $1,000 for April is included in the mortgage payment of $2,000 per month.

- Depreciation is a write-off of fixed assets; it requires no cash flow.

Other information includes:

- Assume that cash at the beginning of April is $5,000.

- Equipment costing $8,000 will be purchased in May on account and is to be paid for in June.

- Cash dividends of $5,000 will be paid to the owners of the Forest Acres Restaurant in June.

Given all the above information, the three-month (April–June, 20XX) cash budget for the Forest Acres Restaurant is shown in Figure 6.8. Explanations for each cash budget line item are shown in Figure 6.9.

Forest Acres Restaurant has positive cash flow; cash at the beginning of the quarter (April 1) of $5,000 is projected to increase to $24,660 by the end of the quarter (June 30). If the owner considers cash at the end of the month to be more than needed, the excess can be invested. For example, the excess may establish a minimum cash balance requirement. Any cash over this can be invested temporarily (if needed for future operations) and/or can be paid to the owners.

Assume the restaurant maintains a cash cushion of $5,000 at the end of each month. Figure 6.10 shows the projected cash available to invest at the end of each month in the quarter. It is projected to have excess cash for investing of $9,110 and $10,650, respectively, in April and May. However, in June, temporary investments of $100 must be liquidated to provide the $5,000 minimum cash balance required at the end of the month.

Estimated April Cash Disbursements
For Various Controllable Expenses
Forest Acres Restaurant

	For March	For April	Total
Direct Operating Expenses	$ 1,500	$ 1,250	$ 2,750
Utility Costs	1,500	1,250	2,750
General and Administrative	1,000	900	1,900
Repairs and Maintenance	1,000	1,000	2,000
Occupancy Expenses	1,500	1,500	3,000
Total	$ 6,500	$ 5,900	$ 12,400

Figure 6.7   Estimate of Controllable Expenses Paid in Cash During April

Cash Budget
Forest Acres Restaurant
April–June 20XX

	April	May	June
Cash—Beginning of Month	$ 5,000	$14,110	$24,760
Estimated Cash Receipts:			
Cash Sales	48,000	52,000	56,000
Collection of Accounts Receivable	12,480	12,200	13,200
Interest Received	2,000	2,000	2,000
Total	62,480	66,200	71,200
Estimated Available Cash	67,480	80,310	95,960
Estimated Cash Disbursements:			
Food Purchases	18,270	19,050	20,550
Salaries, Wages, and Fringe Benefits	18,500	21,000	22,000
Direct Operating Expenses	2,750	2,500	2,500
Marketing	2,200	2,000	2,500
Utility Costs	2,750	2,250	2,000
General and Administrative	1,900	1,750	1,750
Repairs and Maintenance	2,000	2,000	2,000
Occupation Costs	3,000	3,000	3,000
Mortgage Payments	2,000	2,000	2,000
Equipment Purchase	0	0	8,000
Cash Dividends	0	0	5,000
Total	53,370	55,550	71,300
Estimated Cash—End of Month	$14,110	$24,760	$24,660

Figure 6.8   Three-Month Cash Budget for Forest Acres Restaurant

Explanation of Cash Budget Line Items
Forest Acres Restaurant
April–June 20XX

Line Item	MONTHLY BUDGETS		
	April	**May**	**June**
Cash—Beginning of Month (BOM)	$5,000: based on assumption provided	$14,110: cash—EOM, April 20XX	$24,760: cash—EOM, May 20XX
Cash Sales	$48,000: April sales × 0.8 = 60,000 × 0.8 = $48,000	$52,000: May sales × 0.8 = 65,000 × 0.8 = $52,000	$56,000: June sales × 0.8 = 70,000 × 0.8 = $56,000
Collection of Accounts Receivable	$12,480: April sales × 0.2 × 0.2 = 60,000 × 0.2 × 0.2 = $2,400; March sales × 0.2 × 0.8 = 63,000 × 0.2 × 0.8 = $10,080	$12,200: May sales × 0.2 × 0.2 = 65,000 × 0.2 × 0.2 = $2,600; April sales × 0.2 × 0.8 = 60,000 × 0.2 × 0.8 = $9,600	$13,200: June sales × 0.2 × 0.2 = 70,000 × 0.2 × 0.2 = $2,800; May sales × 0.2 × 0.8 = 65,000 × 0.2 × 0.8 = $10,400
Interest Received	$2,000	$2,000	$2,000
Estimated Cash Available	$68,200: cash—BOM + total estimated cash receipts = 5,000 + 63,200 = $68,200	$80,310: cash—BOM + total estimated cash receipts = 14,110 + 66,200 = $81,030	$95,960: cash—BOM + total estimated cash receipts = 24,760 + 71,200 = $95,960
Food Purchases	$18,270: March exp. × 0.3 = 18,900 × 0.3 = $5,670; April exp. × 0.7 = 18,000 × 0.7 = $12,600	$19,050: April exp. × .03 = 18,000 × 0.3 = $5,400; May exp. × 0.7 = $19,500 × 0.7 = $13,650	$20,550: May exp. × 0.3 = 19,500 × 0.3 = $5,850; June exp. × 0.7 = $21,000 × 0.7 = $14,700
Salaries, Wages and Fringe Benefits	$18,500: 16,000 + 2,500 = $18,500	$21,000: 18,000 + 3,000 = $21,000	$22,000: 19,000 + 3,000 = $22,000
Direct Operating Expenses	$2,750: March exp. × 0.5 = 3,000 × .05 = $1,500; April exp. × 0.5 = 2,500 × 0.5 = 2,500 × 0.5 = $1,250	$2,500: April exp. × 0.5 = 2,500 × 0.5 = $1,250; May exp. × 0.5 = 2,500 × 0.5 = 2,500 × 0.5 = $1,250	$2,500: May exp. × 0.5 = 2,500 × 0.5 = $1,250; June exp. × 0.5 = 2,500 × 0.5 = 2,500 × 0.5 = $1,250
Marketing Expenses	$2,200: April exp. − 2,000 = 4,200 − 2,000 = $2,200	$2,000: May exp. − 2,000 = 4,000 − 2,000 = $2,000	$2,500: June exp. − 2,000 = 4,500 − 2,000 = $2,500
Utility Costs	$2,750: March exp. × 0.5 + April exp. × 0.5 = (3,000 × 0.5) + (2,500 × 0.5) = 1,500 + 1,250 = $2,750	$2,250: April exp. × 0.5 + May exp. × 0.5 = (2,500 × 0.5) + (2,000 × 0.5) = 1,250 + 1,000 = $2,250	$2,000: May exp. × 0.5 + June exp. × 0.5 = (2,000 × 0.5) + (2,000 × 0.5) = 1,000 + 1,000 = $2,000
General and Administrative	$1,900: March exp. × 0.5 + April exp. × 0.5 = (2,000 × 0.5) + (1,800 × 0.5) = 1,000 + 900 = $1,900	$1,750: April exp. × 0.5 + May exp. × 0.5 = (1,800 × 0.5) + (1,700 × 0.5) = 900 + 850 = $1,750	$1,750: May exp. × 0.5 + June exp. × 0.5 = (1,700 × 0.5) + (1,800 × 0.5) = 850 + 900 = $1,750
Repairs and Maintenance	$2,000: March exp. × 0.5 + April exp. × 0.5 = (2,000 × 0.5) + (2,000 × 0.5) = 1,000 + 1,000 = $2,000	$2,000: April exp. × 0.5 + May exp. × 0.5 = (2,000 × 0.5) + (2,000 × 0.5) = 1,000 + 1,000 = $2,000	$2,000: May exp. × 0.5 + June exp. × 0.5 = (2,000 × 0.5) + (2,000 × 0.5) = 1,000 + 1,000 = $2,000
Occupation Costs	$3,000	$3,000	$3,000
Mortgage Payment	$2,000	$2,000	$2,000
Purchase of Equipment	$ 0	$ 0	$8,000
Cash Dividends	$ 0	$ 0	$5,000
Estimated Cash—End of Month (EOM)	$14,830: Est. Available cash − est. cash disb. = 67,480 − 53,370 = $14,110	$24,760: Est. Available cash − est. cash disb. = 80,310 − 55,550 = $24,760	$24,660: Est. Available cash − est. cash disb. = $95,960 − 71,300 = $24,660

Figure 6.9 Explanation of Cash Budget Line Items—Forest Acres Restaurant

Projected Cash to Invest
Forest Acres Restaurant
April–June, 20XX

	April	May	June
Cash (Beginning of Month)	$ 5,000	$ 5,000	$ 5,000
Plus: Total Estimated Cash Receipts	62,480	66,200	71,200
Less: Total Estimated Disbursements	53,370	55,550	71,300
Preliminary Cash (End of Month)	14,110	15,650	4,900
Less: Cash Cushion	5,000	5,000	5,000
Excess Cash for Investing	$ 9,110	$10,650	$ (100)*

*If the excess cash is invested in April and May, the restaurant should prepare to liquidate $100 of these investments to maintain the desired cash cushion of $5,000 at the end of June.

Figure 6.10   Projected Cash to Invest—Forest Acres Restaurant

MANAGER'S 10 POINT EFFECTIVENESS CHECKLIST

Evaluate your need for and the status of each of the following financial management tactics. For tactics you judge to be important but not yet in place, develop an action plan including completion date to implement the tactic.

TACTIC	DON'T AGREE (DON'T NEED)	AGREE (DONE)	AGREE (NOT DONE)	IF NOT DONE	
				WHO IS RESPONSIBLE?	TARGET COMPLETION DATE
1. The restaurant has an active cash management program that is reviewed at least quarterly.	❏	❏	❏		
2. An imprest system is used to maintain petty cash banks.	❏	❏	❏		
3. Checking account balances are held to the minimums allowed by the bank.	❏	❏	❏		
4. Monthly differences between income and cash flows are analyzed by management.	❏	❏	❏		
5. A statement of cash flows (SCF) is developed and utilized on the same time frame as that of the income statement.	❏	❏	❏		
6. Analysis is undertaken to manage changes in cash resulting from operating, investing, and financing activities.	❏	❏	❏		
7. A statement of cash flows (SCF) is used to produce a cash budget covering at least a six-month period.	❏	❏	❏		
8. Excess cash is managed/invested to maximize its benefits to the restaurant.	❏	❏	❏		
9. A minimal but appropriate amount of cash is held in all cash accounts.	❏	❏	❏		
10. Excess cash investments are liquid enough to allow for easy conversion back to cash during months of negative cash flow.	❏	❏	❏		

7

UNDERSTANDING COST CONCEPTS
AND BREAK-EVEN

MANAGER'S BRIEF

Restaurant managers must be concerned about controlling costs. In this chapter you will learn about several types of costs. For example, costs can be thought of as fixed, variable, or mixed. A fixed cost remains constant even when sales volume varies. Examples include salaries and interest expense. A variable cost increases or decreases as sales volume increases or decreases. Examples include the costs of food and beverages sold. A mixed (semivariable) cost is one that is partially fixed and partially variable. An example is a building lease where one part of the lease is based on a fixed cost per square foot rented and another part is based upon percentage of revenue.

Costs may also be viewed as either controllable or noncontrollable. Controllable costs can be influenced directly by managers, while noncontrollable costs generally cannot. Additional cost classifications divide costs into differential, relevant, sunk, average/incremental, and standard. Each of these classifications is reviewed in this chapter.

Regardless of the system used to classify costs, managers want to know the precise level of revenue that must be generated to pay all costs. This revenue level is called the break-even point. It is the revenue level needed to pay all fixed and variable costs. Additional sales levels beyond the break-even point then contribute to variable costs incurred and, most important, to profits. In this chapter, you will learn how to compute a break-even point and use it to analyze your own restaurant.

The term **"cost"** can be used in many different contexts with very different meanings. For example: the cost of a dishwasher was $10,000; the labor cost for the period was $10,000; the cost of damages to the restaurant from fire was $10,000. In the first use, "cost" means the purchase price of an asset; one asset (cash) was exchanged for another asset (the dishwasher). In the second use, "cost" refers to an expense; cash (an asset) was paid to employees for services. (In this instance, assets were not directly exchanged; instead, cash was paid for services by employees to generate revenues.) In the third use, the "cost" from the fire refers to a loss: a reduction of assets without the receipt either directly or indirectly of other assets. In this chapter, we will generally use the word "cost" to mean expense.

> **COST** The reduction of an asset generally for the ultimate purpose of increasing revenues. By this definition, "cost" is the same as "expense."

OVERVIEW OF COST

Cost (expense) is the reduction of an asset, generally for the ultimate purpose of increasing revenues. Examples of costs include cost of food (or beverage) sold and expenses for labor, supplies, utilities, marketing, rent, depreciation, insurance, and many other necessities. Since the **profit margin** for most restaurants is less than 10%, more than 90% of a restaurant's revenues (ultimately cash) are used to pay these costs (expenses). It is essential that managers understand the types of costs and their several applications.

> **PROFIT MARGIN** An overall measure of management's ability to generate sales and control expenses; profit margin is calculated by dividing net income by total revenue.

Costs and Sales Volume

One way to consider costs is to think about how they change when there are changes in the activity (sales) of the restaurant. Costs can be seen as fixed, variable, or mixed (partly fixed and partly variable).

Fixed Costs. Fixed costs remain constant in the short run even when sales volume varies. For example, food sales may increase by 5% or beverage sales may decline by 10%; in both cases a fixed cost such as interest expenses remains constant. Figure 7.1 shows a graph that tracks costs and revenue volume. It shows that total fixed costs remain the same even when sales volume increases.

> **FIXED COSTS Costs that do not vary in the short term even when sales volume varies; examples include salaries and interest expense.**

Common examples of fixed costs include salaries, rent and insurance expense, property taxes, depreciation expense, and interest expense. Fixed costs are sometimes classified as either capacity or discretionary. **Capacity fixed costs** relate to the ability to provide goods and services. For a restaurant, capacity fixed costs relate to the number of seats in the dining area and include depreciation, property taxes, interest, and certain salaries. There is a quality dimension related to capacity fixed costs. For

> **CAPACITY FIXED COSTS Charges relating to the property or its capacity to provide goods and services.**

example, if the restaurant were to eliminate its air conditioning system, it could still serve the same number of guests, but at a lower level of service.

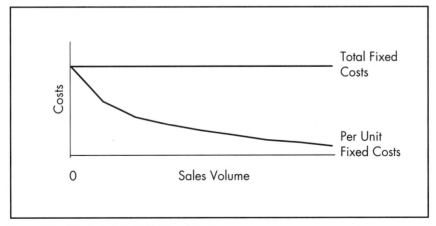

Figure 7.1 Total and Per Unit Fixed Costs

Discretionary fixed costs do not affect a restaurant's current capacity. They are costs managers might avoid in the short run (often to meet budget restraints) because they have no (little) immediate operating impact. However, continued avoidance will generally create problems. Discretionary fixed costs include costs for educational seminars, charitable contributions, employee training programs, and advertising. During a financial crisis, discretionary fixed costs are more likely to be cut than are capacity fixed costs because they are easier to restore and will have less immediate impact.

DISCRETIONARY FIXED COSTS Charges that managers may, in the short term, avoid because they do not affect the restaurant's capacity.

Fixed costs can also be related to sales volume by determining the average fixed cost per unit sold. For example, if fixed costs total $5,000 for a period in which 2,000 meals are sold, the average fixed cost per meal is $2.50 (5,000 ÷ 2,000 meals). However, if 3,000 meals are sold during the period, then the average fixed cost per meal is $1.67 (5,000 ÷ 3,000 meals). As the sales volume increases, the per unit fixed cost decreases even though total fixed costs remain the same. Figure 7.1 illustrates this relationship.

Although constant in the short run, all fixed costs change over longer periods. For example, the monthly lease payment on an equipment item may increase annually. Therefore, from a long-term perspective, all fixed costs may be viewed as variable costs.

Variable Costs. Variable costs change proportionally with changes in business volume. For example, if food sales increase by 10%, the cost of food sold may be expected to increase by 10%. Figure 7.2 shows total variable costs and variable costs per unit as each relate to sales volume. Total variable costs (TVC) are determined by multiplying the variable cost per unit by the number of unit sales. For example, the TVC for a restaurant with a variable cost per meal of $3 and 1,000 projected meal sales is $3,000 ($3 × 1,000 = $3,000).

VARIABLE COSTS Costs that change proportionately with changes in sales volume.

Theoretically, total variable costs vary with total sales, and unit variable costs remain constant. For example, if the cost of food sold is 35%, then the unit cost per $1 of sales is $0.35, regardless of sales volume. Figure 7.2 shows that unit variable costs are really fixed; their cost per sales dollar remains constant. (Although a restaurant might be able to receive volume purchase discounts as its sales increase, and then the cost of sales should increase at a slower rate than sales volume.)

In truth, few costs, if any, vary in exact proportion to total sales. However,

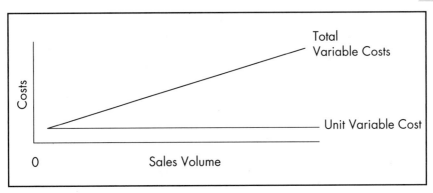

Figure 7.2 Total Per Unit Variable Costs

several costs come close to meeting this definition and are considered variable costs. Examples include the cost of food and beverages sold, some labor costs, and supplies used in production and service operations.

Mixed Costs. Some costs are partly fixed and partly variable; they contain a mix of both fixed and variable costs. Sometimes called semi-variable (or semi-fixed) we will call them **mixed costs.**

> **MIXED COSTS Costs that contain a mixture of both fixed and variable costs.**

The fixed element in a mixed cost is determined independently of sales variance; the variable element varies proportionally with sales volume. (As with variable costs, the variable element in a mixed cost may not vary in exact proportion to sales activity. However, the relationship is generally accepted as linear because the divergences, if any, are usually insignificant.)

Figure 7.3 shows fixed and variable elements in mixed costs. The portion of costs below point A represents fixed costs; the difference between the slopes of the total mixed costs and fixed costs lines reflects the variable costs.

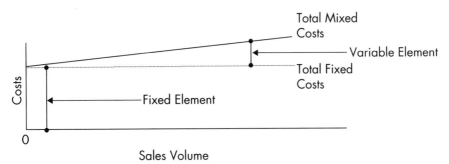

Figure 7.3 Mixed Costs

Figure 7.4 shows a decrease in unit mixed costs as sales volume increases. This decrease is not as dramatic as the decrease in fixed costs per sales unit (Figure 7.1) because the variable element in mixed costs increases with each unit sold; this increases the total mixed costs.

Examples of mixed costs with a brief discussion of their fixed and variable elements are shown in Figure 7.5.

Total mixed costs (TMC) for any cost can be estimated as follows:

$$TMC = \text{Fixed costs} + (\text{Variable cost per unit} \times \text{Unit sales})$$

A restaurant with a franchise fee of $1,000 per month and $0.25 per meal sold would estimate its franchise fees (a mixed cost) for a month with 3,000 projected covers (meals) as follows:

$$\text{Franchise fees} = \$1,000 + (3000 \times 0.25) = \$1,750$$

Total Costs

Total costs (TC) for a restaurant consist of the sum of its fixed, variable, and mixed costs.

$$TC = \text{Fixed costs} + (\text{Variable cost per unit} \times \text{Unit sales})$$

An estimate of TC for a restaurant that sells 1,000 meals and that has total fixed costs of $10,000 and variable costs per meal of $3.00 is $13,000:

$$TC = \$10,000 + (1,000 \times 3)$$

$$TC = \$13,000$$

Total costs are shown in Figure 7.6 on page 162.

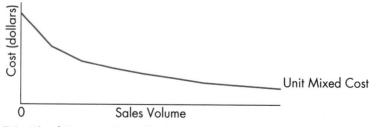

Figure 7.4 Mixed Costs per Unit of Sale

	Elements	
Mixed Cost	**Fixed**	**Variable**
Telephone expense	Cost of system	Cost of calls
Building lease	Fixed rental cost per square foot of space rented	Percentage of revenue in addition to fixed amount
Auto lease	Fixed cost/day	Additional charge per mile auto is driven
Executive compensation	Base pay	Bonuses based on sales
Repair and maintenance	Minimum amount required to maintain (keep) restaurant open	Additional maintenance needed with increased business volume

Figure 7.5 Examples of Mixed Costs

Some products and services can be purchased on either a fixed or variable cost contract. For example, a lease may be either fixed (at a set price per period, such as a month, or per square foot) or variable (at a certain specified percentage of revenues). The decision to select a fixed or variable cost arrangement should be based on the costs and benefits involved. Under a fixed cost arrangement, the cost remains the same regardless of activity. Under a variable arrangement, the amount paid depends on the level of activity. The level of activity at which the period cost is the same under either alternative is the **indifference point.**

> **INDIFFERENCE POINT The level of sales activity at which the cost is the same under either a fixed or a variable cost contract.**

Assume that a restaurant owner can sign either an annual fixed lease of $48,000 or a variable lease set at 5% of revenue. The indifference point is determined as follows:

$$\text{Variable cost percentage} \times \text{Annual revenue} = \text{Fixed lease cost}$$
$$0.05 \times \text{Annual revenue} = 48,000$$
$$\text{Annual revenue} = \frac{48,000}{0.05}$$
$$\text{Annual revenue} = \underline{\$960,000}$$

When annual revenue is $960,000, the lease expense will be $48,000, regardless of whether the lease is fixed or variable. If annual revenue is expected to exceed $960,000, a fixed lease should be selected to minimize lease expense. If annual revenue is expected to be less than $960,000, a variable lease will minimize lease expense.

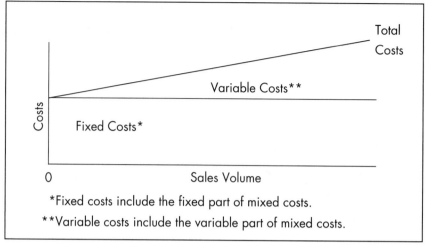

Figure 7.6 Total Costs

OTHER TYPES OF COSTS

There are numerous ways to classify costs. We will look at overhead, controllable, differential, relevant, sunk, and average/incremental costs in this section.

OVERHEAD COSTS All expenses other than costs directly related to a specific profit center. Examples include interest expense, depreciation, rent, property taxes, and fire insurance.

DIRECT COSTS Expenses directly related to the department that incurred them. For example, labor costs for cooks and cost of food sold are direct costs to the food production department; labor costs for bartenders and cost of beverages are applicable to the beverage operation.

Overhead Costs

Overhead costs include all costs other than **direct costs** incurred by **profit centers.** Therefore, overhead costs are indirect costs from the perspective of a specific profit center.

Overhead costs include interest expense, depreciation, rent, property taxes, and fire insurance. Some restaurants **allocate** costs among profit centers in an effort to approximate the profitability of each profit center. A detailed description of the cost allocation process is beyond the scope of this book.

Controllable Costs

Managers should generally hold subordinates responsible only for costs the subordinates can control.

Controllable costs are costs that a person can influence. For example, the chef may be able to influence food usage, cook labor, and food production supplies. Therefore, cost of food sold, cook payroll expense, and food production supplies expense are controllable costs for the chef. By contrast, the chef probably has no control over the restaurant's rent. However, the owner can control the rent expense; therefore, from the owner's viewpoint, rent is a controllable expense.

> **PROFIT CENTER** An operating department within a restaurant that generates revenues and incurs expenses. Examples include the food operation, the beverage operation, and the banquet operation.

Several costs cannot be easily influenced or changed in the short run; these are often considered **noncontrollable costs.** However, these costs can be regulated over the long run and, from this point of view, can be considered controllable. Most costs are controllable given sufficient time and input at a sufficiently high level.

> **ALLOCATE** To distribute expenses as applicable among various departments (profit centers).

> **CONTROLLABLE COSTS** Costs that management can influence.

The owner or general manager should be held accountable for the costs he/she controls. These costs are generally below the "operating income" line on the income statement. Expenses that are primarily influenced by the owner of the restaurant include rent and other occupation costs, interest, depreciation, and income taxes.

> **NONCONTROLLABLE COSTS** Cost that cannot be easily changed or influenced by management in the short run.

Differential Costs

When decisions are made, the difference in costs between two or more alternatives is called **differential costs.** By focusing on differential costs, decision makers can narrow the set of cost considerations to those that really make a difference. Suppose the restaurant manager is considering the installation of a new back-office computer system. Differential costs include the purchase price of the computer and any other costs associated with it that differ from the costs involved in using the existing equipment. (These costs might include labor, utilities, supplies, and insurance.) Costs that remain the same with or without the new computer system are nondifferential; they do not need to be considered in the decision-making process.

> **DIFFERENTIAL COSTS** Costs that make up the difference between two alternatives being evaluated as part of the decision-making process.

Relevant Costs

RELEVANT COSTS Those costs that must be considered when a decision is made; relevant costs are those that are differential, future, and quantifiable.

Relevant costs are those that must be considered in a decision-making situation. For a cost to be relevant, it must be differential, future, and quantifiable. The differential factor was described above. The future factor demands that the cost must not have already occurred, but instead will be incurred only after the decision is made. Finally, relevant costs must be quantifiable. (A subjective preference for Machine A or Machine B is not a cost concern in decision-making.)

An example illustrates relevant costs. A restaurant owner is approached by a salesperson selling ranges who provides the following information:

Cost of new range	= $ 5,000
Estimated life of range	= Six years
Annual operating costs:	
Electricity	= $ 800
Repairs	= $ 200
Labor (operating cost)	= $10,000
Estimated salvage value (six years)	= $ 500

The restaurant owner believes his present range after a major repair will last for six more years. To make a rational, informed decision, the owner compiles the following data on his present range:

Original cost	= $ 2,000
Estimated cost (required major repair)	= $ 1,200
Estimated salvage value (now)	= $ 300
Estimated salvage value (after six years)	= $ 100
Annual operating costs:	
Electricity	= $ 700
Repairs	= $ 500
Labor (operating cost)	= $10,000

The relevant costs are shown in Figure 7.7. All costs shown in that figure are relevant because they are differential, future, and quantifiable. The original

Cost	Alternatives	
	Buy New	**Keep Old**
Cost of new range	$5,000	----
Electricity (annually — 6 years)	$800 × 6 = $4,800	$700 × 6 = $4,200
Repairs (annually)	$200 × 6 = $1,200	$500 × 6 = $3,000
Salvage value of present range now	($300)*	-----
Salvage value of present range (end of 6th year)	$0	($100)*
Salvage value of new range (end of 6th year)	($500)*	$0
Major repair job	-----	$1,200
TOTAL	**$10,200**	**$8,300**

*Cash received by restaurant.

Figure 7.7 Relevant Costs for Range Purchase/Repair Decision

cost of the present range is irrelevant; it is not a future cost (but rather a sunk cost, which is discussed below), and the cost of labor is irrelevant because it is not differential.

Based on the costs for the two alternatives, the restaurant manager should keep the old range, since $8,300 is $1,900 less than $10,200. (For simplicity, the timing of the costs and related tax implications are ignored.)

As a second example, consider the manager who wants to purchase a new mixer to make the chef more productive; the chef's salary will not change after the purchase. Costs related to the purchase of Mixer A and Mixer B are shown in Figure 7.8.

Other information includes:

- Each mixer is expected to have a useful life of ten years, after which it will have no **salvage value.**

    > **SALVAGE VALUE The estimated market value of an asset when it is retired from use; also called residual value.**

- Timing of costs associated with each mixer will be ignored as will any income tax implications.

- The chef likes the appearance of Mixer B better but cannot place a value on this preference.

- The value to the restaurant of the chef's increased productivity is the same regardless of which mixer is purchased.

Costs	Alternatives	
	Mixer A	**Mixer B**
Mixer	$3,450.00	$4,250.00
Attachments	2,000.00	1,800.00
Annual operating costs:		
Electricity	100.00	100.00
Supplies	200.00	200.00
Maintenance contract	200.00	100.00
Repairs (not covered by maintenance contract)	50.00	50.00

Figure 7.8 Relevant Costs for Mixer Purchase

The irrelevant costs are those that do not differ between the two mixer alternatives: electricity, supplies, and repairs. All other costs are relevant, because they are future, differential, and quantifiable. The chef's preference for Mixer B is not directly considered, since it cannot be quantified. The value of the chef's increased productivity has not been quantified, since it does not differ between the two mixers. In either case, the value to the restaurant of his increased productivity will far exceed the cost of the mixer.

Figure 7.9 shows a cost analysis helpful in making the purchase decision. Based on the lower cost, Mixer A should be selected. If the $100 difference between mixers is considered immaterial, then Mixer B should probably be purchased because of the chef's unquantifiable preference for it.

Sunk Costs

SUNK COST A past cost relating to a previous decision that is not relevant to a present decision; for example, the net book value of a fixed asset.

A **sunk cost** is a past cost relating to a past decision. A sunk cost may be differential yet irrelevant because it is not future. In the case of the range purchase/repair decision above, the original cost of the old range ($2,000) is a sunk cost.

In some decision-making situations, managers review financial records to determine the net book value (cost less accumulated depreciation) of a fixed asset rather than its original (sunk) cost. However, in this chapter, we will consider both the original cost and the net book value (sunk) costs. The relevant cost in replacing a fixed asset is the asset's current market value (what it could be sold for). In Figure 7.7, the current ($300) value of the old range and its projected value of $100 at the end

Relevant Cost	Mixer	
	A	B
Purchase costs	$3,450.00	$4,250.00
Attachments	2,000.00	1,800.00
Operating costs—maintenance contract for 5 years		
$200 × 5	1,000.00	----
$100 × 5	----	500.00
Total cost	$6,450.00	$6,550.00

Figure 7.9 Cost Analysis: Mixer Purchase Decision

of six years are both relevant costs, since they are differential, future, and quantifiable. In this case, since both represent cash inflows for the restaurant, they may be viewed as cost savings and have been subtracted in the analysis.

Average/Incremental Costs

The **average cost** of providing products and services is determined by dividing the total production and service costs by the quantity (units) of production. For example, a restaurant may be able to produce a breakfast for an average cost of $4.00. The production costs include fixed, variable, and mixed costs. The calculation follows:

> **AVERAGE COST The total production/service cost divided by the quantity of units produced.**

Cost of food (variable)	$250
Cost of labor (mixed)	250
Cost of supplies (variable)	10
Utilities (mixed)	10
Depreciation (fixed)	10
Other (mixed)	70
Total	$600
Number of breakfasts	150

Average cost = $600 ÷ 150 = $4.00

The cost to produce and serve the next breakfast (number 151) is called the **incremental cost.** Incremental costs include the variable costs of food and

INCREMENTAL COSTS The costs of producing one more unit beyond the quantity of production used to calculate the average cost; includes the variable cost and the variable portion of the mixed cost.

supplies and the variable portion of the mixed costs. Assume there is a $2.00 incremental cost. (In this case, the incremental cost per meal is less than the average per meal cost.) In some cases, fixed costs (or at least the fixed element of a mixed cost) must be included in the incremental cost calculation. For example, if a manager wanted to know the cost of producing and serving 150 additional meals, the cost of additional supervision, etc., would need to be assessed.

A common difference between average and incremental costs concerns income taxes. To illustrate, consider a simplified graduated tax rate as follows:

Taxable Income	Tax Rate
$20,000 and under	10%
Greater than $20,000	20%

The incremental taxes and average taxes paid on each dollar of taxable income up to $20,000 is 10 cents. Taxes on taxable income in excess of $20,000 will be 20 cents per dollar. Therefore, the incremental tax on the 25,000th dollar is 20 cents; the average tax on $25,000 is 12%:

$$\text{Taxes on the first } \$20,000 = \$20,000 \times 0.10 = \$2,000$$
$$\text{Taxes on the next } \$5,000 = \$\ 5,000 \times 0.20 = \underline{\$1,000}$$
$$\text{Total taxes} \qquad\qquad\qquad\qquad = \$3,000$$
$$\text{Average tax} = \$3,000 \div \$25,000 = \underline{\underline{12\%}}$$

Standard Costs

STANDARD COST A forecast of actual cost under projected conditions.

Standard costs are a forecast of what actual costs should be under projected conditions. Standards can serve as a comparison base for control purposes and as a way to evaluate productivity. Generally, standard costs are established on a per unit basis. For example, standard recipe costs consider the planned cost of a food serving such as a dinner or an à la carte item. Assume that the standard recipe cost for a dinner is $7.50. If 100 dinners are served, then the budgeted cost is $750. An actual food cost of $875 reveals a $125 variance. If the variance is significant, it must be investigated to determine the probable causes and appropriate corrective actions.

BREAK-EVEN ANALYSIS

Break-even analysis allows a manager to determine the revenues required for any desired profit level. When properly used, it can provide useful information to answer other questions, such as:

> **BREAK-EVEN ANALYSIS A management tool that can help restaurant managers examine the relationship between various costs, revenues, and sales volume. A break-even analysis allows the manager to determine the revenue required at any desired profit level; also called cost-volume-profit (CVP) analysis.**

- What is the restaurant's break-even point?
- What is the profit at any given level of sales above the break-even point?
- How will a $10,000 increase in property taxes next year affect the restaurant's break-even point?
- How much additional revenue must be generated next year to cover the increase in property taxes and still achieve the desired profit?
- How many meals must be sold to achieve an $80,000 profit?
- What is the impact on profit if prices, variable costs, or fixed costs increase?

A Close Look at Break-even Analysis

Break-even analysis is a management tool that shows relationships between various costs, sales volume, and profits. Let's look at a simple example.

The manager of the Grand Café wants to identify the average selling price that must be charged to make a profit of $2,500 in a 30-day period. Available information follows:

- Variable costs per meal equal $5.
- With an average price between $7 and $9, 2,500 meals can be sold.
- Fixed costs for a 30-day period are $5,000.

With this information the manager can use break-even analysis to determine that the selling price must average $8 to generate a $2,500 profit in a 30-day period:

$$\text{Selling price} = \text{Variable cost per meal} + \frac{\text{Desired profit} + \text{Fixed costs}}{\text{Number of meals to be sold}}$$

$$\$8 \quad = \quad \$5 \quad + \quad \frac{2,500 + 5,000}{2,500}$$

Since the selling price of $8 is within the range of $7 to $9 required to sell the specified number of meals, the manager can attain the goal of a $2,500 profit in 30 days by averaging a selling price of $8. The Grand Café's summarized operating budget for the 30-day period will be:

Food sales (2,500 × $8)		$20,000
Variable costs (2,500 × $5)	$12,500	
Fixed costs	5,000	17,500
Profit		$ 2,500

Assumptions, Limitations, and Relationships

Break-even analysis is based on several assumptions. When these assumptions are not borne out, the analysis may produce incorrect results. Common assumptions follow:

- Fixed costs remain fixed during the period being considered.
- Variable costs change in a linear relationship with revenues; if revenues increase 6%, variable costs also increase 6%.
- Revenues are directly proportional to volume; as unit sales increase by 10%, revenues increase by 10%.
- Mixed costs can be divided into their fixed and variable parts.
- Break-even analysis considers only quantitative factors. Qualitative factors such as employee morale, guests' goodwill, etc., are not considered. Management must carefully assess these subjective factors, of course, before making final decisions.

The break-even analysis model considers the relationship of profit to sales volume and relates both to fixed and variable costs. As the volume of sales increases and reaches the point where the amount of revenues generated by those sales equals the total costs of generating the sales, the restaurant reaches its break-even point. As the volume of sales increases past the break-even point, the amount of revenues generated by those sales increases at a faster rate than the costs associated with those sales. Then the growing difference between revenues and costs measures the increase in profit relative to sales volume.

Examples of Break-even Analysis

The break-even equation expresses the cost-volume-profit relationship and is illustrated in Figure 7.10. At the break-even point, net income is zero, and the equation is shown as:

$$0 = SX - VX - F$$

The break-even analysis equation can be rearranged to arrive at any one of the four variables as follows:

To Determine:

1. Meals at break-even:

$$\text{Units sold} = \frac{\text{Total fixed cost}}{\text{Selling price} - \text{Variable cost per meal}}$$

2. Fixed costs at break-even:

Total fixed costs
$$= (\text{Selling price} \times \text{Meals sold}) - (\text{Variable cost per meal} \times \text{Meals sold})$$

3. Selling price at break-even:

$$\text{Selling price} = \frac{\text{Total fixed cost}}{\text{Number of meals sold}} + \text{Variable cost per meal}$$

4. Variable cost per meal:

$$\text{Variable cost per meal} = \text{Selling price} - \frac{\text{Total fixed cost}}{\text{Number of meals sold}}$$

The break-even equation shows cost-volume-profit relationships as follows:

$$\text{Net income} = \begin{matrix}\text{Selling}\\\text{price}\end{matrix} \times \begin{matrix}\text{Units}\\\text{sold}\end{matrix} - \begin{matrix}\text{Variable cost}\\\text{per unit}\end{matrix} \times \begin{matrix}\text{Units}\\\text{sold}\end{matrix} - \begin{matrix}\text{Total fixed}\\\text{costs}\end{matrix}$$

Therefore: Selling price $\times$ Units sold $=$ Total revenue
Variable cost per unit $\times$ Units sold $=$ Total variable cost

Figure 7.10 Break-even Analysis

Break-even Analysis in Action

Let's assume Michael's Bistro has the following cost and price structure:

- annual fixed costs equal \$108,000
- average per meal selling price is \$15
- variable cost per meal equals \$6

Question: What is the number of meals that must be sold for Michael's Bistro to break even?

$$\text{Units sold} = \frac{\text{Total fixed cost}}{\text{Selling price} - \text{Variable cost per unit}}$$

$$= \frac{\$108{,}000}{\$15 - \$6}$$

$$= \underline{\underline{12{,}000 \text{ meals}}}$$

Question: What is the amount of fixed costs at break-even?

$$\begin{aligned}\text{Fixed cost} &= \text{Selling price} \times \text{Units sold} - \text{Variable cost per unit} \times \text{Units sold}\\ &= (\$15 \times 12{,}000) - (\$6 \times 12{,}000)\\ &= \$180{,}000 - 72{,}000\\ &= \underline{\underline{\$108{,}000}}\end{aligned}$$

Question: What is the selling price at break-even?

$$\text{Selling price} = \frac{\text{Total fixed costs}}{\text{Units sold}} + \text{Variable cost per unit}$$

$$= \frac{\$108,000}{12,000} + \$6$$

$$= \$9 + \$6$$

$$= \underline{\underline{\$15}}$$

Question: What is the variable cost per unit at break-even?

$$\text{Variable cost per unit} = \text{Selling price} - \frac{\text{Total fixed cost}}{\text{Units sold}}$$

$$= \$15 - \frac{\$108,000}{12,000}$$

$$= \$15 - \$9$$

$$= \underline{\underline{\$6}}$$

The owner desires Michael's Bistro to earn $18,000 for the year; how many meals must be sold? This can be determined by modifying the equation for units sold at break-even as follows:

$$\text{Units sold} = \frac{\text{Total fixed cost} + \text{Pretax income}}{\text{Selling price} - \text{Variable cost per unit}}$$

$$= \frac{\$108,000 + \$18,000}{\$15 - \$6}$$

$$= \underline{14,000 \text{ meals}}$$

Note that to earn $18,000 of pretax income in a year, Michael's Bistro must sell 2,000 meals beyond its break-even point (12,000 meals). The profit earned on these additional sales is the result of the selling price less the variable cost per meal multiplied by the excess meals ($15 − $6 = $9; $9 × 2,000 meals = $18,000).

The difference between selling price and variable cost per meal is called the **contribution margin** (CM). In this example, the CM is $9.00; in other words, for each meal sold, $9.00 is available after variable costs are subtracted from the selling price to cover fixed costs and/or contribute to profits. Beyond the break-even point, the sale of 2,000 additional meals results in an $18,000 profit (number of meals sold beyond break-even × CM = profit).

Likewise, if fewer meals are sold than the 12,000 needed for break-even, $9.00 (CM) is lost for every meal that is not sold. For example, we can calculate the loss for one year if Michael's Bistro sells only 11,000 meals. Based on the above information, the answer should be $9,000 (CM × the number of meals sold less than break-even). Using the general formula, the proof follows:

Net income = Selling price × Units sold − Variable cost per unit × Units sold

$$= \$15(11,000) - \$6(11,000) - \$108,000$$

Net loss   = $\underline{\$(9,000)}$

Therefore, a loss of $9,000 would be incurred if only 11,000 meals were sold during the year.

Margin of Safety

The **margin of safety** is the excess budgeted or actual sales over sales at break-even. For Michael's Bistro, the level of sales generated when pretax income of $18,000 is earned is $210,000. Since the break-even sales were $180,000, the margin of safety for Michael's Bistro when $18,000 of profit is generated is $30,000 and 2,000 meals; this is shown below:

	Break-even	Pretax Income of $18,000	Margin of Safety
Sales—$	$180,000	$210,000	$30,000
Sales—Meals	12,000	14,000	2,000

WWW: Internet Assistant

Some managers find break-even computations difficult and time consuming. There are a variety of tools available today to help make this job easier. Many are available over the Internet. To review one such aid, go to

http://www.financialstrategies.com/tools/BreakEven.html

MANAGER'S 10 POINT EFFECTIVENESS CHECKLIST

Evaluate your need for and the status of each of the following financial management tactics. For tactics you judge to be important but not yet in place, develop an action plan including completion date to implement the tactic.

TACTIC	DON'T AGREE (DON'T NEED)	AGREE (DONE)	AGREE (NOT DONE)	IF NOT DONE	
				WHO IS RESPONSIBLE?	TARGET COMPLETION DATE
1. Managers have identified all fixed monthly costs and use this information as a base when preparing budgets.	❑	❑	❑		
2. Indifference points (the level at which cost is the same) are calculated when selecting a fixed or variable cost contract.	❑	❑	❑		
3. Managers have computed the average and incremental cost of meals for each meal period that the restaurant is open.	❑	❑	❑		
4. Standard costs are known and managers compare them to actual operating costs when taking corrective action.	❑	❑	❑		
5. Managers know the importance of computing the restaurant's break-even point.	❑	❑	❑		
6. The number of meals served at the restaurant's break-even is known.	❑	❑	❑		
7. The average meal selling price needed to break even is known.	❑	❑	❑		
8. Fixed costs at the restaurant's break-even point have been computed.	❑	❑	❑		
9. New break-even points are computed whenever there are significant changes in menu prices or operating hours, and/or as significant capital expenditures are considered.	❑	❑	❑		
10. Managers thoroughly educate staff about differences between costs that help generate revenue and those that do not.	❑	❑	❑		

8

PRICING FOR PROFITS

MANAGER'S BRIEF

In this chapter you will learn about the important role that menu pricing plays in the success of your restaurant. If your menu prices are too high, the number of guests attracted to your restaurant may be too low to ensure its long-term success. If your menu prices are too low, your restaurant's profits may be too low to allow it to stay in business.

Ideally, an item's menu price should be related to the total cost of producing the item, as well as ensure that the item contributes to the profitability of the restaurant. First and foremost, the manager should take the restaurant's profit goals into consideration when establishing prices.

Just as there are many types of managers, there are many approaches managers use to determine the selling prices of menu items. Some of these approaches are effective; others are not. In this chapter, the most common methods used by managers to establish menu prices are reviewed, as are the strengths and weaknesses of each approach. Subjective pricing, that is, pricing not directly related to the costs incurred in producing a menu item, should be avoided. In this chapter you will learn how and why such methods are not helpful.

Objective pricing approaches are those that consider both costs and profitability in establishing price. Four objective methods are described in detail in this chapter, and examples are presented that demonstrate how each is used.

The establishment of menu prices will have a profound effect on a restaurant's profitability. In this chapter you will learn how to expertly analyze your operation to assure that your menu prices contribute to, and do not detract from, your financial success.

How a restaurant owner or manager sets selling prices for food and beverage products will affect to what extent profit goals are met. If a price is too high, guests will perceive low value; complaints and reduced repeat business will be likely. If the selling price is too low, costs may not be recovered; profits will obviously suffer. Likewise, improper pricing that yields a lower-than-reasonable selling price can have a negative market impact; the public may reason "you can't get something for nothing" and question the quality, cleanliness, and service standards of the restaurant if prices are set too low. Specials that offer significant value can be an effective marketing tool. Taken to the extreme, however, consistently low selling prices can connote low value in spite of the manager's best intentions.

THE ART OF PRICING

Some experienced managers talk about the "art" of pricing. They are referring to the role that their intuition, knowledge of the guests' wants and needs, competition (its products and prices), and "having a feel for costs" play when pricing decisions are made. While these factors may be involved in the pricing decision at some point, managers must also be aware of their profit requirements and the costs associated with providing the products and services as selling prices are established. Those who only use an intuitive, subjective approach to pricing and neglect profit concerns run the risk of falling short of investors' expectations.

SUBJECTIVE PRICING METHODS

When a restaurant is well established, its pricing strategy is usually well developed. However, when costs escalate and guests' demand for "value" from the dining dollars they spend rises, the bottom line can suffer; to adapt to such changes, old methods of establishing selling prices must often be reexamined.

The following pricing methods are used in many restaurants, but are probably best avoided:

- *The "reasonable" price method.* A manager using this method subjectively establishes selling prices based upon a personal belief about price levels that represent value for the guests. This emphasis is often ineffective; many managers do not know about their guests' real concerns; clearly, this approach does not relate to the profit requirements of the restaurant.

- *The "highest price" method.* Also based on the manager's perceived ability to "outguess the guest," this method suggests that selling prices be set as high as possible and then reduced slightly to allow for a margin of error in management's judgment about the guests' ability to pay.

- *The loss-leader pricing method.* With this tactic, the menu selling price for one or more items is set at the lowest possible price (even below cost) with the thought that guests will be attracted who will then purchase other products at regular (or even higher) prices. Managers using this approach think, for example, that "we will give away the food, and we'll make it up in beverage sales" (or vice versa).

- *The intuitive pricing method.* This approach actually involves little more than guessing about menu selling prices and then establishing other prices "if the first plan doesn't work."

- *The "no pricing" method.* This worst of all possible pricing practice is used all too often. When it is used, the service staff and cooks—not the managers—set selling prices. It occurs, for example, when menu substitutions are made and/or when menu items are prepared to special order. In the absence of a management-established price, prices are set as they are quoted to guests.

None of the above pricing methods incorporate profit requirements or even product costs into the pricing plan.

COSTS AND PRICING

ALLOCATION The process of rationally identifying and distributing applicable overhead (indirect) costs incurred by specific departments within the restaurant.

Costs should be a central concern in any pricing decision. Accounting systems used by some restaurants do not identify all costs, and even if they do, they may not use an **allocation** process to spread overhead (indirect) costs between food and beverage departments. If costs are not accurately identified and allocated, information that might otherwise be available to managers cannot be used; decisions based upon poor information are often poor ones.

The pricing method used by a restaurant must incorporate both profit requirements and all costs. In contrast, the method used in many "real world" restaurants works as follows:

A new food item is to be offered. The manager "determines" that a 40% food cost is necessary. If the cost of all ingredients in the new menu item is $3.15, a base selling price of $7.88 results [$3.15 × (100% ÷ 40%) = $7.88]. Since this "does not sound good," a more realistic price of $7.95 (or $8.25 or $8.55 or ?) results.

How was the 40% food cost established? In the manager's mind, it may represent "the state or national average" or "what my food cost has been in the past" or simply "intuition." How are the restaurant's profit requirements and nonfood costs considered when this approach is used?

The pricing method used for the beverage department is often even more simplified. The manager "matches up" a drink item with one of the existing beverages categories offered to determine a selling price. For example, if a drink is a "highball" (one type of liquor with a mixer such as water, tonic, or soda) it sells for the same price as all other highballs. If a drink is a cocktail (martini, old fashioned, or manhattan), the cocktail price applies. Then beverage sales prices are gradually raised "when they need to be." Beverage pricing for new facilities is often based only on competition or "what the market will bear."

Subjective pricing methods such as those discussed above do not directly and objectively incorporate the restaurant's profit requirements defined in its operating budget into the pricing decision. Further, they do not consider product (food and beverage) costs that are incurred as these items are sold.

More objective pricing methods can be used that do incorporate required profit and product cost factors. Much of the rest of this chapter addresses cost-based pricing methods. Several modifying factors must be considered as these methods are used.

Modifying Factors

When menu pricing is based on an objective **cost approach,** four modifying factors—historical prices, perceived price/value relationships, competition, and price rounding—must be evaluated. These price modifiers relate to the pricing of nearly all products and services by the restaurant manager.

> **COST APPROACH (TO PRICING)**
> **A method of establishing selling prices that factors in product costs.**

First, the restaurant's past prices must be considered. A dramatic change dictated by a cost approach may seem unreasonable to guests. For example, if a breakfast currently priced at $3.49 needs to be raised to $5.49 to cover costs, the manager may need to move slowly, introducing several smaller price increases over a period of time.

Second, guests must perceive products/services to be reasonably priced to yield a good value. Today's guests are increasingly value-conscious. Most are willing to pay higher prices than they did a few years ago, but they also demand value for the prices they pay. Note: Perceived value includes the entire dining experience: not only food and beverage products but also the restaurant's atmosphere, location, service quality, level of sanitation/cleanliness, and other, often intangible, factors.

Third, the competition cannot be ignored. If an operation's product is viewed as substantially the same as a competitor's, then everything else being equal, selling prices must be similar. For example, assume that a manager's cost-based calculations for a Caesar salad suggest a $6.50 selling price; if a strong, nearby competitor is charging $3.50 for a similar product, everything else being the same, then competition will probably force a price reduction. (Note: It is very difficult for *everything* else to be the same. The location is at least slightly different, one salad may be fresher, service may differ, etc. Effective managers attempt to differentiate their products/services from the competition to make them more favored by guests.)

Finally, the price may be modified by price rounding. That is, many managers round up calculated prices to the nearest $0.25 or, possibly, to $X.95.

Elasticity of Demand

One of the most important considerations in the pricing decision relates to the impact that selling prices have on sales volume. Often, restaurants that offer products at low prices are more dramatically affected by price increases than are their counterparts selling items at higher prices. When prices are low, guests often believe they are paying for the product itself—not the service, atmosphere, and other elements present in a more extensive "dining experience." Therefore, as selling prices increase, guests may believe that they are paying more for intangible aspects of the product/service/atmosphere mix being purchased; resistance may occur.

ELASTICITY The relationship between the impact of selling price increases or decreases on total revenues.

Conversely, the guest paying a higher price may not relate the price directly to the product being purchased. He/she may be less price-conscious than the guest in the low–selling price restaurant; the purchase decision may involve intangible (nonproduct) elements, the value of which is more difficult to quantify.

ELASTIC DEMAND The situation that occurs when a reduction in selling price yields the sale of enough additional units to increase total revenues.

Elasticity is a term relating to the effects of selling-price increases or decreases on total revenues. **Elastic demand** describes a situation in which a reduction in selling price yields sales of enough additional units (meals or beverages) to increase total revenues, or a situation in which an increase in price yields lower sales, and therefore a decrease in total revenues. By

INELASTIC DEMAND The situation that occurs when a decrease in selling price leads to a decrease in revenues.

contrast, **inelastic demand** describes the situation that occurs when a decrease in selling price leads to a decrease in total revenues, or when increased prices result in increased revenue.

The formula to measure elasticity of demand is:

$$\frac{\text{Change in quantity demanded} \div \text{Base quantity}}{\text{Change in price} \div \text{Initial price}}$$

The above formula looks complicated, but basically, when the calculation yields a number greater than 1, demand is elastic (total revenues *increase* when the unit selling price is *decreased*); when it is less than 1, demand is inelastic (total revenues decrease when the unit selling price is decreased). When the elasticity of demand is equal to 1, the price change produces no effect on total revenues. This is called **unit elasticity.**

UNIT ELASTICITY The situation that occurs when a price change produces no effect on total revenues.

Consider the following:

A menu item sells for $6.95; 350 servings are sold during an average week. The manager lowers the selling price to $6.25; 410 servings are sold weekly. What is the impact of the selling-price reduction on total revenues? What is the elasticity of demand?

The total change in revenues can be easily calculated:

Before price change: 350 servings at $6.95 each = $2,432.50
After price change: 410 servings at $6.25 each = $2,562.50

As a result of the decreased selling price, total revenue increased by $130.00 ($2,562.50 − $2,432.50). There is elastic demand, as can be seen by the formula just presented:

$$\frac{\text{Change in quantity demanded} \div \text{Base quantity}}{\text{Change in price} \div \text{Initial price}}$$

$$\frac{(410 - 350) \div 350}{0.70 \div 6.95} = \frac{0.171}{0.101} = \underline{\underline{1.69}}$$

Note that the outcome is 1.69; we stated earlier that a result of 1.0 or greater means the demand is elastic (total revenues increase when the selling price is decreased).

THE MANAGER AND MENU PRICING

Who should establish menu selling prices? Generally, responsibility for menu pricing should rest with the official who develops and implements the operating budget. (Note: The operating budget will be discussed at length in chapter 9.) As will be seen, profit requirements are included in the budget, and profit requirements should be carried forward to the pricing decision. In effect, then, a **profit pricing** approach should be used.

> **PROFIT PRICING** An approach to establishing menu selling prices that incorporates the restaurant profit requirements into the pricing strategy.

A restaurant's general manager may ultimately be responsible for attaining budget goals of the entire property. However, the food and beverage department heads both have an impact on revenues. Also, both these managers should control costs incurred by their departments. Therefore, each may be required to generate a mutually agreed upon part of the total profit requirement. Thus, department managers, working in conjunction with the general manager, may mutually establish selling prices for a given budget period.

The concept of **integrated pricing** should be noted. Food and beverage products generally should not be priced independently of each other. All products should be priced in a complementary manner so as to best ensure that the restaurant's total profit goals, including those of the specific departments, are attained.

INTEGRATED PRICING   The tactic of pricing food and beverage products in a complementary relationship to each other.

This principle can also be thought of as the concept of **derived demand;** sale of food (or beverage) products in one department is likely to affect activity in other departments. Consider, for example, the "spin-off" effects of increased drink sales in the lounge on food sales in the restaurant. As sales in one department

DERIVED DEMAND   A recognition that the sale of food (or beverage) products in one department is likely to impact activity in other departments of the restaurant.

increase (or decrease), a similar effect may carry over to the other department.

The concepts of integrated pricing and desired demand again support the need for a management team approach when pricing decisions are made.

SUBJECTIVE PRICING PROCEDURES SHOULD BE AVOIDED

The subjective pricing methods discussed earlier are understood by many in the restaurant industry and are simple to implement. However, they ignore the need to both identify and consider profit requirements and all costs, including direct food and beverage costs. When past operating percentages (from previous budgets) and current selling prices are used as the base from which to establish new prices, the manager assumes that past food/beverage operations were efficient and profit was optimized. (Yet in fact, without proper analysis of required profit, there is not even certainty that profit was "satisfactory"!) If this assumption is incorrect (past operations were not optimally effective) these pricing methods, in effect, extend past operating problems into new fiscal periods.

Managers should recognize that profits are in part a function of sales. With fixed costs constant, total cost percentages are reduced as sales rise; higher profit levels result. In addition, larger purchases of food and beverages may result in quantity discounts: Economies of scale may result from lower per unit prices as higher quantities of product are purchased because of increased sales. There is, then, a need to correlate profit and costs with sales levels. Many common pricing methods fail to do this.

Managers who rely totally upon subjective methods to set selling prices often do not control their operation. They do not allow financial statements and accounting records to provide useful information about operations. By contrast, an effective pricing system incorporates management control information into pricing decisions. This, in turn, provides more internal consistency than do systems that yield autonomous, independent decisions about selling prices, incurred expenses, and profit expectations.

PROFIT PRICING: PAY YOURSELF FIRST

Profit must be planned; costs must be identified and controlled. These standards should be incorporated into the pricing system used by the restaurant. These ideas can be combined into a single focal point if the manager merely regards profit as a "cost of doing business." Stated another way, revenue should be sufficient to cover all incurred costs, as well as to generate required profit. The manager should think about the following relationship:

$$\text{Profit} + \text{Incurred Costs} = \text{Revenue}$$

A useful pricing system must consider the profit needs of the owner/investor "up front" of incurred costs. This approach provides a different emphasis and perspective than does the following more traditional formula:

$$\text{Revenue} - \text{Incurred Costs} = \text{Profit}$$

Any mathematician knows that the two formulas are the same; a good businessperson knows they are conceptually "worlds apart." Profit should *not* be "what's left after costs are subtracted from revenue." Managers should plan to, in effect, "pay themselves first" (generate profit) and then operate the restaurant effectively with remaining revenues without sacrificing quality requirements. One way to do this is to think about profit as a cost and build this cost (profit) into the selling price. Some refer to this approach as "bottom-up" pricing.

BOTTOM-UP PRICING

A bottom-up method can be used to determine the average meal price for a restaurant. Seven steps in the process follow:

Step 1:   Determine desired net income by multiplying the owners' investment by the desired return on owners' investment (ROI).

Step 2:   Determine the pretax profit by dividing the desired net income by 1 minus the tax rate.

Step 3:   Determine interest expenses.

Step 4:   Determine operating expenses.

Step 5:   Determine required food revenue by adding figures from Steps 2–4 and then dividing this sum by 1 minus the desired food cost percentage.

Step 6:   Determine meals to be served by multiplying days open by number of seats by seat turnover for the day.

Step 7:   Determine the required price of the average meal by dividing the total food revenue by the estimated number of meals to be served.

To illustrate the above process, let's look at Segee's Place. Applicable information is found in Figure 8.1.

Given this information we can calculate the average meal price needed to generate required profits.

Step 1:   Determine Desired Net Income.

$$\text{Owners' Investment} \times \text{Desired ROI}$$
$$\$500,000 \quad \times \quad 12\% \quad = \$60,000$$

Step 2:   Determine PreTax Profit.

$$\frac{\text{Net income}}{1 - \text{Tax rate}} = \frac{\$60,000}{1 - .25} = \$80,000$$

Step 3:   Determine Interest Expense (funds borrowed).

$$\$1,000,000 \times .10 \times 1 = \$100,000$$

Item	Amount	Other
Owners' investment	$ 500,000	Desired ROI = 12%
Funds borrowed	1,000,000	Interest rate = 10%
Tax rate	---	25%
Operating expenses	800,000	Annual amount
Cost of food sold percentage	---	40%
Seat turnover	---	2 times per day
Days open	---	365 days
Number of seats	---	100 seats

Figure 8.1 Factors to Assess Average Meal Price at Segee's Place

Step 4: Determine Operating Expenses.

$800,000 (Note: This was provided in Figure 8.1.)

Step 5: Determine Required Food Revenue.

$$\frac{\text{Pretax profit} + \text{Interest expense} + \text{Operating expenses}}{1 - \text{Food cost percentage}}$$

$$\frac{\$80,000 + \$100,000 + \$800,000}{1 - 40\%} = \$1,633,333$$

Step 6: Determine Meals to Be Served.

Days open $\times$ Number of seats $\times$ Seat turnover
365     $\times$ 100 seats $\times$ 2 turns = 73,000 meals

Step 7: Determine Price of Average Meal.

$$\frac{\text{Total Revenue}}{\text{Total Meals}} = \frac{\$1,633,333}{73,000} = \$22.37$$

The above calculations indicate an average per meal selling price of $22.37 will generate the level of revenue needed, first, to meet the owners' investment requirement (profits), and second, to meet costs required for interest and operating expenses (including cost of sales: food).

If management could turn the seats over faster (everything else being the same), the average meal price required to provide the owners with the desired 12% return on their investment would be reduced. For example, if the seat turnover could be increased to 3, then the average meal selling price would be:

$$\text{Average meal price} = \frac{\text{Food revenue}}{\text{Meals sold}} = \frac{\$1,633,333}{365 \times 100 \times 3} = \$14.92$$

By contrast, a less frequent seat turnover requires a higher average meal price if other factors are the same. For Segee's, a seat turnover of 1.5 would require an average meal price of $29.83.

Our discussion of the bottom-up approach to pricing meals has, to this point, centered on average meal prices. Few, if any, restaurants establish one price for all meals, and many restaurants offer meals at more than one meal period. For example, if the restaurant serves lunch and dinner, the average meal price for both meal periods can be calculated as follows:

- Calculate the revenue per meal period by multiplying the total food revenue by the estimated percentage of the total earned during that meal period.

- Divide the revenue per meal period by the meals sold per meal period. (The number of meals sold per meal period is calculated by multiplying the days the restaurant is open by the seat turnover by the number of seats.)

Once again, let's use Segee's to illustrate. Assume that management estimates the total food revenue to be divided between lunch and dinner revenue as 40% and 60%, respectively. Further, assume the luncheon seat turnover is 1.25 and the dinner seat turnover is 0.75. Using the total revenue for Segee's as calculated above, the average meal prices by meal period are:

Revenue Per Meal Period:

Lunch:	40% × $1,633,333 =	$ 653,333
Dinner:	60% × $1,633,333 =	980,000
Total		$1,633,333

Meals Sold Per Meal Period:

Lunch: $365 \times 100 \times 1.25 = \underline{45,625}$

Dinner: $365 \times 100 \times 0.75 = \underline{27,375}$

$$\text{Average Meal Prices by Meal Period} = \frac{\text{Meal Period Revenue}}{\text{Meals Sold}}$$

$$\text{Lunch} = \frac{\$653,333}{45,625} = \underline{\$14.32}$$

$$\text{Dinner} = \frac{\$980,000}{27,375} = \underline{\$35.80}$$

Now that we have considered what the average per meal selling price must be for the restaurant to generate required profit and to have funds remaining to pay all other costs, let's look at some specific methods that incorporate price concerns into base selling prices.

OBJECTIVE MENU PRICING METHODS

Methods emphasizing mark-up pricing, contribution margin pricing, ratio pricing, and simple prime cost pricing are objective approaches, as is the "bottom-up" approach just discussed; that is, they address profit concerns and help to assure that guests receive value for the dollars they spend in the restaurant.

Mark-Up Pricing

A mark-up factor can be planned to cover all costs and to yield desired profit. For example, the ingredients mark-up method considers all product costs. The three steps are as follows:

Step 1: Determine the cost of the ingredients in the menu item being priced.

Step 2: Determine the multiplier to be used in marking up the ingredients' costs.

Step 3: Establish a **base selling price** by multiplying the ingredients' costs by the multiplier.

> **BASE SELLING PRICE** The starting point for determining a menu item's actual selling price that results from an objective pricing method incorporating profit goals and product ingredient costs.

Note: A base selling price is not necessarily the final selling price. Rather, it is a starting point from which other factors must be assessed. These include the modifying factors discussed earlier, such as value (price relative to quality from the guest's perspective), supply and demand, production volume concerns, and prices charged by competitors.

PRE-COSTING The process of determining the actual purchase costs of all ingredients comprising a menu item. Pre-costing must be kept current by changing costs of ingredients as their purchase price changes.

Step 1: Determine the ingredients' costs. Assume that a chicken dinner has a cost of $3.32. This cost represents the total food costs of all items comprising the dinner (chicken entrée, potato, vegetable, etc.) when prepared according to applicable standard recipes after **pre-costing** with current ingredient costs.

Step 2: Determine the **multiplier.** The multiplier (also called "mark-up") used to mark up the ingredient costs can be based upon the food cost percentage from an effectively developed operating budget. (Menu items priced, on average, to yield the budgeted food cost

MULTIPLIER A number to be multiplied by a menu item's ingredient cost to yield a base selling price; also called "mark-up."

percentage create a foundation to generate revenue sufficient to cover food, other costs, and profit requirements.) For example, assume:

- Budgeted revenues − $875,000
- Budgeted food cost − $325,000
- Budgeted food cost % (food cost ÷ food revenues) = 37.1%

$$\text{Multiplier} = \frac{1}{\text{Budgeted food cost percentage}} = \frac{1}{0.371} = 2.7 \text{ (rounded)}$$

Step 3: Multiply ingredient costs by multiplier.

$$\text{Ingredient costs} \times \text{Multiplier} = \text{Base selling price}$$
$$\$3.32 \quad \times \quad 2.7 \quad = \quad \$8.96$$

If this base selling price appears reasonable, the chicken dinner would be sold for about $9.00. Note: Price multipliers will be discussed in more detail later in this chapter.

Contribution Margin Pricing

The **contribution margin** is found by subtracting a menu item's food cost from its selling price. It is the amount the item "contributes" to nonfood costs and profit.

Note: Earlier we defined the term "contribution margin" to be: Revenue − Variable cost. This definition is a typical accounting-related explanation of the term. In the context of food cost control, however, "contribution margin" has a slightly different meaning: Revenue − Food costs. Food costs are one type of variable cost, so in the context of food cost control our definition is more specific.

The two steps used in contribution margin pricing are:

Step 1: Determine the average contribution margin per guest.
Step 2: Determine the base selling price for the menu item.

Assume that the approved operating budget for the restaurant indicates that all nonfood costs will be $395,000, that required profit is $50,000, and that 85,000 guests are expected to be served during the budget period.

Step 1: Determine the average contribution margin per guest. This is done by dividing all nonfood costs plus profit by the number of expected guests.

$$\frac{\text{Nonfood costs} + \text{Profit}}{\text{Number of expected guests}} = \text{Average contribution margin per guest}$$

$$\frac{\$395,000 + \$50,000}{85,000} = \$5.24$$

Step 2: Determine the base selling price for the menu item. This is done by adding the average contribution margin per guest (Step 1) to the item's ingredient cost. The base selling price for a menu item with a $3.60 ingredient cost would be $8.84 ($3.60 + $5.24 = $8.84).

This method is easy to use when reasonably accurate information is available from the operating budget. It is practical when costs associated with serving each guest are basically the same with the exception of varying food costs. This method tends to reduce the range of selling prices on the menu, since the only difference is reflected in the actual food cost incorporated into the selling price.

Wise restaurant managers know that, regardless of the amount spent by a guest, that guest should receive the same quality of service, environmental ambiance, cleanliness, and "dining experience." The only variable, then, is the menu item that is ordered with its associated food (ingredient) cost. Therefore, the contribution margin pricing method recognizes that each guest should pay his/her "fair share" of nonproduct costs and contributions to the restaurant's profits.

Ratio Pricing

The ratio pricing method assesses the relationship between ingredient costs and all noningredient costs (all other controllable costs except food and all fixed costs) plus profit requirements and then uses this ratio to develop base selling prices for menu items. The steps to ratio pricing are:

Step 1:   Calculate the ratio of ingredient costs to nonfood costs and profit.
Step 2:   Calculate the total noningredient costs and profit for the menu item.
Step 3:   Determine the base selling price.

Assume that the operating budget of a family-style restaurant (no alcoholic beverages are sold) indicates:

Total ingredient (food) costs	—	$235,000
Total noningredient costs	—	$560,000
Budgeted profit	—	$80,000

Note: "Noningredient" costs include all expenses incurred by the restaurant other than food.

Step 1:   Calculate the ratio of ingredient costs to noningredient costs plus profit. The following formula is used:

$$\frac{\text{Noningredient costs + Profit}}{\text{Ingredient costs}} = \text{Ratio}$$

$$\frac{\$560,000 + \$80,000}{\$235,000} = 2.72 \text{ (rounded)}$$

This ratio means that for each $1 of revenue required to cover food costs, an additional $2.72 in revenue is needed for noningredient costs and to meet profit requirements.

Step 2: Calculate the total noningredient costs and profit for the menu item. This is done by multiplying the ingredient costs of the menu item by the ratio (from Step 1). For example, if the ingredient cost is $3.75, the amount of noningredient costs and profit required is $10.20 [$3.75 × 2.72 = $10.20 (rounded)].

Step 3: Determine the base selling price for the menu item. This is done by adding the required noningredient cost and profit (from Step 2) to the ingredient cost of the menu item. The base selling price for the item above with a $3.75 ingredient cost is approximately $13.95 [$3.75 + $10.20 = $13.95].

The ratio method of menu pricing is simple and can be based upon information in the operating budget. However, a restaurant offering food and beverages must separate nonfood costs and profit requirements in the two revenue centers.

Simple Prime Cost Pricing

"Prime cost" refers to the largest costs incurred by most restaurants: food and labor. Prime cost pricing involves assessing food and labor costs for the restaurant and factoring these costs into the pricing equation. The steps follow:

Step 1: Determine the labor costs per guest.
Step 2: Determine the prime costs per guest.
Step 3: Determine the base selling price.

Assume the manager knows the following from the operating budget:

Labor costs	—	$210,000
Number of expected guests	—	75,000
Desired prime cost percentage	—	62%
(food cost % + labor cost %)		

Step 1: Determine the labor costs per guest. Divide labor costs by the number of expected guests:

$$\text{Labor cost per guest} = \frac{\text{Labor costs}}{\text{Number of expected guests}}$$

$$\$2.80 = \frac{\$210,000}{75,000}$$

Step 2: Determine the prime cost per guest. The labor cost per guest ($2.80) is added to the menu item's ingredient cost. Assume an ingredient cost of $3.75[13]:

$$\begin{array}{ccccc}
\$3.75 & + & \$2.80 & = & \$6.55 \\
\text{(ingredient cost)} & & \text{(labor cost per guest)} & & \text{(prime cost per guest)}
\end{array}$$

Step 3: Determine the menu item's base selling price. This is calculated by dividing the prime cost per guest (Step 2) by the desired prime cost percentage:

$$\text{Base selling price} = \frac{\text{Prime cost per guest}}{\text{Desired prime cost \%}}$$

$$\$10.56 = \frac{\$6.55}{0.62}$$

The objective pricing methods discussed above are relatively easy to use because they incorporate information from the approved operating budget ("profit plan") of the restaurant. Perhaps the single most challenging calculation in all the above methods is that involving ingredient costs. The manager must have a standard recipe pre-costed with current financial information to use any pricing method based at least in part on product cost. However, the need for standard recipes permeates all aspects of operating control, and pre-costing has become much easier with the advent of applicable software.

---

[13]This ingredient cost is the estimated food cost when all menu items are prepared according to standard recipes.

MORE ABOUT MULTIPLIERS AND PRICING TACTICS

Multipliers were briefly noted above in our review of mark-up pricing. We noted that a rational way to determine the multiplier was to use information from the operating budget (budgeted food costs divided by budgeted revenue). This approach is relatively simple for a restaurant having only one revenue center. (For example, a "family-style" restaurant that serves no alcoholic beverages.) It is obvious that 100% of all profit must be obtained from the food products sold. Likewise, all costs must be recovered from the applicable revenue.

Food-Only Restaurants

It is often easier to control product costs (food or beverage) than other costs. Since pricing mark-ups are generally based upon product costs it seems reasonable to estimate the amount that can be spent for product purchases. To determine the maximum (allowable) amount that can be spent to purchase products if the restaurant serves only food the following approach can be used:

$$\text{Total forecasted revenue} - \left[\text{Total nonproduct costs} + \text{Required profit}\right] = \text{Allowable product (food) costs}$$

If total forecasted food revenues approximate those in the calculations, if nonproduct costs do not exceed budget estimates, and if allowable product costs are not exceeded, revenue should be available to meet both nonproduct costs and the restaurant's profit requirements.

The same process can be used in a beverage-only (bar) operation to determine the amount that can be spent on beverage products.

The following example reviews the three-step process to price for profit that can be used by a restaurant selling only food.

Assume the following from the restaurant's annual operating budget:

- Total annual food revenues will be $750,000.

- All expenses other than food ("nonfood" costs) will be $375,000. (These include all overhead and variable costs except cost of goods sold: food.)

- Profit required is $65,000 (before tax).

- The food cost of a menu item when prepared according to a pre-costed standard recipe is $4.40.

Step 1:   Calculate allowable food cost.

Total forecasted revenue − [All nonfood costs + Profit] = Allowable food cost
$750,000   −   [$375,000 + $65,000]   = $310,000

The above example indicates that if estimated revenue will be $750,000, and if nonfood costs and profit needs will be $440,000 ($375,000 + $65,000), the manager cannot spend more than $310,000 to purchase food.

Step 2:   Calculate multiplier.

$$\frac{\text{Budgeted food sales}}{\text{Allowable food costs}} = \text{Multiplier}$$

$$\frac{\$750,000}{\$310,000} = 2.42$$

Note: The multiplier can also be calculated as follows:

$$\frac{1}{\text{Budgeted food cost} \div \text{Budgeted revenue}} = \frac{1}{0.413} = 2.42$$

Step 3:   Calculate base selling price of menu item.

Multiplier × Standard recipe cost = Base selling price
2.42   × $4.40   = $10.65 (rounded)

The base selling price of the menu item ($10.65) must be adjusted as the actual selling price is determined. Factors that affect the determination of the actual selling price include:

- perceived guest value
- competition
- "price rounding"
- traditional prices charged

This approach to pricing allows the manager to carry profit needs from the operating budget on into the calculations to set selling prices.

Food and Beverage Restaurants

If the restaurant sells food and beverage products (as is often the case), the required profit can be generated from the sale of either (and/or both) products. More planning becomes necessary in the pricing decision because both profit and costs must be allocated between the two departments.

Allocating Required Profit. How can profit requirements be allocated between departments? If 75% of total revenue is generated by the food operation, it may be unlikely to expect that 75% of the required profit should be generated by this department; there is generally a higher percentage of profit per dollar of sales from the beverage operation. To require the food department to generate a higher level of profit than necessary is probably unreasonable: The selling price of food items would need to be unreasonably high. Then there would be less value in the dining experience from the guests' perspective and revenue/profits would be likely to decrease. What is an alternative?

One approach is to require the foodservice department to pay for food costs that it directly incurs and to then allocate nonfood and nonbeverage costs between the departments. With this plan the amount of profit, if any, generated by food sales is first assessed. The beverage operation is then managed to recover the remaining required profit. This method is discussed below.

Allocating Costs.   Food and beverage costs should be charged to the food and beverage departments, respectively. (Details regarding food and beverage transfers, costs of employee meals, complimentary food and beverage assessments, and other matters that affect the cost of goods sold in actual practice have been omitted in this discussion for simplification.) Nonproduct costs must then be allocated between both departments. A simple but, unfortunately, not very accurate proration method would consider the percentage of total sales (if 75% of all revenues are from food sales, then 75% of all costs other than food and beverage will be applicable to foodservice; 25% of nonproduct costs will be applicable to the beverage operation).

It is also possible (and more accurate) to prorate nonproduct costs on some basis other than revenues. Unfortunately, more accurate allocation methods that involve separate allocations for each cost are more time consuming, and for this reason are of less interest to many managers. However, a compromise that involves careful allocation of large expenses by a rational means and the combined allocation of small expenses on the basis of simple revenue percentages may be useful.

Establishing Selling Prices.   The following example reviews a five-step process that can be used to determine a base selling price for food and beverage items. To simplify, all nonproduct costs will be allocated on the basis of revenue percentage.

Let's assume:

- The restaurant must generate $60,000 before-tax profit.
- The annual operating budget estimates that:

    —Total food revenue will be $600,000.

    —Total beverage revenue will be $125,000.

    —Food costs will be $216,000.

    —Total nonproduct costs will be $399,000. (This includes overhead and all variable costs except direct food costs and beverage costs.)

- The standard recipe indicates that the food cost for one portion of a menu item is $4.85.
- The beverage cost of a drink, prepared according to a standard recipe, is $1.10.

Step 1:   Calculate profit from sale of food.

$$\text{Food revenue} - \left[\text{Food costs} + \frac{\text{Prorated share of nonfood}}{\text{beverage costs}}\right] = \text{Profit from sale of food}$$

$$\$600,000 - [216,000 + 83\%^{14}\,(399,000)] = \text{Profit from sale of food}$$

$$\$600,000 - [216,000 + 331,170] = \$52,830$$

These calculations tell the manager that, with the cost allocation process used, $52,830 of the required $60,000 before-tax profit will be generated from

----

[14]Since cost allocation is on the basis of food revenue to total revenue, then

Total revenue = $725,000 ($600,000 in food revenue + $125,000 in beverage revenue)

Food revenue = $600,000

$$\text{Ratio of food revenue to total revenue} = \frac{\$600,000}{\$725,000} = 83\%\ (\text{rounded})$$

sale of food. The remainder of required profit must be generated by beverage sales.

You have learned that information developed to this point can help establish a base selling price for a menu item. Since the operating budget estimates that food revenues will approximate $600,000 and food costs will be $216,000, a mark-up is established:

$$\text{Mark-up} = \frac{\text{Budgeted food revenue}}{\text{Budgeted food costs}} = \frac{\$600,000}{\$216,000} = 2.78 \text{ (rounded)}$$

The base selling price of our menu item can now be calculated:

$$\text{Base selling price} = \text{Price multiplier} \times \text{Standard food cost}$$
$$\$13.48 \quad = \quad 2.78 \quad \times \quad \$4.85$$

These procedures are identical to those illustrated in the pricing model suggested above for a restaurant selling only food (no alcoholic beverages).

Step 2: Calculate profit from sale of beverage.

$$\text{Total required profit} - \text{Profit from food sales} = \text{Profit from beverage sales}$$
$$\$60,000 \quad - \quad \$52,830 \quad = \quad \$7,170$$

Step 3: Determine allowable beverage cost.

$$\begin{array}{c}\text{Total beverage}\\\text{revenue}\end{array} - \left[\begin{array}{c}\text{Prorated share of}\\\text{nonfood/beverage} +\\\text{expenses}\end{array}\begin{array}{c}\text{Profit from}\\\text{beverage sales}\end{array}\right] = \begin{array}{c}\text{Allowable beverage}\\\text{cost}\end{array}$$

$$\$125,000 - 17\%^{15}\,(399,000) + \$7,170 = \text{Allowable beverage cost}$$

$$\$125,000 - \quad [67,830 + 7,170] \quad = \quad \$50,000$$

---

[15]Note: Proration is on the basis of beverage revenue to total revenue.

Total revenue = $725,000 ($600,000 in food revenue + $125,000 in beverage revenue)

Beverage revenue = $125,000

$$\text{Ratio of beverage revenue to total revenue} = \frac{\$125,000}{\$725,000} = 17\%$$

Step 4:　Calculate the mark-up.

$$\text{Mark-up} = \frac{\text{Budgeted beverage income}}{\text{Allowable beverage cost} - \$50,000} = \frac{\$125,000}{\$50,000} = 2.5$$

Step 5:　Calculate base selling price of drink.

$$\text{Mark-up} \times \text{Standard recipe cost} = \text{Base drink selling price}$$
$$2.5 \quad \times \quad \$1.10 \quad = \quad \$2.75$$

The price of the drink ($2.75) would now be adjusted to fit the needs of the restaurant; for example, if base drink selling prices for other popular house drinks average about $2.50, and if they were of approximately equal popularity, an actual selling price ranging from $2.60 to $2.70 might be established for all drinks in this drink category. (The drink price might be rounded to the highest $0.05 to make it easier for service personnel to remember prices and to make change.)

Adjusting the Allowable Beverage Cost.　The preceding plan assumes that the food department will make a significant contribution to the required profit. If it is operating efficiently, and if menu pricing is done correctly, this should be the case. Managers must constantly ensure that required control procedures are utilized. The pricing plan also assumes that profit requirements will not be met by the sale of food alone; rather, the beverage department will make an additional contribution. This necessary contribution is better ensured by adjusting the allowable beverage cost. (In other words, if more profit is required, beverage costs must be lower; if less profit is needed, allowable beverage costs can be higher.)

A problem occurs when allowable beverage costs (which cannot be exceeded if necessary profit levels are to be attained) are not high enough to provide desired standards of beverage service. There are several ways to resolve this problem. For example, the manager can examine the food operation to see if costs can be reduced and/or revenues can be increased. This practice should always be followed, but becomes critical when anticipated revenue will not be sufficient to cover both expected expenses and required profit. An increase in profits from the food operation will increase the amount that can be spent on beverages. (Since increased food profits decrease beverage profit requirements, revenue is released for beverage purchases that would otherwise need to be reserved for profits.)

Likewise, managers can examine nonproduct costs incurred by the beverage operation; if these can be reduced it will free additional dollars to spend on beverage purchases.

It is also possible to consider increasing the selling prices of food and/or beverages; if this is done (and if gross revenues do not decrease because of guests' resistance) additional revenue will be generated that can be used to increase beverage purchases. Note: Extreme caution is necessary if this alternative is considered. Restaurants often see raising selling prices as an "easy" option; nothing must be done (except print new menus!); it is more difficult and time consuming to carefully analyze the existing operation and to first reduce costs to provide additional funds for beverage purchases. But as prices are increased, the guests' perception of reduced value may result in a loss of customers and decreased revenue. It is difficult to judge when guests will react negatively to price increases. Therefore, it is generally better to look within the operation for ways to decrease costs before increasing selling prices.

Another alternative for increasing allowable beverage costs is to increase revenues (food or beverage) by expanding to a larger market and/or by developing additional repeat business. Creative advertising, in-house guest interest-building activities, and other internal/external marketing/promotional techniques may increase revenues. As revenues increase, a smaller percentage of revenues is needed to meet cost obligations; profit increases, and again, additional funds are available to purchase beverages.

It is also possible to "live with" the allowable beverage cost. Some managers opt to purchase lower quality products, offer smaller portions, etc., to stay within allowable beverage restraints. These tactics may be met with guest resistance; knowledge of what the market will and will not tolerate becomes important.

A final alternative is to consider accepting a reduced profit return. While this alternative is obviously unattractive, it is frequently a better choice than raising prices. Likewise, if ways to increase revenue and/or reduce costs are not found, and if required quality standards cannot be met with reduced allowable beverage costs, few other alternatives remain. Many restaurants must accept a low (or no) profit return during their early years of operation. This alternative may be reasonable in the short term, then, but becomes less feasible as the restaurant matures. An effective cost identification and control system is the best assurance that profit requirements will be consistently met by the restaurant.

MANAGER'S 10 POINT EFFECTIVENESS CHECKLIST

Evaluate your need for and the status of each of the following financial management tactics. For tactics you judge to be important but not yet in place, develop an action plan including completion date to implement the tactic.

TACTIC	DON'T AGREE (DON'T NEED)	AGREE (DONE)	AGREE (NOT DONE)	IF NOT DONE WHO IS RESPONSIBLE?	IF NOT DONE TARGET COMPLETION DATE
1. Managers review menu prices on a predetermined time schedule and allow for more frequent revision, if necessary.	❑	❑	❑		
2. The manager avoids use of subjective pricing strategies when assigning menu prices.	❑	❑	❑		
3. Managers routinely review competitors' pricing structures for comparison purposes.	❑	❑	❑		
4. The impact, if any, of elasticity of demand is considered prior to any changes in menu item prices.	❑	❑	❑		
5. The restaurant's profit requirements are first considered when establishing menu prices.	❑	❑	❑		
6. The manager uses objective pricing strategies when determining menu selling prices.	❑	❑	❑		
7. Managers regularly compute product ingredient costs for each menu item.	❑	❑	❑		
8. Data from the operating budget is used to determine allowable product (food) costs when developing menu selling prices.	❑	❑	❑		
9. When operated as two separate departments, food and beverage costs are allocated to each of these units when selling prices are determined.	❑	❑	❑		
10. Managers investigate all possible areas of operating expense reduction prior to increasing menu prices.	❑	❑	❑		

9

OPERATING BUDGETS

MANAGER'S BRIEF

In this chapter you will learn how operating budgets can help you better manage your restaurant. You will learn that a budget is a valuable control tool that enables you to predict your revenues, estimate your expenses, and ensure that profits meet intended levels.

Whether your restaurant is yet to be built or is already in operation, you will see that budgets for capital improvements, cash management, specific operating departments, and overall operations are critical for success. To develop a budget, the manager must be able to develop an accurate revenue forecast, plan for profit, estimate expenses, and analyze actual operating results to evaluate differences between planned results and actual outcomes.

This chapter addresses factors to be considered before estimating future revenues. In addition, the concept of planning for profit is discussed. Profit is not just what is "left over" after all expenses are paid. Rather, profit must be viewed as an expense; in fact, it is a vital expense, because only with adequate profit is the restaurant's continued operation ensured. A significant part of the budgeting process involves estimating operating expenses, and we will discuss this in great detail. Budget preparation procedures are presented in this chapter in an easy-to-read, step-by-step format including sample budgets.

Most managers recognize that budgets by themselves do not make an operation profitable. The manager's skillful use of the budget makes it an important managerial tool. The chapter concludes with a detailed description of how a manager can (a) determine budget variances, (b) analyze variations between intended and actual results, (c) determine the causes of variations, and then, when appropriate, (d) take corrective action.

> **OPERATING BUDGET A detailed plan developed by restaurant managers that indicates estimated revenues and expenses for each department within the restaurant.**

An **operating budget** should be at the heart of the planning and control system of every restaurant. An operating budget is a plan that estimates the amount of revenue and expenses necessary to meet profit requirements. The budget establishes performance standards necessary to implement a control system. It also provides the base of comparison against which profit levels can be measured. It is an integral aspect of the management system and should not be viewed as an obstacle to efficient performance mandated by top managers.

PARTICIPATIVE BUDGET PROCESS IS BEST

All too often budgets are primarily used because of required operating procedures, routines, or "because the boss says so." These are situations in which **pro forma income statements,** operating budgets, and other financial management tools are developed because the lender and/or the investors require them, and without these mandates, managers would neither require nor use them.

> **PRO FORMA INCOME STATEMENT An estimate of income and expenses developed for a restaurant operation before it actually opens.**

By contrast, consider an operating budget that (a) is developed because its importance is realized, (b) is constructed with collective input and give-and-take decision-making by managers in all departments, and (c) is used as an integral part of the restaurant's management and control process. Those managers responsible for specific aspects of the budget participate in its development. They have an opportunity to explain, defend, and justify initial budget proposals and to plan/implement alternative plans as the budgetary control cycle evolves.

All restaurants need an operating budget, and careful thought must be given to its development. Actual accounting data is required. Used in comparison with other financial statements, the operating budget can provide timely help to managers desiring to know where, if at all, corrective action must be taken. Viewed this way, the budget becomes a profit plan, designed to help meet the restaurant's profit goals.

TYPES OF BUDGETS

There are several types of budgets restaurants can use. A **capital budget** outlines the restaurant's plans to invest in projects involving fixed assets such as equipment, land, and property improvements. A **cash budget** estimates cash receipts and disbursements during a specified time period for the property; cash flow requirements (the ability to pay bills when due [see chapter 6]) are of critical concern to all managers. A **departmental budget** shows, for the food, beverage, and/or catering or other departments, the estimated revenue and allocated expenses anticipated for each department. A **master budget** can be used to show each department's operating, capital, and cash plans.

The restaurant's primary need is for a short-term (one-year) operating budget, detailed on a monthly basis, that addresses items on the income statement. It becomes a constant reminder that if estimated revenue is not generated and/or if expense limits are exceeded, profits will decrease.

As the budget period evolves, managers will know the amount spent and the amount remaining

CAPITAL BUDGET A budget that relates to the acquisition of equipment, land, property improvement, and other fixed assets.

CASH BUDGET A budget that estimates cash receipts and disbursements during a specified time period.

DEPARTMENTAL BUDGET A budget that estimates revenue and allocated expenses for a specific department within the restaurant.

MASTER BUDGET A budget that combines operating, capital, and cash budgets for each specific department within the restaurant.

from the total which has been budgeted for each expense category. Information from the current budget, along with actual accounting information, becomes the basis for developing the next fiscal year's budget. Since operating budgets identify financial objectives for revenues and expenses, they are integral to the restaurant's control system: Actual data from the accounting system can be compared to budget plans to assess where, if at all, corrective action must be taken.

ADVANTAGES OF OPERATING BUDGET

Ideally, all managers help in developing the budget. This way, coordination and communication is improved; the entire management team is aware of the "game plan." Also, the budget helps managers consider alternative plans. How, for example, can the restaurant increase revenues? How can it reduce excessive costs? The budget sets performance standards that help managers tell how effective the restaurant actually is in meeting its goals. Since a step in the budget control process compares budget plans with actual operating results, managers can evaluate past efforts and plan future corrective actions. Finally, the budget helps pinpoint responsibility. Managers in each department become responsible for meeting assigned revenue goals and for maintaining food, beverage, and other operating costs within budgeted limits.

A CLOSE LOOK AT BUDGET CONTROL

CONTROL The management task that involves determining standards, assessing actual operating results, comparing expected and operating results, taking corrective action when predetermined variances are exceeded, and evaluating results of corrective action.

The manager who uses a carefully developed operating budget has access to a very effective **control** tool. The task of control is an important component of the management process and involves five steps:

Step 1: Establish standards (allowable or anticipated revenue and expense levels).

Step 2: Assess actual operating results (the income statement developed under an accrual accounting system does this).

Step 3: Compare standard (expected) revenues and expenses with actual revenues and expenses to determine causes of differences.

Step 4:   Take corrective action when actual revenue is less than expected and/or when actual expenses exceed allowable expenses by more than a predetermined variance.

Step 5:   Evaluate the results of the corrective action process.

The operating budget defines revenue and expense plans. In control terms, it expresses standard (expected) revenues and expenses, enabling the manager to compare financial plans with actual operating data reported in the income statement. If actual revenues are less than operating budget estimates, and/or if actual expenses are greater than those anticipated in the operating budget, corrective action may be necessary. The purpose of the corrective action will be to increase revenues or decrease expenses to budget limits. The effectiveness of the corrective action is then evaluated by noting the extent to which data in subsequent income statements more closely approximate those in the operating budget.

BUDGET DEVELOPMENT PROCEDURES

When developing a budget, expected revenue levels are first determined; then the estimated expenses to be incurred in generating these revenues are calculated. One of the "costs" to be assessed is the profit requirement. (The concept of treating profit as a cost is explained later in this chapter.)

In small restaurants, the owner/manager develops the budget. In larger operations, other staff members provide important assistance. Department heads and others who are expected to stay within budget limitations should do budget planning for their areas of responsibility in consultation with senior managers. In still larger restaurants, a committee of managers may review departmental income and expense plans before a final restaurant-wide budget is approved.

Annual operating budgets are developed before the start of the fiscal year. For example, in some large restaurants, managers may begin developing budgets as early as April or May of the preceding year to finalize the process by October or November for the budget period that will begin in January.

The budget is developed by projecting revenue, profit, and expense information on a monthly basis and then combining this information for the year. As the budget year evolves, remaining months may need revision to account for changes in revenue and/or expense levels. (Consider, for example, the impact on a restaurant of a major employer closing a plant after a natural disaster that could not have been anticipated.)

Calculating Projected Revenues

A restaurant's primary economic goal is to generate a level of profit that meets the owners' investment requirements. The ability of a manager to meet this goal rests in some measure on an ability to accurately estimate revenues. This is the first step in the budget development process and, as will be seen, sets the pace for planning allowable expense levels. If revenues can accurately be estimated (trending and indexing can be helpful and are discussed in the next section), and if profit requirements are mandated, then expense levels must be adjusted to stay within estimated revenue limits.

Food, beverage, and other revenue forecasts should generally be prepared separately. As noted above, revenue calculations should be made monthly (perhaps even weekly) and then be combined for an annual sales forecast. With monthly projections, actual revenues can be compared with budgeted revenues for the month and actual expenses can be compared to budgeted expenses for the month so timely corrective action, if needed, can be taken. Generally, monthly income statements from previous years can be used as a basis for estimating future revenue for the applicable month. Computerized systems used by many restaurants report monthly cumulative sales statistics. This makes it relatively easy to collect revenue figures and to note trends in each fiscal period.

Factors to consider when determining revenue estimates include:

- *Sales histories.* Past sales levels can be analyzed to identify trends helpful in projecting sales for the new budget period. For example, if food and/or beverage sales have increased by about 8% for the past five years, current sales plus 8% might be the base for estimating sales for the upcoming fiscal period. (The effects of "real" increases—for example, number of covers sold—as opposed to revenue increases generated merely by selling price increases, need to be factored into these estimates.)

- *Current and anticipated changes.* New competition, street improvement projects, or necessary remodeling projects may affect revenue levels, and estimates may need adjustment because of them.

- *Economic variables.* Inflation can change the public's habits and lifestyles. Perhaps people will visit the property more or less often.

Perhaps guests will demand greater value for their eating and drinking dollar at the same time that costs increase; selling price adjustments for food and beverage products may need to be evaluated.

- **Consideration of all departments.** Restaurants offering food, beverage, and other products or services should estimate total revenue levels separately for each department.

Determining Profit Requirements

Revenues projected in the budget will be used for two purposes:

- to provide required profits
- to pay necessary expenses

Many managers assess expense levels after revenue is estimated. Profit is then "what's left" of revenue after deducting expenses. It is also possible to calculate profit levels before expense requirements, so that in effect, the restaurant "pays itself" first. Funds remaining after profit requirements have been deducted from revenue are then used to pay incurred expenses. This approach treats profit as a cost, and keeps the manager focused on it. The manager must also assure that sufficient funds will be generated to meet expenses without sacrificing quality standards. (Note: The concept of profit in budget development is explained more fully later in this chapter.)

Calculating Projected Expenses

Many expenses are directly related to revenue volume and vary as revenue volume changes. For example, food and beverage costs increase when revenues increase because more food and beverage products must be purchased. Once revenue volumes are known, the expenses required to generate the projected level of revenues can be estimated.

Perhaps the most common method of forecasting the **variable costs** of a restaurant uses a simple mark-up with the current expense level as a base. This amount is then increased (or infrequently decreased) to arrive at the

> **VARIABLE COSTS Expenses that change in direct proportion to the related revenue.**

expense level for the new operating budget. For example, if the current year's food expense is $235,000, and a 6% increase in food sales is anticipated, the adjusted food expense for the new budget period is $249,100 ($235,000 × 6% + $235,000).

A similar calculation for beverage purchases and for all other categories of variable expenses can yield the total projected variable costs for the restaurant's new budget period. One potential problem with the mark-up method is that it assumes all costs were reasonable during the past year. If, in fact, some costs were too high because of waste, theft, etc., inefficiencies are extended into the new budget period.

Mark-up procedures are generally not effective when estimating fixed costs (which are not tied to revenue levels as are variable costs). Some fixed costs may not vary between budget periods; they are constant for many years. (Examples include rent specified in long-term leases, interest, and license fees.) Since these costs are often established by a contract, they are easily estimated and figured into the operating budget.

Another method for forecasting restaurant operating expenses involves calculating the current percentage of each expense relative to revenue (for example, current beverage cost ÷ current beverage revenue = current beverage cost percent). Percentages of revenue are then used to estimate costs for the new budget. For example, if the current beverage cost percentage is 24% of revenues, the new budget will be developed with beverage costs equal to 24% of new estimated revenues. This method also carries the disadvantage of preserving inefficiencies if the current cost percentage is higher than it should be.

Another method, which unfortunately takes more time, involves starting at a zero expense level for each category of cost and building up, through a justification process, to the estimated expense level. This method, called zero-based budgeting, yields current, necessary expense information designed specifically for the period covered by the operating budget. This approach may be most useful for budget overhead expenses such as repairs and maintenance.

Beverage Budget: Special Concerns

There are several special concerns involved in developing the beverage budget. For example, the sale of liquor, beer, wine, and soft drinks generates revenues and incurs expenses. This impact may need to be considered when the budget is developed. Few, if any, small restaurants develop specific budget plans for individual products. Rather, they assume that each beverage product will generate the same percentage of total beverage revenues in each budget period. For example, if liquor has generated 70% of beverage revenues in past years, it is assumed it will contribute 70% to future beverage sales. However, beverage managers should carefully review trends in sales statistics. Tastes change, and wine, sparkling water, and gourmet coffee may be generating a larger portion of beverage sales than they did in the past; if so, other products such as liquor may be contributing a reduced percentage of revenues.

Decisions about the percentage of total beverage revenue generated by each product are easy to make, since modern electronic data equipment records beverage revenues by product. Administrative judgment (and, perhaps, a trial period for keeping careful product revenues records) may be necessary in small restaurants that do not use sophisticated equipment or keep such records.

Different costs for different beverage products may also be considered during the budget development process. For example, suppose 70% of the anticipated beverage revenues of $125,000 are estimated to be from liquor sales; the liquor cost is 28%. The total cost of liquor is estimated to be $24,500 ($125,000 $\times$ 0.70 $\times$ 0.28).

The same process is used to estimate costs of beer, wine, and soft drinks. The sum of the costs for the separate beverage products will represent the total estimated beverage cost.

Budget Standards

Once the budgeted food and beverage cost (and any other category of expense) is expressed as a percentage (budgeted food or beverage cost ÷ by budgeted food or beverage revenues), it can be compared with actual operating results to measure

---

WWW: Internet Assistant

The ability to develop an accurate budget in a reasonable time-frame is a skill that can be learned by any effective manager. Using a computerized budgeting program for budget preparation is one technique that will speed up, simplify, and improve the accuracy of the budgeting process.

A variety of such budgeting programs are available to small businesses. To see one example, and a free demonstration of one complete program, go to

www.budget.com

Also, try your nearest office supply or software store to see other tools that can help you to better understand the budgeting process.

effectiveness. This simple process is very important and provides the basis for the subsequent operating control system.

Managers have at least two special concerns as they establish standards in the operating budget. First, the standards must be attainable. Personnel will get frustrated if standards are too difficult to attain. Second, standards must not compromise established quality requirements. For example, while lower food costs might be achieved by raising prices, reducing portion sizes, and/ or purchasing lower-quality products, these procedures may not be acceptable.

AN EXAMPLE OF BUDGET DEVELOPMENT

The focus in this section is on developing a budget for the food department; however, the same procedures can be used to plan a budget for the beverage department.

Step 1: Calculate projected revenue levels. Assume the restaurant is in its third year of operation. Budget Worksheet A: Food Revenue History Analysis (Figure 9.1) shows monthly food revenues as reported in past income statements. (Note: Revenues for October, November, and December of the current year are estimated, since the budget is being developed in October for the next calendar year.) The worksheet reports revenues for each month and the increase in dollars and percentages over the same month in the preceding year.

To calculate the amount of monthly revenue increase in dollars, subtract revenues for a specific month from the revenues of the same month in a previous year. For example, in January:

$$\$139,950 \quad - \quad \$129,750 \quad = \quad \$10,200$$

January revenue:	January revenue:	Monthly increase
current year −	past year =	in dollars
(column 5)	(column 2)	(column 6)

To calculate the monthly percentage of revenue increase, divide the increase of $10,200 (column 6) by January revenues for the previous year ($129,750 in column 2). This percentage (column 7) is:

| Month | 2 Years Ago | 1 Year Ago | | | Current Year | | |
	Revenue Amount	Revenue Amount	Difference (previous year)	%[b]	Revenue Amount	Difference (previous year)	%[b]
	1	2	3	4	5	6	7
Jan.	125,500	129,750	4,250	3	139,950	10,200	8
Feb.	124,300	135,500	11,200	9	149,000	13,500	10
Mar.	122,200	133,750	11,550	9	147,500	13,750	10
Apr.	130,500	139,500	9,000	7	148,250	8,750	6
May	124,750	139,850	15,100	12	148,000	8,150	6
June	124,900	136,100	11,200	9	147,000	10,900	8
July	122,000	132,400	10,400	9	148,500	16,100	12
Aug.	129,500	139,750	10,250	8	148,000	8,250	6
Sept.	124,900	136,900	12,000	10	149,500	12,600	9
Oct.	124,200	135,900	11,700	9	148,750[a]	12,850	9
Nov.	123,100	134,950	11,850	10	148,000[a]	13,050	10
Dec.	123,000	135,500	12,500	10	147,750[a]	12,250	9
Totals	1,498,850	1,629,850	131,000	8	1,770,200	140,350	8

[a]Estimate (the opening budget is being developed in October for the coming calendar year).
[b]Percentages in column are rounded.

Figure 9.1 Budget Worksheet A: Food Revenue History Analysis

$$\frac{\$10,200}{\$129,750} = 8\% \text{ (rounded)}$$

To calculate annual percentage of revenue increases, use the totals at the bottom of the columns for the same computation:

$$\frac{\text{Total increase in revenue from previous year (column 6)}}{\text{Total revenue in previous year (column 2)}} = \% \text{ increase}$$

For example, the current year increase over last year is calculated as follows:

$$\frac{\$139,850 \text{ (column 6)}}{\$1,630,350 \text{ (column 2)}} = 9\% \text{ (rounded)}$$

Analysis of the revenue history in Budget Worksheet A shows that food revenues in the second year of operation (one year ago) increased 8% over the first year (two years ago) while food revenues in the current year increased 9% over the second year (one year ago).

The projected food revenue of $1,947,240 for the operating budget in Figure 9.2 is a 10% increase ($177,040) over the current year. It is the base of revenue estimated to be available to both generate expected profits and meet expenses in the coming year.

With this knowledge, the restaurant manager should study current economic and related factors to estimate revenues for the next year. Suppose the manager believes the upward trend will continue and that sales will increase by 10% during the coming year. Note: Some restaurants generate revenues on a level basis throughout the year; there are no "peaks and valleys" representing seasonal busy and slow periods. Other restaurants do experience monthly revenue fluctuations. In this example, we will assume that the 10% expected revenue increase will be evenly spread throughout the year. The manager can then distribute monthly food revenue projections in Figure 9.2 by adding 10% to each month's revenues. Alternatively, the manager can review revenue trends on a monthly basis over several years of operating expense to establish more exact estimates of monthly increases.

The manager should consider why the percentage of revenue increases declined in some months such as April, May, June, and August (see Figure 9.1). Other questions include whether January revenues will always be among the lowest of the year as they have been for the past two years, and how much of the revenue increase is "real" growth and how much is due only to an increase in menu item selling prices.

Step 2: Calculate profit required from the food and beverage departments. This involves:

- calculating total profit required from the food and beverage departments
- calculating profit from food sales
- determining profit required from beverage sales

To assess profit levels for food and beverage profit centers, costs must first be allocated as follows:

Month	Revenues in Current Year	Increase by 10%[b]	Estimated Revenue: New Operating Budget
January	$ 139,950	$ 14,000	$ 153,950
February	149,000	14,900	163,900
March	147,500	14,750	162,250
April	148,250	14,830	163,080
May	148,000	14,800	162,800
June	147,000	14,700	161,700
July	148,500	14,850	163,350
August	148,000	14,800	162,800
September	149,500	14,950	164,450
October	148,750[a]	14,880	163,630
November	148,000[a]	14,800	162,800
December	147,750[a]	14,780	162,530
Totals	$1,770,200	$177,040	$1,947,240

[a]The budget is being planned in late summer/early fall; these are estimates.
[b]Increase is to the nearest $10.

Figure 9.2   Budget Worksheet B: Food Estimated Monthly Revenue for New Operating Budget

- Food and beverage costs are charged, respectively, to the food and beverage departments. Food and beverage transfers, employee meal costs, complimentary food and beverage charges, etc., complicate the application of this standard. (These procedures are discussed in detail in chapter 10.)

- Other large expenses are prorated between the food and beverage departments according to the amount of expense incurred. For example, labor costs could be prorated between food and beverage departments according to the staff members whose primary duties are in generating food or beverage revenues. Wages for employees involved in both food and beverage operations (for example, the bookkeeper and purchasing agent) can be prorated based on the percentage of revenues. For example, if 75% of the total food and beverage revenues come from food, then 75% of these indirect labor costs are allocated to the food department.

- Other expenses, such as those for laundry, supplies, or licenses, might be allocated on the basis of a simple sales percentage, or a square feet ratio. Other allocation bases could be cubic footage, the value of fixed assets, or, for example, pounds of laundry.

		Amount Prorated To			
		Food		Beverage	
Type of Cost	Total Annual Current Cost	(Revenue = $1,770,200)	% of Sales[b]	(Revenue = $466,550)	% of Sales[b]
1	2	3	4	5	6
Food	$ 619,570	$ 619,570	35%	—	—
Beverage	120,000	—	—	120,000	26%
Payroll	489,850	424,850	24%	65,000	14%
Payroll taxes and employee benefits	41,900	35,400	2%	6,500	1%
Direct operating expenses	111,010	88,510	5%	22,500	5%
Music/entertainment	75,000	—	—	75,000	16%
Advertising	45,400	35,400	2%	10,000	2%
Utilities	98,510	88,510	5%	10,000	2%
Administration/general	90,800	70,800	4%	20,000	4%
Repairs/maintenance	26,700	17,700	1%	9,000	2%
Rent	163,910	123,910	7%	40,000	9%
Real estate/property taxes	26,700	17,700	1%	9,000	2%
Insurance	44,150	35,400	2%	8,750	2%
Interest expense	77,800	70,800	4%	7,000	1%
Depreciation	68,110	53,110	3%	15,000	3%
Totals	$2,099,410	$1,681,660	95%[a]	$417,750	90%
	$2,099,410 =	$1,681,660	+	$417,750	

Food Cost	$ 619,570		Beverage Cost	$120,000
Nonfood Cost	$1,062,090		Nonbeverage Cost	$297,750
	$1,681,660			$417,750

[a]Column does not add due to rounding.
[b]Rounded to the nearest 1%.

Figure 9.3 Budget Worksheet C: Recap and Allocation of Current Costs between Food and Beverage Operations

Figure 9.3 indicates the total amount (column 2) of each cost (column 1) identified in the restaurant's accounting system. Costs have been allocated between the food and beverage operations, and their percentage relationship to respective sales is shown.

Current food sales of $1,770,200 are taken from Worksheet B (Figure 9.2). Assume current beverage sales of $466,550 have been determined by another Budget Worksheet B developed for the beverage department. These figures appear at the top of columns 3 and 5 on Worksheet C. Percent of Sales (columns 4 and 6) is calculated for each cost by dividing the amount of costs allocated to the department by the total sales. (For each item, the percentage is stated to the nearest 1%.)

For example, the food cost calculation is

$$\frac{\$619,570}{\$1,770,200} = 35\%$$

Total profit before taxes for the restaurant is computed as follows: Total revenues of $2,236,750 (food revenues of $1,770,200 plus beverage sales of $466,550) minus total costs of $2,099,410 (food department costs of $1,681,660 [column 3] plus beverage department costs of $417,750 [column 5]) equals $137,340. The profit percentage is determined by dividing the profit by total revenue.

$$\frac{\$137,340}{\$2,236,750} = 6.1\%$$

Suppose that the 6.1% current profit level is not acceptable; the owner desires a before-tax profit of 10% of total food and beverage revenues for the next year to compensate for the risk associated with the investment. The manager can use a common procedure to plan for this. As was already done for food in Worksheet B, we can estimate next year's beverage revenues by multiplying current revenues by the amount of increase predicted; assume that beverage revenues are also expected to increase by 10%.

$$\$466,550 \quad \times \quad 0.10 \quad = \quad \$46,655$$

| Current beverage revenues | × | Estimated revenue increase % | = | Total revenue increase |

$$\$466,550 \quad + \quad \$46,655 \quad = \quad \$513,205$$

| Total current revenues | + Increased revenue = | Estimated beverage revenue for new budget year |

Total revenue and required profit for the new budget period can now be calculated. For the new budget period:

Food revenue (Budget Worksheet B—Food)	$1,947,240
Beverage revenues (per above)	$ 513,200
Total revenues	$2,460,440

$$\text{Required profit} = 0.10 \times \$2,460,444 = \$246,044$$

Two points should be made about the required profit level. First, determining profit requirements on the basis of revenues alone is not generally appropriate, since the dollar amount of profit decreases as revenue levels decrease. It is better to express profit requirements as a specified percentage return on investment (ROI), assets (ROA), or other measure.

Second, although the required profit can be generated by either the food or beverage departments or both, normally the beverage department yields a higher profit per dollar of revenues. One approach to spreading required profit between the food and beverage program is to do the following:

- Charge the food department for direct product (food) costs.
- Allocate nonproduct costs between the food and beverage departments.
- Calculate profit required from food sales: Food revenues − [Food cost + Allocated share of nonproduct costs] = Profit from food sales.
- Calculate profit required from beverage sales: Total required profit − Profit from food sales = Profit required from beverage sales.

The current budget example allocates nonproduct costs to the food department for the new budget year. The beverage manager then uses this information to calculate the beverage budget.

Step 3:   Calculate food department costs. At this point, for the new budget period, the manager knows:

- estimated food revenues
- profit required from food and from beverage department sales

To project costs applicable to the food operation, the manager multiplies the current percentage of each cost as determined in Figure 9.3 (Budget Worksheet C) by the estimated revenue for the new budget period. This is done in Figure 9.4 (Budget Worksheet D: Calculation of Food Department Costs for New Budget).

Figure 9.4 (Budget Worksheet D) indicates that estimated costs for the next year's food operation are $1,849,860. This estimate assumes that the percentages of the expense to total food revenues in each category will be the same for the new budget year as they are in the current year.

Category of Cost	% of Food Revenues: Current Year[a]	Estimated Revenue: Budget Year	Estimated Cost: Budget Year[b]
1	2	3	4
Food cost	35%	$1,947,240	$ 681,530
Payroll	24%	1,947,240	467,340
Payroll taxes/employee benefits	2%	1,947,240	38,940
Direct operating expenses	5%	1,947,240	97,360
Music/entertainment	---	1,947,240	---
Advertising	2%	1,947,240	38,940
Utilities	5%	1,947,240	97,360
Administration/general	4%	1,947,240	77,890
Repairs/maintenance	1%	1,947,240	19,470
Rent	7%	1,947,240	136,310
Real estate/property taxes	1%	1,947,240	19,470
Insurance	2%	1,947,240	38,940
Interest expense	4%	1,947,240	77,890
Depreciation	3%	1,947,240	58,420
Total estimated cost			$1,849,860

[a]Percentage from column 4 in Figure 9.3 (Budget Worksheet C).
[b]Amounts are rounded to the nearest $10.

Figure 9.4 Budget Worksheet D: Calculation of Food Department Costs for New Budget

Now that costs for the food department are known, subtracting food-related costs from food revenues will yield food department profits:

$$\$1,947,240 \quad - \quad \$1,849,860 \quad = \quad \$97,380$$

Budgeted food sales − Budgeted food costs = Budgeted food profits

Once profit generated by the food department is known, the manager can calculate the profit required from the beverage department by subtracting profit from the food department from total required profit. If total required profit is $246,040, beverage profit needed is:

$$\$246,040 \quad - \quad \$97,380 \quad = \quad \$148,660$$

Required profit − Budget food profit = Required beverage profit

Putting It All Together

For the operating budget to be a meaningful and workable planning tool, it must be in an easy-to-use format such as Budget Worksheet E: Food Department Operating Budget (Figure 9.5). Worksheet E is completed monthly. The sample is only for January—the first month of the new budget year.

- Column 1 lists food revenue, cost of goods sold (food cost), operating expenses, and profit (before tax) in a format similar to an income statement.

- Column 2 indicates the percentage of food revenue represented by each item as indicated in Budget Worksheet D.

- Column 3 lists budgeted revenues and expenses by month. Food revenue of $153,950 is obtained directly from Budget Worksheet B. To calculate the amount of each type of expense listed in column 1, multiply the budget percentage (column 2) by total monthly revenue of $153,950. For example, the payroll expense for January is:

$$\$153,950 \qquad \times \qquad 24\% \qquad = \qquad \$36,948$$

$$\underset{\text{(column 3)}}{\text{January food revenue}} \times \underset{\text{(column 2)}}{\text{Budgeted payroll expense}} = \underset{\text{(column 3)}}{\overset{\text{Budgeted payroll}}{\text{costs for January}}}$$

Note: Budget planners typically omit cents and round estimates, often to the nearest ten or one hundred dollars; our examples are rounded to the nearest ten dollars.

- Column 4 lists budgeted revenues and expenses for the entire year. Food revenue of $1,947,240 is obtained directly from Budget Worksheet B. Each operating expense (for example, payroll of $467,340) is obtained directly from Worksheet D.

- Column 5 lists the actual revenue and expenses for the month, obtained from the same source documents used to develop information for monthly accounting statements. (They can be taken from the statements themselves if they are developed on a timely basis.)

Month: January

Item	Budget %[a]	Budget		Actual		Monthly Percentage Calculation %[a]
		Month	Year	Month	Year	
1	2	3	4	5	6	7
Food revenue	100%	$153,950	$1,947,240	$160,100	$160,100	100%
Cost of goods sold:						
Food costs	35%	53,880	681,530	57,640	57,640	36%
Operating Expenses:						
Payroll	24%	36,950	467,340	37,500	37,500	23%
Payroll tax/benefits	2%	3,080	38,940	3,250	3,250	2%
Direct operating expenses	5%	7,700	97,360	8,700	8,700	5%
Advertising	2%	3,080	38,940	3,080	3,080	2%
Utilities	5%	7,700	97,360	8,100	8,100	5%
Administration/general	4%	6,160	77,890	5,500	5,500	3%
Repairs/maintenance	1%	1,540	19,470	1,110	1,110	1%
Rent	7%	10,780	136,310	10,780	10,780	7%
Real estate/property taxes	1%	1,540	19,470	1,540	1,540	1%
Insurance	2%	3,080	38,940	3,080	3,080	2%
Interest expense	4%	6,160	77,890	6,160	6,160	4%
Depreciation	3%	4,620	58,420	4,620	4,620	3%
Total operating expenses	60%	92,390	1,168,330	93,420	93,420	58%
Total expenses	95%	146,270	1,849,860	151,060	151,060	94%
Profit (before tax)	5%	7,680	97,380	9,040	9,040	6%

[a]Rounded to the nearest 1%.

Figure 9.5 Budget Worksheet E: Food Department Operating Budget

- Column 6 tallies actual information on a cumulative, year-to-date basis. Normally, column 6 (last month) + column 5 (this month) = column 6 (this month). However, since this is January, the first month of the new budget year, column 6 = column 5.

- Column 7 provides the same information in percentages of actual total food revenues. For example, consider the food cost percentage (food costs ÷ food revenues):

$$\frac{\text{Food costs}}{\text{Food revenues}} = \text{Food cost \%}$$

$$\frac{\$57,640}{\$160,100} = 36\%$$

Information in Budget Worksheet E tells the manager:

- what food revenues, costs, and profits should be
- what food revenues, costs, and profits actually are

Important information is shown in Budget Worksheet E.

- The actual food revenues for January were greater than anticipated ($160,100 actual food revenues minus $153,950 planned food revenues represents an increase in revenues of $6,150).

- Food costs were $3,760 greater than planned ($57,640 actual food costs minus $53,880 budgeted food costs). Some additional food costs are expected since food revenues were also greater than planned. However, the actual cost percentage of 36% (column 7) is greater than the planned food cost percentage of 35% (column 2).

- Operating expenses (excluding food costs) were $1,030 greater than planned ($93,420 actual operating expenses minus $92,390 budgeted operating expenses).

- Profit was $1,360 more than planned ($9,040 actual profit minus $7,680 planned profit). When reviewing these budget results, the manager should look within several operating expense categories to determine whether higher revenues can explain the higher-than-budgeted costs. If any category of higher costs cannot be quickly and easily explained, further analysis is in order.

When comparing budgeted and actual costs, direct operating expenses appear somewhat out of line, since the actual expense was $1,000 greater than budgeted for January. The cost review and control process should begin with these expenses. Also, since the food cost percent was slightly greater than anticipated, some analysis may be appropriate here. However, it is difficult to generalize about budget costs after only one month. More accurate and meaningful analysis becomes possible with data from several months. Information gained from this analysis may be helpful in revising budget projections for the remainder of the year. Likewise, recall that a separate budget process is used for the beverage profit center. Analysis of that operation may indicate where, if at all, corrective action is necessary to generate expected profit requirements through the beverage program.

VARIANCE ANALYSIS

Operating budgets should be the standard of comparison for actual revenues and expenses. Generally, actual operating results are compared to budgeted amounts at the end of each month. Major variances are determined and analyzed, and corrective action is taken if necessary.

The recommended variance analysis process consists of five steps:

Step 1: Determine budget variances.
Step 2: Determine significant variances.
Step 3: Analyze significant variances.
Step 4: Determine cause(s) of problems.
Step 5: Take corrective action.

A comparison of actual monthly numbers against the budget for the month often reveals **budget variances.** This comparison is part of the accounting process and is shown on the monthly income statement. There will likely be budget variances for most expenses, since the operating budget is based on estimates. No budgeting process, however sophisticated, is perfect.

> **BUDGET VARIANCE** The difference between budgeted and actual amounts in any revenue or expense account; analysis should be undertaken when this difference (in dollars and/or percentage) exceeds a pre-established amount.

Step 1 of the budget variance process indicates the need to determine budget variances. Each time a budgeted line item differs from its actual number counterpart, a variance exists. In **Steps 2 and 3** of the process, significant variances are, respectively, determined and analyzed. A variance is considered significant if it exceeds a pre-established dollar amount *and* if it exceeds a pre-established percentage of the budget amount. For example, assume the restaurant's utilities expense is budgeted for $5,000 for the month and the dual factors for determining variance significance are $400 and 5%. Further, assume that the actual utilities expense for the month is $5,500. The budget variance for utilities expense is $500, which is 10% of the budgeted amount ($500 ÷ $5,000). Therefore, the budget variance is significant, since it exceeds the pre-established factors of $400 and 5%. The variance in this illustration is *unfavorable,* since it is an expense, and the actual expense exceeds the budgeted amount. (A revenue item that exceeds the budget estimate would be considered favorable.) By contrast, when an actual expense is less than that budgeted, it is considered favorable and when an actual revenue item is less than that budgeted, this suggests an unfavorable variance. Whether the budget variances are favorable or unfavorable, they should be analyzed, causes should be determined and applicable corrective action should be taken if unfavorable. Alternatively, if possible, procedures to continue the financial result should be implemented (favorable variance).

In *Step 3* of the process, significant variances are analyzed to determine information useful for detecting the cause(s) of the variance *(Step 4)*, and finally, in *Step 5*, corrective action is to be taken.

Significant revenue and expense variances should both be analyzed. However, we will limit our discussion to variable expenses.

A generic approach to analyzing expense variances involves determining the usage and rate variances. This process will be briefly discussed and illustrated. The basic model for analysis is:

For Usage Variance:

$$UV = AR \times (BU - AU)$$

Usage variance = Actual rate (Budgeted usage − Actual usage)

For Rate Variance:

$$RV = BU \times (BR - AR)$$

Rate variance = Budgeted usage × (Budgeted rate − Actual rate)

The sum of the usage variance and the rate variance must equal the budget variance for the expense item.

To illustrate, consider the Mountain View Restaurant, which has a variable wages budget of $15,000 for June 20XX. This budget was based on 1,875 employee hours, with an average hourly wage paid to applicable employees of $8.00.

The actual variable labor expense totaled $13,767.80, which is $1,232.20 less than what was budgeted. Figure 9.6 contains the analysis of the favorable budget variance.

	Hours	Hourly Rate	Total
Budget	1,875	$8.00	$15,000.00
Actual	1,679	$8.20	$13,767.80
Budget variance			$ 1,232.20 (F)

UV = $8.20 (1,875 − 1,679)
UV = $8.20 (196)
UV = $1,607.20 (F)

RV = 1,875 ($8.00 − $8.20)
RV = 1,875 (−0.20)
RV = −$375 (U)

Budget variance = UV + RV
Budget variance = $1,607.20 (F) − $375 (U)
Budget variance = $1,232.20 (F)

Figure 9.6 Labor Budget Variance Analysis for Mountain View Restaurant

The results include a favorable usage variance of $1,607.20, which is determined by multiplying the 196 unused hours by the average hourly rate of $8.20. The unfavorable rate variance of $375 is determined by multiplying the 1,875 budgeted hours by the excessive hourly rate of $0.20 per hour.

This analysis suggests that the restaurant manager should review the causes of the usage and rate variances and take corrective action as necessary. For example, the $0.20 per hour usage rate difference could be caused by overtime pay. Only a thorough investigation will reveal if this occurred. In addition, the manager should investigate the underutilization of variable labor by 196 hours for the month. Relevant questions include, but are not limited to, the following:

- Did service standards suffer?
- Were the number of meals served less than projected, leading to apparent cost savings?

For the budgetary control process to be successful, corrective action must be taken when required. The failure to take corrective action may result in future variances that impact both the restaurant and its bottom line.

BUDGET REFORECASTING

Operating budgets establish financial goals and are driven by revenue forecasts. What happens when revenue estimates are off-target? This can happen, for example, when budgets are planned many months in advance of the applicable operating period, and then economic or other factors lead to decreased (or, sometimes) increased revenues.

Budget reforecasting is the process by which revenue and expense data in an operating budget are updated to reflect current (updated) economic conditions. The process can be time consuming, but is eased by the fact that most expenses are variable; as defined earlier, they vary in direct proportion to revenues. Therefore, for example, if revenue estimates for the remainder of a year are 20% under the original budget forecast:

> **BUDGET REFORECASTING The process by which revenue and expense data in an operating budget are revised to reflect current (updated) economic conditions.**

- Revised revenue levels for each remaining month (20% less than the original budget) can be determined.

- Variable costs can be assessed by multiplying the revised (lowered) revenue estimate by the variable cost percent.

- Fixed costs can be assessed (since, by definition, fixed costs do not change even when revenue changes, these costs will be the same in both the original and the reforecasted budgets).

- Adjustments must then be made to compensate for the fact that fixed costs will require a larger percentage of the lowered revenue estimates. Often, tactics to reduce variable costs (hopefully without sacrificing product/service quality standards) are implemented, and at the same time, profit (pretax net income) expectations are reduced.

Once reforecasting is complete, managers normally compare actual financial results with both the original and the reforecasted budget data.

MANAGER'S 10 POINT EFFECTIVENESS CHECKLIST

Evaluate your need for and the status of each of the following financial management tactics. For tactics you judge to be important but not yet in place, develop an action plan including completion date to implement the tactic.

TACTIC	DON'T AGREE (DON'T NEED)	AGREE (DONE)	AGREE (NOT DONE)	IF NOT DONE WHO IS RESPONSIBLE?	IF NOT DONE TARGET COMPLETION DATE
1. A pro forma income statement is prepared by managers prior to opening a new restaurant.	❑	❑	❑		
2. Preparation of the operating budget includes the development of capital *and* cash budgets.	❑	❑	❑		
3. When the annual operating budget is developed, revenues are first estimated, then required profits, and finally estimates for other applicable expenses.	❑	❑	❑		
4. Sales histories and current and future economic and competitive conditions are fully considered as budgeted revenues are estimated.	❑	❑	❑		
5. Expense goals established by managers are realistic and attainable.	❑	❑	❑		
6. Food and beverage departmental revenues, profit expectations, and expense estimates are expressed as a percentage of the total revenue on the budget.	❑	❑	❑		
7. The restaurant's required profit levels are established in terms of ROI, ROA, or another appropriate measure when operating budgets are developed.	❑	❑	❑		
8. Estimated profit margins for the food and beverage departments are separately computed to reflect the unique profit contributions of each department.	❑	❑	❑		
9. The operating budget is compared, on a regular basis, with actual operating results to identify major variances and to take corrective action as necessary.	❑	❑	❑		
10. Significant differences between budgeted and actual expense results are reviewed for both usage and rate variances.	❑	❑	❑		

10

ACCOUNTING ASPECTS OF FOOD AND BEVERAGE CONTROL

MANAGER'S BRIEF

Many of the accounting techniques used in a restaurant are also used in other businesses. Restaurants do, however, employ some unique accounting techniques, and these are presented in this chapter. For example, restaurants generally offer a menu of items for sale. The actual cost of these items along with each item's popularity and selling price combine to influence the overall profitability of the restaurant. The technique used to evaluate a menu's profitability is called menu engineering. Knowing how it works improves a manager's ability to plan, design, and price menu items. The menu engineering process is detailed in this chapter.

The purchase and preparation of food is another activity unique to restaurants. Food must be purchased, accepted from suppliers, and placed into storage, all of which requires special record-keeping techniques; these are presented in a step-by-step manner. Inventoried food products have a value, and a variety of methods used to establish that value are presented. Restaurants can use either a physical or a perpetual inventory to record the number and value of stored items. The importance of taking a physical inventory is discussed, as are procedures for using the information to compute the restaurant's inventory turnover rate. Calculated at the conclusion of each accounting period and then compared with other time periods, this measure of management effectiveness helps ensure that inventories are maintained at proper levels.

Lastly, procedures for issuing food from storage areas and calculating an accurate cost of sales for food and beverage are presented. With this information managers can compare actual operating results with forecasted results and take corrective action if necessary.

Virtually all of the accounting concepts discussed throughout this book are applicable to the general world of business, regardless of the product being produced and/or the service being provided. There are, however, some aspects of financial management that are unique to restaurants and other types of food/beverage operations. Most of these relate to developing, collecting, and using financial information to help control the costs of food and/or beverage products. Examples of these special financial management concerns include:

- menu engineering
- purchasing (source document flow)
- receiving
- inventory (food/beverage) control and valuation
- issuing
- calculation of actual food/beverage costs

These are the topics of this chapter.

MENU ENGINEERING

Menu engineering provides the manager with information about a menu item's profitability and popularity to aid menu planning, design, and pricing decisions.

It allows the manager to consider financial management (the restaurant's need for a profit) and marketing concerns (guest preferences) at the same time.

MENU ENGINEERING A process that provides the manager with information about a menu item's profitability and popularity to aid menu planning, design, and pricing decisions.

Basic Control Tools Needed

Before menu engineering analysis can be undertaken, three critical control tools must be in place:

- *Standard recipes.* All recipes used to produce food items must be standardized; that is, the same type and amount of ingredients must be used to produce a specified portion size.

- *Recipe pre-costing.* Within the limits of practicality, the costs of all ingredients used to produce one portion of a menu item according to its standard recipe must be known. A process called "pre-costing"—which can be done either manually or, increasingly, electronically—is used for this purpose.

PRE-COSTING The process of determining the current market cost for the quantity of ingredients used in a standard recipe. Pre-costing is necessary to determine what one portion of a menu item prepared according to its standard recipe will cost.

- *Consistent recipe use.* Standard recipes, after they are made available and have been pre-costed, must be used consistently as menu items are produced.

WWW: Internet Assistant

In the past, creating and costing standardized recipes for a restaurant was a time-consuming and therefore often neglected activity. With today's technology, establishing standardized recipes and keeping their actual cost per serving up to date is easy. To view a restaurant software program that will help, go to

http:www.cbord.com

To view a similar program designed specifically for the healthcare industry, go to

http://www.computrition.com

Managers Make Menu Decisions

Restaurant managers can use menu engineering strategies to help make their menus highly effective sales tools. In other words, menu engineering allows managers to recognize the items they desire to sell (those that are the most profitable and popular). The menu engineering worksheet (see Figure 10.1) is used for the analysis. There are 16 steps involved in completing the worksheet:

- identify competing menu items
- tally number of items sold
- assess menu mix percentages
- record menu item food costs
- list menu item selling prices
- calculate menu item contribution margins
- determine menu item food costs
- calculate total menu revenues
- determine total menu costs (box I)
- determine total menu revenues (box J)
- assess total contribution margin (box M)
- calculate potential food costs (box K)
- calculate average contribution margin (box O)
- assess popularity index (box Q)
- assign menu mix category
- classify menu items

Menu engineering addresses the concept of profitability by emphasizing the **contribution margin:** food revenue minus food costs. The contribution margin (CM) can be determined for one menu item such as a steak dinner

CONTRIBUTION MARGIN (CM)
Food revenue − Food costs.

(menu selling price for dinner − total food costs for all items comprising the steak dinner). The CM for an entire menu can also be calculated (total revenue received from the sale of all food items − the food costs incurred to produce all menu items that generated the revenue).

Date: _____ 10/15/20X2 _____

Restaurant: _____ Midtown Plaza _____   Meal Period: _____   Dinner

A	B	C	D	E	F	G	H	L	P	R	S
Menu Item Name	Number Sold (MM)	Menu Mix %	Item Food Cost	Item Selling Price	Item CM (E-D)	Menu Costs (D*B)	Menu Revenues (E*B)	Menu CM (H-G)	CM Category	MM% Category	Menu Item Classification
1. Beef Stew	350	17.5	4.10	10.00	5.90	1,435.00	3,500.00	2,065.00	Low	High	Plowhorse
2. Chow Mein	210	10.5	4.40	11.25	6.85	924.00	2,362.50	1,438.50	High	Low	Puzzle
3. Ham Cheese Sandwich	100	5.0	4.80	10.50	5.70	480.00	1,050.00	570.00	Low	Low	Dog
4. BLT Sandwich	450	22.5	4.90	12.50	7.60	2,205.00	5,625.00	3,420.00	High	High	Star
5. Hamburger Platter	510	25.5	4.45	11.45	7.00	2,269.50	5,839.50	3,570.00	High	High	Star
6. Chicken Sandwich	380	19.0	2.75	8.50	5.75	1,045.00	3,230.00	2,185.00	Low	High	Plowhorse
Column	N					I	J	M			
Total	2,000					8,358.50	21,607.00	13,248.50			

Additional computations: K = I/J   O = M/N   Q = (100%/items) (70%)

     6.62   11.7%

Figure 10.1 Menu Engineering Worksheet

233

Note: This definition of "contribution margin" (Food revenue − Food costs) differs from the term's definition for general accounting purposes (revenues − all variable costs).

Menu engineering addresses an item's popularity by considering the percentage that each menu item represents of all menu items sold. It then assumes that an item is popular if it sells 70% of expected sales. For example, if a menu offered 25 competing items and if the items were all equally popular, each item would represent 4% of sales. (100% ÷ 25 items. Note: The term "sales" refers to number of units, *not* number of revenue dollars generated.) A menu item would then be considered popular if it represented at least 2.8% of total sales (4.0% × 0.70 = 2.8%).

In terms of profitability and popularity, then, menu engineering suggests that items that are "profitable" (that is, items that have a CM equal to or greater than the average CM for the menu) and "popular" (items that sell 70% or more of what they are expected to sell) are the most desirable items.

All About Contribution Margins

As noted above, the menu engineering model utilizes the contribution margin as the determinant of profitability. Historically, restaurant managers have used the food cost percentage to measure profitability. A rule of thumb was: the lower the food percent, the greater the profitability.

The problem with relying on the food cost percentage is suggested by the data in Figure 10.2 As you review Figure 10.2, note that the item with the lowest food cost percent (36.8% for chicken) has a contribution margin of only $6. By contrast, the item with the highest food cost percent (lobster—45.2%) has the highest contribution margin. Since, by definition, contribution margin represents the amount of revenue dollars remaining after food cost is deducted (in

Menu Item	Total Food Cost	Menu Price	Food Cost %	Contribution Margin
Chicken	$3.50	$ 9.50	36.8%	$ 6.00
Steak	$7.50	$18.00	41.7%	$10.50
Lobster	$9.50	$21.00	45.2%	$11.50

Figure 10.2   Food Cost Percentage or Contribution Margin: Which Is the Best Profitability Indicator?

other words, "what's left" to pay for all other expenses and to contribute to profit), it is clear that the key to increased profitability is to *increase* the contribution margin, not to *decrease* the food cost percent.

A Close Look at a Menu Engineering Worksheet

A sample menu engineering worksheet is shown in Figure 10.1. For simplicity, let's assume the restaurant menu has only six menu items that compete with each other. Now let's study Figure 10.1 carefully and review row 1:

- Column A—Menu Item Name: Beef Stew

- Column B—Number Sold (MM): 350 servings of beef stew were sold during the time period covered by the analysis.

- Column C—Menu Mix %: The 350 portions of beef stew sold (see column B) represent 17.5% of the total number of items sold during the time period covered by the analysis (2000 items in box N).

- Column D—Item Food Cost: One portion of beef stew prepared according to the standard recipes after current ingredient costs have been calculated will yield a $4.10 food cost.

- Column E—Item Selling Price: The menu selling price for beef stew is listed at $10.00.

- Column F—Item CM (E−D): The contribution margin for beef stew is $5.90 ($10.00 − $4.10).

- Column G—Menu Costs (D*B): The total food costs to produce 350 servings of beef stew is $1,435 (350 portions at $4.10 each).

- Column H—Menu Revenues (E*B): The total revenue generated from the sale of all 350 portions of beef stew is $3,500 (350 portions at $10.00 each).

- Column L—Menu CM (H-G): The total contribution margin generated by beef stew is $2,065 ($3,500 − $1,435).

- Box N—As explained above, 2,000 menu items were sold during the period of this analysis.

- Box I—The total menu (food) costs incurred (column G) to produce all 2,000 menu items (box N) was $8,358.50.

Menu Item Name	Item CM	Desired CM	CM Category	Menu Mix %	Desired Menu Mix %	Menu Mix % Category	Menu Item Name
(Col. A)	(Col. F)	(Box O)	(Col. P)	(Col. C)	(Box Q)	(Col. R)	(Col. S)
1	$5.90	$6.62	Low	17.5%	11.7%	High	Plowhorse
2	$6.85	$6.62	High	10.5%	11.7%	Low	Puzzle
3	$5.70	$6.62	Low	5.0%	11.7%	Low	Dog
4	$7.60	$6.62	High	22.5%	11.7%	High	Star
5	$7.00	$6.62	High	25.5%	11.7%	High	Star
6	$5.75	$6.62	Low	19.0%	11.7%	High	Plowhorse

Figure 10.3 Menu Item Classifications

- Box J—The total revenue generated (column H) from the sale of all 2,000 menu items sold (box N) was $21,607.00.

- Box M—The contribution margin generated (column L) from the sale of all 2,000 items sold (box N) was $13,248.50 ($21,607.00 − $8,358.50).

- Box O—This is the average contribution margin of a menu item. It is calculated by dividing the total menu contribution margin ($13,248.50 in box M) by the total number of items sold (2,000 in box N).

- Box Q—This is the menu's popularity factor: Since there were six items on the menu (column A), if each item were equally popular it would represent 16.67% of the total sales (100 ÷ 6). Menu engineering considers an item popular if it represents 70% of its share of expected sales (16.67 × 0.70 = 11.7%).

To this point, we have calculated the menu's profitability factor (profitable items are those that have a contribution margin of $6.62 or more) and popularity (items are popular if they represent at least 11.7% of total sales).

Figure 10.3 shows how columns P, R, and S in Figure 10.1 are completed. Note, for example, that menu item 1 has a "low" contribution margin category. (Its CM [$5.90 in column F] is lower than that desired [$6.62 in box O].) Further, its menu mix category (column R) is high, because its menu mix (column C—17.5%) is higher than the desired menu mix percent (11.7% in box Q). The menu item classification (column S) uses terms developed by the menu engineering model:

- Plowhorses—items that are less profitable (low CM) but that are popular (high MM)

- Puzzle—items that are more profitable (high CM) but unpopular (low MM)

- Dog—items that are less profitable (low CM) and are not popular (low MM)

- Star—items that are more profitable (high CM) and popular (high MM)

A graph of the menu engineering results (see Figure 10.4 on page 238) can help show how each menu item relates to the others. It shows that items in the same classification (star, puzzle, plowhorse, dog) can still be very different. Look, for example, at hamburger platter (item 5) compared with BLT sandwich (item 4). Both are stars. However, the platter sells more (25.5% of sales) but has a lower CM ($7.00) than does the BLT sandwich (22.5% and $7.60, respectively). What can the manager do to increase the CM of the "more popular" star? Tactics such as offering a dinner with a dessert at a selling price increase which is more than the dessert's cost and perhaps using a less expensive garnish, will create a higher CM. However, the manager cannot consider such tactics unless menu engineering is first undertaken to determine potential problem areas.

Strategies for better managing other items should also be considered. For example, what can be done to improve the sales of chow mein (item 2)? As a puzzle, it is more profitable than some items but not as popular as others. Will lowering its selling price slightly increase sales? Can suggestive selling by servers and/or point-of-sale advertising increase guest orders? Again, managers can use the results of the menu engineering analysis to make menu management decisions.

PURCHASING: SOURCE DOCUMENT FLOW

It is often said that restaurant operations are made up of very closely related sub-systems; what occurs in one sub-system impacts the others. This is certainly true for the purchasing, receiving, storing, and issuing sub-systems. The person(s) responsible for each of these tasks tracks and uses financial information that impacts the other sub-systems.

In the past a significant amount of paperwork was necessary for persons in the purchasing, receiving, storeroom, issuing, and production departments to

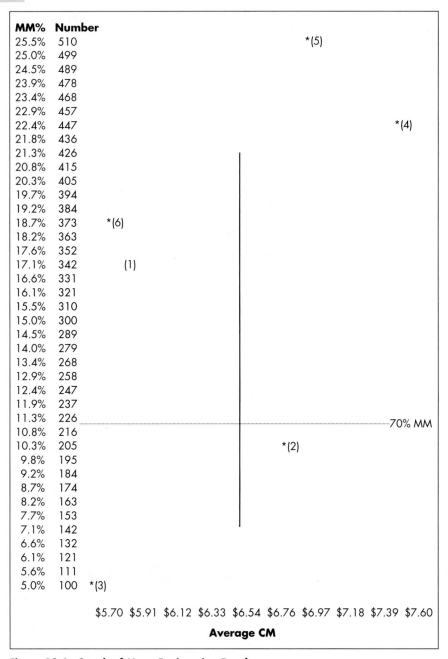

MM%	Number										
25.5%	510						*(5)				
25.0%	499										
24.5%	489										
23.9%	478										
23.4%	468										
22.9%	457										
22.4%	447									*(4)	
21.8%	436										
21.3%	426										
20.8%	415										
20.3%	405										
19.7%	394										
19.2%	384										
18.7%	373	*(6)									
18.2%	363										
17.6%	352										
17.1%	342	(1)									
16.6%	331										
16.1%	321										
15.5%	310										
15.0%	300										
14.5%	289										
14.0%	279										
13.4%	268										
12.9%	258										
12.4%	247										
11.9%	237										
11.3%	226										70% MM
10.8%	216										
10.3%	205						*(2)				
9.8%	195										
9.2%	184										
8.7%	174										
8.2%	163										
7.7%	153										
7.1%	142										
6.6%	132										
6.1%	121										
5.6%	111										
5.0%	100	*(3)									

$5.70 $5.91 $6.12 $6.33 $6.54 $6.76 $6.97 $7.18 $7.39 $7.60

Average CM

Figure 10.4 Graph of Menu Engineering Results

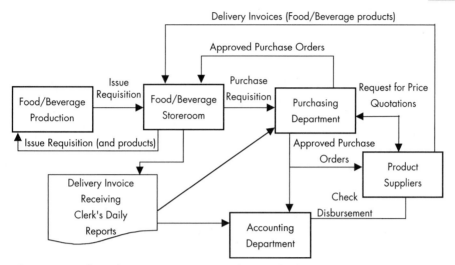

Figure 10.5 Flow of Source Documents During Purchasing Process

communicate with each other (internal information) and with suppliers (external information). The flow of source documents through the purchasing process might look like that in Figure 10.5 in a large restaurant operation.

As shown in Figure 10.5,

- The food/beverage production departments use an issue requisition to request products from applicable storeroom areas.

- Products, along with the applicable issue requisitions, are distributed to the production departments.

- Food/beverage storeroom employees use a purchase requisition to request that the purchasing department purchase additional products.

- The purchasing department requests price quotations from product suppliers and approves product purchases based upon numerous factors including product quality (specifications), experience with suppliers, and product price.

- Copies of the approved purchase orders are routed from the purchasing department to the accounting department and to the food/beverage storeroom.

- When food and beverage products are delivered to the food/beverage storeroom by the approved supplier, an applicable delivery invoice is also provided.

- The delivery invoice, along with the receiving clerk's daily report (this is discussed later in this chapter), is forwarded to the purchasing department and, in some operations, to the accounting department.

- The purchasing department matches purchase requisitions, purchase orders, and delivery invoices. This paperwork is forwarded to the accounting department where it can be compared with copies of purchase orders initially sent from the purchasing department.

- Finally, checks are disbursed to the suppliers by accounting department personnel.

It is important that, whenever possible, financial management and control systems be established that make it difficult for one person working alone to circumvent the system. For example, in a small restaurant, the chef might plan the menu, establish purchasing specifications for the products needed, select suppliers, and purchase, receive, store, and issue necessary products. It would be much better if the restaurant owner/manager assumed the duties of supplier selection, purchasing, and receiving. As another example, there may be only one person in a slightly larger restaurant that is responsible for purchasing and accounting. As systems become smaller, financial management tasks must be combined, and the possibility of employee theft/pilferage increases. By contrast, as operations grow larger, tasks become more specialized, and **collusion** between two or more staff members becomes necessary to carry out most theft schemes.

COLLUSION   A secret agreement between two or more persons to defraud the restaurant.

JUST-IN-TIME (JIT) DELIVERY   A system in which food/beverage products are delivered at least daily (sometimes more frequently) to reduce the need for product storage and issuing tasks. Under a JIT system, products may be delivered directly to production areas for immediate preparation.

Today, technology is replacing many of the purchasing procedures that were once done manually. For example, when predetermined product order points are reached, eligible suppliers can be contacted under a **just-in-time (JIT)** system in which there are frequent (daily or more often) deliveries to reduce product storage space and costs for the restaurant. Delivery invoices may be matched with copies initiated at the time of purchasing and electronically transmitted from the purchasing to the accounting department. In extreme cases where there is little or no storage space, products are delivered directly to production areas, and the entire task of issuing is almost eliminated. "Paperless" purchasing can occur as production departments electronically notify purchasing department personnel about required needs, as purchasing staff interact with product supplier personnel, and as production, storage, purchasing, and accounting personnel communicate with each other about purchasing needs and supplier delivery.

RECEIVING AND FINANCIAL MANAGEMENT

Some restaurants, especially larger ones, use data collected at time of product receiving to calculate a daily food cost. Restaurant managers must calculate food costs on at least a monthly basis. (Procedures for doing this are discussed later in this chapter.) In addition, they may wish to calculate a daily food cost to provide information on a more frequent basis so potential problems can be detected and resolved as soon as possible.

When a daily food cost system is in place, information from a daily receiving report is frequently used, as is information from the product issuing systems (also discussed later in this chapter).

Figure 10.6 shows a sample form that can be used to collect information for calculating daily food costs. Before reviewing this form, two terms should be defined:

- *Stores*—items that are expensive and therefore closely controlled. Examples include fresh and frozen meats, poultry, and seafood. The source document for the cost of stores used on a specific day is an issue requisition.
- *Directs*—items that are less expensive, such as dairy and bakery products and produce. The source document for directs is the daily receiving report with accompanying delivery invoices.

When reviewing Figure 10.6, note that for each supplier, a delivery invoice number is recorded, as is each product covered by the invoice, along with its unit cost, number of units purchased, and total cost. Each item is

Date: _____ 6/1/20XX _____

Supplier	Delivery Invoice	Product	Unit Cost	Number of Units	Total Cost	Stores	Directs
Bill's Dairy	10711	Milk	$2.50/gal.	8 gal.	$ 20.00		$ 20.00
Joe's Meat Co.	9812	Hot Dogs	$1.80/lb.	90 lbs.	$162.00		$162.00
		Sirloin Steaks	$4.70/lb.	112 lbs.	$526.40	$526.40	

Figure 10.6   Daily Receiving Report

then classified as either a store or a direct using the restaurant's definitions of these categories.

Information from the daily receiving report can be used to calculate the estimated daily food cost. Figure 10.7 can be used for this purpose.

Let's look at Figure 10.7 to determine how daily food cost information is calculated:

- Column 1—Date: The date is recorded.

- Column 2—Stores Cost: The cost of stores issued today, based upon issue requisitions.

- Column 3—Direct Costs: The cost of items delivered today that are not classified as stores.

- Column 4—Total Daily Food Cost: The total of stores issued ($6,575) and directs received today ($1,050) equals today's food cost ($7,625).

- Column 5—Daily Food Cost To Date: Since this is the first day of the month, today's food costs (column 4) equal the "to-date" food costs (column 5) of $7,625.

- Column 6—Revenue Today: Total revenue generated from food sales today.

Date	Stores Cost	Directs Cost	Total Daily Food Cost	Daily Food Cost To Date	Revenue		Food Cost %	
					Today	To Date	Today	To Date
1	2	3	4	5	6	7	8	9
7/1	$6,575	$1,050	$7,625	$ 7,625	$16,400	$16,400	46.5%	46.5%
7/2	$3,840	$ 590	$4,430	$12,055	$14,750	$31,150	30.0%	38.7%

Figure 10.7 Daily Food Cost Worksheet

- Column 7—Revenue to Date: The sum of all revenues generated. Since today is the first day of the month, today's revenues equal revenues to-date.

- Column 8—Food Cost Percent (Today): This figure (46.5%) is calculated by dividing today's daily food cost ($7,625 in column 4) by today's revenue ($16,400 in column 6).

- Column 9—Food Cost Percent (To Date): This figure (46.5%) is determined by dividing the daily food cost to date (column 5) by the revenues to date (column 7). Since this is the first day of the month, the food cost percent to date equals the food cost percent today.

After the first several days of the month, the manager will be able to determine a reasonably accurate to-date food cost that can be used in decision-making long before the monthly food cost percent calculation is made. The to-date food cost percentage (column 9) can be compared with the forecasted food cost percentage from the approved operating budget. If there is a variance that is significant and that does not become lower as the accounting period evolves, some type of corrective action may be warranted.

INVENTORY MANAGEMENT

After food and beverage products are purchased and received, they must be effectively stored. Two accounting concerns involve controlling the quantity and assessing the value of products in storage. Both directly affect the profitability of the restaurant. If, for example, the quantity of products in storage is excessive, cash flow can be affected (cash is tied up in inventory), the chance for spoilage increases (which requires additional purchases to compensate for products that have been purchased but from which no revenue was generated), and opportunities for employee theft increase. By contrast, when inadequate levels of inventory are maintained, there is an increased chance of stockouts, which can result in employee frustration, guest dissatisfaction, and increased food costs if, for example, replacement products must be purchased at retail market prices.

Inventory valuation also has a significant impact upon the restaurant's profitability. For example, high inventory values result in lower food costs, which, on paper, generate higher levels of profit and higher levels of income taxes. By contrast, lower inventory values result in higher food costs, lower levels of profit on paper, and lower income taxes. Note: The calculation of food and beverage costs are discussed later in this chapter.

Inventory Valuation Methods

Inventory valuation can be complicated, and a detailed discussion is beyond the scope of this book. However, some basic standards of inventory valuation must be incorporated into accounting systems for restaurants. These include the following:

1. *A consistent method of inventory valuation should be used.* Since food and beverage products are purchased essentially on an as-needed basis, inventory levels are generally low; inventory turnover rates can be high since products are used as they are purchased. There are four basic ways that values of inventory can be assigned:

   - *FIFO.* The first in–first out (FIFO) method assumes that products are withdrawn from inventory in the order in which they were received and entered into storage. Therefore, the products that remain in storage are judged to be the most recently purchased items. The value assigned to products in inventory becomes that of the most recently purchased products.

   - *LIFO.* The last in–first out (LIFO) method assumes the reverse of the FIFO method; the products most recently purchased are used first. The value of inventory is then represented by the unit cost of items in inventory the longest.

- *Actual cost.* This method of inventory valuation considers the actual price paid for each product in inventory. The inventory value is the sum of these actual individual unit costs.

- *Weighted average.* This method of inventory valuation considers the quantity of each product purchased at different unit prices. As the name implies, the inventory value is based on the average price paid for each product. The average price is weighted according to the quantity of products available in inventory that are purchased at each price.

Here is an example of how each of these inventory valuation methods affects the cost of inventory. Assume that on February 28, there are 28 cases of bar bourbon with a value of $72.00 per case in inventory. There are, then, also 28 cases of bar bourbon available on March 1 (the next day and the date of beginning inventory for March). Assume also that 15 cases of bar bourbon that cost $74.80 per case were purchased during the month (this amount can be assessed from delivery invoice records; it will also be entered into perpetual inventory records for the product if this control measure is used; perpetual inventory systems are discussed later in this section). The inventory count on March 31 reveals that there are 20 cases available. What is the value of bar bourbon in inventory?

a. Using the FIFO method (value based upon the most recent purchase), the calculation is:

$$
\begin{array}{rl}
\text{Most recent costs} = & 15 \text{ cases at } \$74.80/\text{case} = \$1,122.00 \\
\text{March 1 inventory costs} = & 5 \text{ cases at } \$72.00/\text{case} = \$\ \ 360.00 \\
& \text{Value of bar bourbon in inventory} = \underline{\$1,482.00}
\end{array}
$$

b. Using the LIFO method (value based upon the earliest purchase), the inventory value is:

$$
\text{Earliest cost} = 20 \text{ units at } \$72.00/\text{unit} = \underline{\$1,440.00}
$$

c. Using the actual cost method, the manager dates each case of bar bourbon when received. Inventory costs are calculated by counting the number of cases available at each purchase price. According to actual count there are 14 cases at $74.80/case and 6 cases at $72.00/case. The actual value of bar bourbon inventory is:

$$14 \text{ cases at } \$74.80/\text{case} = \$1,047.20$$
$$6 \text{ cases at } \$72.00/\text{case} = \underline{\$\ \ 432.00}$$
$$\text{Value of bar bourbon in inventory} = \underline{\underline{\$1,479.20}}$$

d. Using the weighted average method (average based upon the number of units acquired at each price) the value of inventory for the bar bourbon is computed as follows:

$$\text{March 1 inventory} = 28 \text{ cases at } \$72.00/\text{case} = \$2,016.00$$
$$\text{March purchase} = \underline{15} \text{ cases at } \$74.80/\text{case} = \underline{\$1,122.00}$$
$$43 \text{ cases} = \underline{\underline{\$3,138.00}}$$

$$\text{Average price} = \$3,138.00/43 \text{ cases} = \$72.98$$

$1,459.53	= 20	× $72.98
Value of inventory	No. of cases in inventory–March 31	Average case price

It can be seen, then, that the method used to measure inventory can have a significant effect on the calculated value. In review, the value of bar bourbon in inventory is either:

FIFO method	$1,482.00
LIFO method	$1,440.00
Actual method	$1,479.20
Weighted average	$1,459.53

There is a range from $1,482.00 (FIFO method) to $1,440.00 (LIFO method). This difference of $40.00 represents only a small quantity of one product (bar bourbon). The difference can be several thousand (or more) dollars in inventory costs as values of large quantities of all beverages are assessed.

The manager must determine the method of inventory valuation that will be used and must assure that the agreed upon method is consistently used. There are tax implications and restrictions applicable to changing inventory valuation methods. Also, the need to develop consistent information for accounting purposes has been stressed throughout this book.

2. *Inventory valuation affects profit levels.* As stated above, when the value of inventory increases, with no other changes, the value of actual food or beverage costs decreases. As the amount of costs decreases, profit levels increase. The income tax paid on profits is affected. (It increases.) It is important that the manager solicit advice from an accountant to determine the most appropriate method of inventory valuation for the specific restaurant.

3. *Inventory valuation is important.* In some restaurants managers delegate the task of "taking inventory" to almost anyone. They see it as a "routine procedure" that must be done "because the accountant requires it." A manager should understand why knowledge about inventory values are important. They are a basic element in the process used to "match" costs of food (or beverage) sold with food (or beverage) revenue.

Physical and Perpetual Inventories

All restaurants must undertake a physical inventory to determine costs of goods used. Larger restaurants will, additionally, benefit from use of a perpetual inventory system.

Physical Inventory. A physical inventory involves making an actual physical count and valuation of inventory on hand at the close of an accounting period. This is necessary because value of inventory is a component in calculating the actual costs of goods (food or beverage) sold, which is reported on monthly financial statements. A sample physical inventory form is shown in Figure 10.8 on page 248. The process basically involves counting the number of units of each item in inventory and multiplying the number of units by unit costs (recall the discussion of inventory valuation above).

Unless the person taking the inventory is the manager, inventory counts should not be taken by the employee responsible for maintaining the storeroom.

Item	Storage Unit	Number of Units	Unit Cost	Inventory Value
Applesauce	6 cases (#10)	3.5	$48.00	$168.00
Beans, Green	6 cases (#10)	4.5	$43.50	$195.75
Flour, AP	50 lb. Bag	3	$27.75	$ 83.25

Figure 10.8 Physical Inventory Form

The purpose of inventory valuation is, in part, to confirm the quantity of products that should be available in inventory. A basic principle of control is that an employee should not monitor procedures which are that employee's responsibility. Frequently, the head cook (who is not involved in storage or issuing) might work with the accountant/bookkeeper to undertake the task. In the beverage operation, the head bartender (likewise not involved in storage/issuing) may undertake the inventory count with the accountant/bookkeeper. In small operations, the owner/manager working alone may conduct inventory counts, or, alternatively, a representative from the bookkeeping service employed by the restaurant may perform this task.

Perpetual Inventory.   Some restaurants use a perpetual inventory system for some (usually the most expensive) inventory items. A sample item under a perpetual inventory system is illustrated in Figure 10.9. A perpetual inventory system allows a running balance to be kept of the quantity of items in stock at any point in time. For example, when the delivery of a product is made, the balance is increased. Likewise, as products are removed (issued) from storage areas, the balance is decreased.

It is not necessary for perpetual inventory records to maintain a running balance of the cost of products in inventory. Even when a perpetual inventory record is maintained, an end-of-fiscal-period physical count (see above) of inventory items must still be made to verify the accuracy of perpetual inventory records. Costs of products available in inventory are determined once each month when the physical inventory is taken, rather than continuously through the month (as would occur if a perpetual inventory system incorporating costs of products in storage were maintained). Since the cost of products in stock during the fiscal period is not a component in most control systems, this informa-

Product: _____Sirloin Steaks_____   Purchase Unit: _____Pound (#)_____

Date	Received	Issued	Quantity in Storage
7/3	80#	28#	154#
7/4		35#	119#
7/5	25#		144#

Figure 10.9 Perpetual Inventory System

tion should not be collected; time can be better spent on other phases of restaurant management.

As noted earlier in this chapter, new technologies are emerging that can minimize the time and maximize the accuracy in inventory counts and valuations. As these become more available, managers will find it easier to gather timely and accurate information for financial management decision-making.

Inventory Turnover Rate

The term **"inventory turnover rate"** refers to the number of times the total value of inventory is purchased and replaced in an accounting period. Each time the cycle is completed, it is said that the inventory has "turned." For example, if the manager normally has $1,000.00 of food inventory on hand at any given time and the monthly usage of products is $5,000.00, the inventory has been replaced (turned) five times during the month.

Inventory turnover is computed as follows:

> **INVENTORY TURNOVER RATE—** The number of times in a given accounting period that inventory is converted (turned) into revenue. The inventory turnover rate measures the rate at which inventory is turned into food or beverage costs required to generate food or beverage revenue.

$$\frac{\text{Cost of food (or beverage) consumed}}{\text{Average inventory value}} = \text{Food (beverage) turnover}$$

"Average inventory value" is calculated as follows:

$$\frac{\begin{array}{c}\text{Beginning} \qquad\quad \text{Ending} \\ \text{inventory value} + \text{inventory value}\end{array}}{2} = \begin{array}{c}\text{Average food (or beverage)} \\ \text{inventory value}\end{array}$$

The following example illustrates the process. Assume:

Food inventory value (July 1)   = $ 22,700
Food inventory value (July 31) = $ 24,100
Cost of food consumed   = $126,000

$$\text{Average food inventory (daily)} = \frac{\text{July 1 inventory value} + \text{July 31 inventory value}}{2}$$

$$\$23,400 = \frac{\$22,700 + \$24,100}{2}$$

$$\frac{\text{July food inventory}}{\text{turnover rate}} = \frac{\text{Cost of food consumed in July}}{\text{Average food inventory (July)}}$$

$$5.38 \text{ times} = \frac{\$126,000}{\$23,400}$$

As seen above, the value of inventory was used approximately 5.38 times per month. In other words, approximately 5.38 times the average amount of daily inventory must be purchased during the month to provide the products required for the restaurant production.

Restaurant managers must track the inventory turnover rate separately for food and beverage products. A specific rate for a specific month may not be meaningful. However, trends (for example, the beverage turnover rate decreasing each month over a period of several months and the food inventory turnover rate increasing each month over several months) may suggest that the restaurant manager should question procedures used to purchase, receive, store, and issue food and beverage products.

PRODUCT ISSUING

Large restaurants may have a full-time storeroom clerk and may require that any product removed from storage areas be included in a formalized issue requisi-

Date: _____7/16/20XX_____

Item Withdrawn from Inventory	Storage Unit	Number of Units Withdrawn	Storage Unit Cost	Total Cost
Strip Steaks	8 oz.	15	$4.85	$ 72.75
Ground Beef	lb.	45	$2.20	$ 99.00
Veal Patties	lb.	30	$4.10	$123.00

Figure 10.10   Issue Requisition Form

tion process. Smaller restaurants can use an **issuing** system for, at least, the "A" items (those relatively few products that are the most expensive and theft-prone; fresh meats, frozen seafoods, and alcoholic beverages are examples).

> **ISSUING   The process of removing food or beverage products from inventory and moving them into the pre-production or production cycles.**

As noted earlier in this chapter, restaurants calculating daily food costs use an issue requisition as a source document to determine the value of "stores" that have been issued from storage. (Recall that daily food costs are the sum of stores reported on issue requisition forms and directs reported in the daily receiving report.)

Figure 10.10 shows a sample document that can be used for this purpose. Items to be formally issued with the requisition form should be maintained under lock and key and will likely be included in the restaurant's perpetual inventory system (see above). The issue requisition form provides the source document for reducing the quantity of a specific product in the perpetual inventory system, and when included with all other issue requisitions for the day, is used to calculate daily food costs.

CALCULATION OF ACTUAL FOOD/ BEVERAGE COSTS

Calculating the actual food and beverage costs for a restaurant's income statement requires determining the "cost of sales." We discussed some basics for this calculation earlier (see chapter 4). It is critical that the manager know the cost of

PRIME COSTS Product (food and beverage) and labor costs, which represent the two largest expenses of virtually all restaurants.

sales for each accounting period to control product costs, which, along with labor costs (see chapter 11), represent one of the two most significant costs incurred by the restaurant. Note: Product and labor costs are often referred to as **prime costs** for this reason.

All restaurants using an accrual accounting system use the same basic calculation to determine cost of sales. This calculation is:

Beginning inventory + Purchases − Ending inventory = Cost of sales

Note: Procedures for valuing beginning and ending inventories were presented earlier in this chapter. The value of purchases is represented by the sum of all delivery invoices for products received during the month plus or minus any adjustments required as delivery invoices are audited by restaurant personnel. In addition, any delivery costs paid by the purchasing restaurant are added to the cost of purchases.

If a restaurant uses the above definition of cost of sales consumed, the actual food and beverage costs for the accounting period can be determined as follows:

	Food	Beverage	Source Document
Beginning inventory value	$_____	$_____	Physical inventory forms (first day of period[16])
+ Value of purchases	$_____	$_____	Delivery invoices
− Ending inventory value	$(_____)	$(_____)	Physical inventory forms (last day of period[16])
= Cost of sales	$_____	$_____	

[16]Note: The value of inventory taken on the last day of a period becomes the inventory value on the first day of the next period; inventory values must only be calculated once each accounting period.

$$\frac{\text{Cost of sales: food}}{\text{Food revenues}} = \text{Food cost percentage}$$

$$\frac{\text{Cost of sales: beverage}}{\text{Beverage revenues}} = \text{Beverage cost percentage}$$

When reviewing the above, note that the beginning inventory for food and for beverage plus the value of purchases for these two products equals the total amount of product (food and beverage) available. When the value of ending inventory for food and beverage products is subtracted from this amount, the cost of sales for each product results. Note also that the source documents (physical inventory forms for beginning and ending inventory values and delivery invoices for the value of purchases) indicate where data for these calculations will be found.

In chapter 1 we learned about the Generally Accepted Accounting Principle (GAAP) involving "matching"; that is, the revenue generated from a sale of a food or beverage product should be matched with the expense incurred while generating the revenue. Adjustments to the cost of sales calculations presented above are necessary to apply this matching principle.

- Some food products may actually generate revenues for the beverage operations: complimentary food provided in the bar/lounge to encourage beverage sales.

- Some beverages might be used to generate food revenue: wine used in cooking and liqueur used to prepare desserts.

- Some food and beverage items may not generate food or beverage revenues at all: complimentary meals/drinks given to persons considering the future booking of functions at the restaurant (this is more accurately a marketing expense) and food provided as a meal (benefit) to employees (this is more accurately a labor/benefit expense).

The GAAP of matching, then, is recognized by making adjustments to the basic cost of sales calculations noted above. The calculations to do this follow:

	Food	Beverage
Beginning inventory value	$_____	$_____
+ Value of purchases	$_____	$_____
− Ending inventory value	$(_____)	$(_____)
= Unadjusted "cost of sales"	$_____	$_____

(continued on page 254)

	Food	Beverage
+ Transfers to kitchen	$_____	$(_____)
− Transfers from kitchen	$(_____)	$(_____)
− Complimentary (marketing) sales	$(_____)	$(_____)
− Employee meal costs	$(_____)	$(_____)
= Net cost of sales	$_____	$_____

$$\frac{\text{Net cost of sales: food}}{\text{Food revenues}} = \text{Food cost percentage}$$

$$\frac{\text{Net cost of sales: beverage}}{\text{Beverage revenues}} = \text{Beverage cost percentage}$$

When reviewing the above calculations, note that the process of making adjustments to food and beverage costs begins the same way as when no adjustments are made: the value of beginning inventory is added to the value of purchases to yield the total value of food available; the ending inventory value is subtracted to yield what is now referred to as "unadjusted cost of sales." That is, the cost of sales before adjustments are made to incorporate concerns raised by the matching principle.

The first series of adjustments relate to transfers to and from the kitchen. Transfers *to* the kitchen increase the food cost and decrease the beverage cost; transfers *from* the kitchen decrease the food cost and increase the beverage cost.

The next two adjustments (complimentary [marketing] sales and employee meal costs) decrease the food cost (if, for example, complimentary meals were served) and decrease the beverage cost (if complimentary beverages were provided). The marketing/promotion expense account should be charged for the value of these complimentary meals/beverages.

The value of employee meal costs is also subtracted from the food cost and, if applicable, the beverage costs. Note: The calculation of employee meal costs can be complicated. For example, the value of meals to an individual employee must be excluded when income tax calculations are made and when FICA (social security) taxes are assessed. (Procedures for determining the value of employee meals and for correcting and reporting this information should be discussed with the restaurant's tax adviser.)

Date: _____7/10/20XX_____

To: _____Bar_____   From: _____Kitchen_____

Item	Storage Unit	Number of Storage Units	Storage Unit Cost	Total Cost
Maraschino Cherries	QT	1	$27.50	$27.50
Celery	Bunch	2	$ 2.50	$ 5.00

Figure 10.11 Sample Food/Beverage Transfer Memo

After the above adjustments are made, the result is a "net cost of sales," which can be divided by, respectively, food revenue and beverage revenue to yield the food cost percentage and beverage cost percentage.

Figure 10.11 can be used to record transfers of food from the kitchen to the bar or beverages from the bar to the kitchen. Once completed, these transfer memos can be retained and then given to the accountant/bookkeeper at the end of the accounting period to make necessary adjustments.

WWW: Internet Assistant

One important part of accounting for transfers from a kitchen to a bar area is the consideration of "yield." Yield is the amount of product remaining after an ingredient is trimmed, cleaned, or cooked prior to being added to a recipe. For example, celery that is purchased by the stalk must be washed and trimmed before it can be used in a bar area as a drink garnish.

To view a "Book of Yields," consisting of the yields of over 900 common recipe ingredients, as well as to see how it can be utilized in purchasing, go to

http://www.chefdesk.com

Select "View Sample Screens."

MANAGER'S 10 POINT EFFECTIVENESS CHECKLIST

Evaluate your need for and the status of each of the following financial management tactics. For tactics you judge to be important but not yet in place, develop an action plan including completion date to implement the tactic.

TACTIC	DON'T AGREE (DON'T NEED)	AGREE (DONE)	AGREE (NOT DONE)	IF NOT DONE WHO IS RESPONSIBLE?	IF NOT DONE TARGET COMPLETION DATE
1. A standardized recipe has been developed and is consistently used for *every* menu item.	❑	❑	❑		
2. Standardized recipes are costed and ingredient costs are updated at least two times per year.	❑	❑	❑		
3. Purchase orders are prepared and used as a check against delivery invoices when receiving food and beverage product deliveries.	❑	❑	❑		
4. Managers use a consistent method of inventory valuation to help assess actual food costs.	❑	❑	❑		
5. An inventory turnover rate is calculated at the end of each accounting period.	❑	❑	❑		
6. Food transfers to the beverage area are documented daily.	❑	❑	❑		
7. Beverage transfers to the food area are documented daily.	❑	❑	❑		
8. The value of employee meals is calculated and recorded daily.	❑	❑	❑		
9. An accurate food (and, if appropriate, beverage) cost is computed at the end of each accounting period.	❑	❑	❑		
10. Actual food and beverage costs for the accounting period are compared to forecasted product costs to identify areas of variation worthy of investigation and correction.	❑	❑	❑		

11

PAYROLL ACCOUNTING

MANAGER'S BRIEF

For virtually all restaurants, labor costs are the largest or second largest (after food costs) expense. In this chapter, you will learn how to properly account for this significant portion of your operation's budget.

A restaurant's total labor expense is made up of many individual items. The largest of these is payroll: the salaries and wages paid to the restaurant's employees. Some portions of payroll are considered fixed payroll costs. A manager's salary, for example, is generally the same (fixed) each month; other payroll expenses, like that of hourly paid service staff, will often increase or decrease based on changes in revenue. Payroll costs like these are considered variable and are likely to be within the direct control of managers.

There are some labor costs that are not as easy to control. Taxes, benefits, employee meals, vacation time, and holiday pay are just some of the labor-related expenses that must be accounted for properly, and this chapter will show you how to account for all of them.

Payroll-related data required by government agencies is discussed in this chapter. Sample forms and techniques to help you understand how to record such information are provided. For example, employees who work over 40 hours in a week must be paid overtime, and the calculations for overtime pay, including those for salaried staff members, are clearly presented. Lastly, journal entries required to record labor-related expenses are described, as is information about the manager's responsibilities for employee tip reporting.

> **PRIME COSTS The total of product (food and beverage) and labor costs; these are the two largest expense categories in virtually all restaurants.**

Labor costs, along with product (food and beverage) costs, are at the top of every restaurant manager's list of concerns when it comes to the need for special controls to maintain quality and at the same time minimize expenses. In fact, these costs, which make up the majority of costs in virtually all restaurants, are referred to as **prime costs.**

IMPORTANCE OF LABOR CONTROLS

> **CONVENIENCE FOOD A food item that has some or all of the labor "built in" that otherwise would need to be provided on-site.**

In today's age of expanding technology, production and service labor in restaurants remains an area in which people—not machines—are required. Increasingly, guests want quality service delivered by "real" people; they do not want service by robots or assembly lines. Further, the concept that "fresh is best" means that, at least for many restaurants, the use of **convenience foods** to reduce on-site labor is not a tactic that can be used to drastically reduce labor costs.

Figure 11.1 recaps labor-related information from a recent year and quantifies what all restaurant managers know: Labor is a significant expense and must be effectively controlled.

	Type of Restaurant	
	Full-Service	**Limited Service**
Salaries/wages and employee benefits as a percent of food/beverage revenues	35%	31%

	Dollars Per FTE* Employee	
Full-Service Restaurants	**Total Revenues**	**Total Payroll Benefits**
Check average = $25.00 or more	$57,268	$18,140
Check average = $15.00–$24.99	$45,012	$19,959
Check average = Less than $15.00	$40,112	$14,332

Full-Service Restaurants	**Cost of Benefits as Percentage of Payroll**
Check average = $25.00 or more	16.5%
Check average = $15.00–$24.99	16.5%
Check average = Less than $15.00	13.2%

Number of Employees – Full-Service	**Food/Beverage**	**Food Only**
Per Restaurant (check average = $25.00 or more)		
Full-time	14	n/a
20–34 hours	10	n/a
Less than 20 hours	5	n/a
Full-time equivalent employees (per 100 seats)	15	n/a
Per Restaurant (check average = $15.00–$24.99)		
Full-time	15	n/a
20–34 hours	14	n/a
Less than 20 hours	6	n/a
Full-time equivalent employees (per 100 seats)	28	16
Per Restaurant (check average = less than $15.00)		
Full-time	10	10
20–34 hours	12	10
Less than 20 hours	7	5
Full-time equivalent employees (per 100 seats)	21	18

*FTE = Full-Time Equivalent

[a]Deloitte & Touche, Restaurant Industry Operations Report 2001 (Washington, D.C., 2001). (Note: Data is for 2000.)

Figure 11.1   Restaurant Labor Statistics[a]

A CLOSE LOOK AT PAYROLL AND OTHER LABOR EXPENSES

PAYROLL The term generally used to refer to salaries and wages paid to restaurant employees.

The term **"payroll"** generally refers to the salaries and wages paid to restaurant employees. By contrast, **labor expense** includes these salaries and wages but also consists of a potentially wide range of other labor-related costs.

LABOR EXPENSE Salaries, wages, and all other labor-related costs related to restaurant employees, including payroll taxes and employee benefits.

Payroll relates to the gross pay received by an employee in exchange for his/her work. If an employee earns $8.00 per hour and works 40 hours for a restaurant, the gross paycheck (the employee's paycheck *before* any mandatory or voluntary deductions) would be $320 ($8.00 per hour × 40 hours = $320). This amount is considered a payroll expense.

If the employee earns a salary, that salary amount is also a payroll expense. A salaried employee receives the same income per week, month, or other pay period regardless of the number of hours worked. If a salaried employee is paid $500 per week (or other pay period), $500 is part of the payroll expense. Payroll, then, is one part of labor expense.

Fixed Payroll Versus Variable Payroll

MINIMUM STAFF The smallest number of employees or payroll dollars required to operate a restaurant or department within the restaurant.

Some employees are needed to provide for minimally anticipated business. An example may be a manager and one server and one cook. In this case, the cost of providing payroll to these three individuals is called a **minimum-staff** payroll. The term "minimum staff" is used to designate the least number of employees or payroll dollars required to operate a restaurant or department within the restaurant.

Suppose, however, the manager anticipates a much greater volume on a given day. The increased number of guests expected drives the need for more cooks, servers, added cashiers, more dishroom personnel and, perhaps, more supervisors to handle the additional workload. These additional employees and positions create a work group that is far larger than the minimum staff.

Some managers confuse minimum-staff requirements with fixed payroll and variable payroll. **Fixed payroll** refers to the amount the restaurant pays in

salaries. This amount is fixed in that it normally remains unchanged from one pay period to the next.
Variable payroll consists of compensation paid to
hourly employees. Therefore, variable payroll is the
amount that "varies" with changes in volume.

> **FIXED PAYROLL** The amount
> the restaurant pays in
> salaries. It normally remains
> unchanged from one pay pe-
> riod to the next.

Generally, as the manager anticipates increased
business volume levels in the restaurant, there is a need
to add additional hourly employees. When lower levels
of volume are anticipated, the number of hourly employees scheduled will likely decrease. In a similar
manner, if increased business volume levels are antici-

> **VARIABLE PAYROLL**
> Compensation paid to hourly
> employees; the amount
> varies with changes in
> volume.

pated to remain steady over a long period of time, the manager may determine
that additional salaried employees would be beneficial. The distinction between
fixed and variable labor is an important one. The manager may sometimes have
little control over fixed labor expenses, while, at the same time, he/she can exert
significant control over variable labor expenses that are above minimum-staff
levels.

Labor Expense

As noted above, "labor expense" refers to the total of *all* costs associated with
maintaining the restaurant's workforce. As such, labor expense is always larger
than payroll expense. As the cost of providing employee benefits increases
and/or as employment taxes go up, labor expense will increase, even if payroll
expense remains constant.

> **CONTROLLABLE LABOR
> EXPENSES** Payroll expenses
> over which a manager has
> total control.

Most managers have total control over their payroll expenses. They are, therefore, often referred to as a
controllable labor expenses. Those labor expenses, on
the other hand, over which the manager has little or no
control are called **noncontrollable labor expenses.**
These expenses include such items as federal- or state-
mandated payroll taxes and insurance premiums. (In
reality, however, a manager can exert some control
even over these noncontrollable labor expenses.

> **NONCONTROLLABLE LABOR
> EXPENSES** Labor expenses
> over which a manager as lit-
> tle or no control.

Consider, for example, a manager who works hard to provide a well-trained
workforce with a safe environment and achieves a lower rate on accident and
health insurance for the employees.)

Components of Labor Expense

As noted earlier, labor expense includes salaries, wages, and other labor-related costs. In addition to salaries and wages, the following expenses are also related to employment and, therefore, are considered labor expenses:

- FICA (social security) taxes
- unemployment taxes
- workman's compensation
- group life insurance
- health insurance
- pension/retirement plan payments
- employee meals
- employee on-job training expenses
- employee transportation costs
- employee uniforms, housing, and other benefits
- vacation/sick leave
- employee incentives and bonuses

Not all restaurants incur all of the above costs. Some have additional types of costs. All restaurants, however, incur some labor-related expenses in addition to payroll costs.

ACCOUNTING FOR PAYROLL

Planning and implementing basic payroll-related processes are an important aspect of the restaurant's financial management system.

Payroll Controls

Several important controls are needed to effectively manage payroll and should be in place before financial management tactics are implemented. These controls include:

- Payroll functions should be segregated when possible. This can be a problem in small restaurants with few employees to handle payroll-related tasks. (In these cases the owner/manager should be involved in all steps in the payroll process.) The following activities should be done by separate staff members when staffing permits:

Activity	Position Responsible
❏ Authorizing employment/establishing wage rates	Owner/manager
❏ Reporting hours worked by employees	Employee #1
❏ Preparing the payroll	Employee #2
❏ Signing payroll checks	Owner/manager
❏ Distributing checks to employees. (Checks should not be distributed to employees by those working in the payroll department.)	Owner/manager
❏ Reconciling payroll bank accounts	Independent party

- In larger restaurants with human resources departments, personnel from this unit should be the only persons authorized to add or delete individuals from payroll records. In addition, only this department should provide the payroll department with the employees' wage rates.

- Proper procedures for recording time worked, including the use of electronic equipment where possible, should be in use.

- Employees should only be paid by check. In addition, a special **imprest payroll account** should be used. An imprest payroll account is one in which the exact amount needed for a given payroll period (and no other funds) is deposited. Payroll checks totaling that deposit are then written on that account. After all the checks clear the bank, there is a zero balance in the account.

> **IMPREST PAYROLL ACCOUNT**
> An account into which only the exact amount of a given payroll period (and no other funds) is deposited. Payroll checks totaling that deposit are then written on that account. The account will have a zero balance after all checks clear the bank.

- Payroll sheets and employee paychecks should be independently audited.

- Unclaimed payroll checks should be returned to an accounting department official or the restaurant manager, who should hold them until the employees return to work and pick up their checks.

Payroll Records

W-4 FORM A form that provides the employer with the employee's marital status, withholding allowances, and other information that helps the employer calculate the amount of taxes to be withheld from the employee's payroll check.

The Fair Labor Standards Act (FLSA) is commonly thought of as the federal wage and hour law. It addresses concerns such as equal pay for equal work, record-keeping requirements, minimum wage rates, and overtime pay. Most restaurants are covered by this act. Managers must keep records of the time worked by hourly employees. Time cards or time sheets are generally used and can be administered manually or with an electronic time clock. An example of an employee time card is shown in Figure 11.2.

Restaurants typically maintain a master payroll file that includes important employee information such as name, address, Social Security number, and wage rate along with payroll deduction information.

SALARIES AND WAGES WORK-SHEET AND CHECK REGISTER A payroll record that lists, among other things, each payroll check issued by the restaurant with gross pay and deductions for federal, state, city, and Social Security taxes; employee health care contributions; and other contributions such as union dues. Some restaurateurs refer to this record simply as a payroll journal.

One document that employees must complete and provide to their employer is the Internal Revenue Service (IRS) **W-4 form.** This form provides the employer with the employee's marital status, withholding allowances, and other information that helps the employer calculate the amount of income taxes to be withheld from the employee's payroll check. A second payroll record is the **salaries and wages worksheet and check register** shown in Figure 11.3. This lists each payroll check issued by the restaurant with gross pay and deductions for federal, state, city, and Social Security taxes, employee health care contributions, and other contributions such as union dues. The IRS **W-2 form,** which employers must provide to employees annually, recaps compensation, taxes withheld, and other wage and tax-related information.

W-2 FORM (IRS) A form provided by the employer to the employee that recaps wages, taxes withheld, and related information for the calendar year.

Another form, **employee earnings record,** is also maintained for each employee. A sample is shown in Figure 11.4. This record compiles information that employers use to report wages to the various levels of government levying income taxes on employees (federal, state, and sometimes local governmental units).

Week Ending: _____   20_____

Name: _____   Employee Number: _____

Date	AM		PM		Other		Total
	In	Out	In	Out	In	Out	

Total Time: _____ hours

Hourly Rate: $_____

Total Weekly Wages: $_____

Figure 11.2 Sample Employee Time Card

Some taxes apply to earnings up to a specified dollar amount; this record is used to assure that these maximums are not exceeded.

Regular and Overtime Pay

The FLSA requires that regular pay for an employee be based upon a 40-hour work week. The **regular hourly rate** is the wage rate per hour used to compute regular pay. The FLSA also requires that overtime pay be given for any hours worked in excess of 40 hours in a week. The **overtime hourly rate** is the wage rate per hour used to compute overtime pay. The FLSA requires that overtime be paid at the rate of 1.5 times the employee's regular hourly rate.

To calculate the overtime pay for some employees may require that a weekly wage be converted into an hourly rate. For example, assume an employee is

EMPLOYEE'S EARNINGS RECORD A payroll record that compiles information for government reporting of employees' wages. Some taxes apply to earnings up to a specified dollar amount; this record is used to assure that those maximums are not exceeded.

REGULAR HOURLY RATE The wage rate per hour used to compute regular pay.

OVERTIME HOURLY RATE The wage rate per hour used to compute overtime pay.

Period from _____ to _____

Check No. or ID No.	Name of Employee	Position	Dept. No.	Wage Rate		Hours Worked		Salaries and Wages	Tips & Service Charges	Total Paid by Employer
				Regular	OT	Regular	OT			
1.										
2.										
3.										
4.										
5.										
6.										
7.										
8.										
9.										
10.										
11.										
12.										
13.										
14.										
15.										
16.										
17.										

[a]National Restaurant Association, *Uniform System of Accounts for Restaurants* (Washington, D.C.)

Figure 11.3 Salaries and Wages Worksheet and Check Register[a]

Period from _____ to _____

Memo Only		Wage and Hour Total		Withholding Tax	Deductions		Total Deductions	Net Pay	Check Number
Employee Meals	Reported Tips		FICA		Other				
					Code	Amount			
1.									
2.									
3.									
4.									
5.									
6.									
7.									
8.									
9.									
10.									
11.									
12.									
13.									
14.									
15.									
16.									
17.									

Figure 11.3 *(Continued)*

Employee Earnings Record

Name: _____

_____

Address: _____

_____

Social Security Number: _____

_____

Pay Period Ending	Earnings				Memo Only				Deductions					
	Regular	Overtime	Gross	Distributed Tips and Service Charges	Wages for WH	Meals and Lodging	Reported Tips	Wages for FICA	FICA	Federal Income Tax	State Income Tax	Retirement Contribution	Health Insurance	Net Pay

Figure 11.4   Sample Employee's Earnings Record

hired at a weekly wage of $218 for a 40-hour workweek. The regular hourly rate for this employee would be $5.45:

$$\text{Regular hourly rate} = \frac{\text{Weekly wage}}{\text{Number of hours in regular workweek}}$$

$$= \frac{\$218}{40}$$

$$= \$5.45$$

After the regular hourly rate has been calculated, the overtime rate can be determined. Since the FLSA requires an overtime rate of 1.5 times the regular hourly rate, the hourly overtime rate is $8.18:

$$\text{Overtime hourly rate} = \text{Regular hourly rate} \times 1.5$$

$$= \$5.45 \times 1.5$$

$$= \$8.18$$

Sometimes salaried staff may be eligible for overtime. Specific federal and state regulations apply; restaurant managers cannot arbitrarily determine whether overtime provisions are applicable to a specific worker. In restaurants, exemptions from overtime provisions are usually reserved for "executives." To be classified as an executive and therefore exempt from overtime pay requirements, a staff member must meet certain conditions:

- The employee's primary responsibility must involve managing the restaurant.

- The employee must directly supervise other staff.

- The employee can hire and fire and must be involved in other employee-related decisions.

- The employee must have discretion when performing his/her duties.

- The employee's salary must exceed a legally mandated amount.

How is the overtime rate calculated for a nonexempt salaried employee? Assume Joe is paid a salary of $30,000 per year or $2,500 per month ($30,000 ÷ 12 months = $2,500). In May (31 days; 4.43 weeks [31 days ÷ 7 days/week]) he works 185 hours. Overtime (1½ times the hourly rate) must be paid for all hours worked after 177.2 hours (4.43 weeks × 40 hours = 177.2 hours). Joe must, then, be paid overtime for 7.8 hours (185 hours − 177.2 hours). His base hourly rate is $14.11 ($2,500 per month ÷ 4.43 weeks ÷ 40 hours). His overtime hourly rate is $21.17 ($14.11 × 1.5). Total compensation due for the 7.8 hours of overtime is $165.13 (7.8 hours × $21.17 hourly overtime rate).

Payroll Journal Entries

There are two major journal entries involving payroll. One entry is needed to record payroll and a second entry to record payroll taxes.

Entry to Record Payroll.   Think of the payroll entry as a "check stub" entry: If the restaurant had only one employee and that employee's check stub were in front of the manager, he/she could use the information on the stub to journalize the entry. The following items are included in the payroll entry:

- **Gross pay.** Gross pay is calculated by multiplying the hours the employee worked for the pay period by the hourly rate including any overtime premium. (In the case of salaried employees, gross pay for a month, for example, would be 1/12 of the annual salary.)
- **Federal income tax (FIT).** Withholding amounts for federal income tax vary depending on marital status and the tax rate(s) in effect.

  The amount of an employee's withholding taxes to be paid is based upon:

  —marital status

  —frequency of compensation payments (weekly, monthly, etc.)

  —number of withholding allowances (dependents)

  —gross wages

  Assume a married employee with four allowances is paid $500.00 weekly. How much FIT must be withheld? The applicable section of the current Internal Revenue Service (IRS) documents (Circular E) should be consulted. (A sample section is illustrated in Figure 11.5.) It indicates that the amount of income, social security, and Medicare taxes for a married person with four dependents who is paid $500.00 weekly is $62.63. This is the amount that must be withheld for transfer to the IRS.

And the wages are		And the number of withholding allowances claimed is—									
At least	But less than	0	1	2	3	4	5	6	7	8	9
460	470	86.57	78.57	69.57	61.57	53.57	44.57	36.57	35.57	35.57	35.57
470	480	89.34	80.34	72.34	64.34	55.34	47.34	38.34	36.34	36.34	36.34
480	490	91.10	83.10	74.10	66.10	58.10	49.10	41.10	37.10	37.10	37.10
490	500	93.87	84.87	76.87	68.87	59.87	51.87	42.87	37.87	37.87	37.87
500	510	95.63	87.63	78.63	70.63	**62.63**	53.63	45.63	38.63	38.63	38.63
510	520	98.40	89.40	81.40	73.40	64.40	56.40	47.40	39.40	39.40	39.40

Figure 11.5 Married Persons—Weekly Payroll Period

- *Social Security taxes.* Social Security taxes result from the Federal Insurance Contributions Act (FICA). The rate for FICA taxes is actually a combination of two rates; a specified percentage on an annually increasing base level of income plus an additional percent on all income.

- *State income tax (SIT).* States vary widely in the amount of state income tax assessed. Rates range from zero percent in several states to North Dakota's rate of about 12 percent.

- *Miscellaneous deductions.* Other deductions from an employee's pay might be made for local income tax, the employee's contribution to health care benefits, union dues taken by the employer for remittance to the union, the employee's charitable contributions, etc.

  Note: All current liabilities, such as FIT, SIT, FICA, and miscellaneous deductions, are eventually remitted to the agencies to whom they are owed. From the time when they are deducted from an employee's wages until they are remitted, these current liabilities are considered current liabilities for the restaurant.

- *The amount of the employee's net pay.* Net pay is gross pay minus the deductions. It is the amount for which the payroll check is written.

> **NET PAY** **An employee's gross pay minus the deductions.**

Let's assume, for a given pay period, that a restaurant had salaries and wages of $40,000 and $25,000, respectively. Let's also assume that the total federal income tax withheld for this pay period amounted to $15,600, the state income tax withheld was $2,650, the FICA deduction was $4,973, and the health insurance deduction $1,020. (The net pay, then is $40,757.) The entry recording this transaction follows:

Salaries	$40,000	
Wages	25,000	
FIT payable		$15,600
SIT payable		2,650
FICA payable		4,973
Health insurance payable		1,020
Salaries/wages payable		40,757

This entry would be made on the date payroll was computed. On the date payroll was actually paid to the employees, the amount of net pay would be transferred into the payroll imprest fund. The journal entry would be:

Salaries/wages payable $40,757
Cash—Payroll $40,757

Note the large difference in this case between the gross payroll ($65,000) and the net pay to the employees ($40,757).

Entry to Record Payroll Taxes.   The second major payroll entry involves the restaurant's payroll taxes. Payroll taxes are paid by the employer based on employee wages. The three major elements of payroll taxes are the employer's FICA tax contribution and the contributions required under the Federal Unemployment Tax Act (FUTA) and the State Unemployment Tax Act (SUTA).

FICA taxes have already been discussed relative to the first payroll entry. FICA requires employers to match the amounts withheld from employees' pay for Social Security taxes. As a result, the dollar amount of the credit to FICA Tax Payable in the first journal entry (to record the payroll) will be the same as the dollar amount in this second journal entry. Employers are required to report the amounts of FICA taxes for employees on Federal Form 941, which is filed quarterly. Note: Employers can also report FICA taxes electronically by touch-tone phone with Form 941 Telefile.

The Federal Unemployment Tax Act (FUTA) establishes a tax on the employer to pay for the administration of unemployment programs to aid those who have lost their jobs. This fund is financed through taxes levied on employees' wages up to a specified amount.

States contribute to the federal unemployment fund by levying state unemployment taxes. Tax rates vary by state, but whatever that rate is, employers may use the state tax rate as a credit against the federal rate. For example, assume that a state levied a 5.4% state unemployment tax while the federal rate was 6.2%. With the credit in place, the federal unemployment tax rate would be reduced to only 0.8%:

$$6.2\% - 5.4\% = 0.8\%$$

With the information given in the earlier example for a restaurant's payroll and using a federal unemployment rate of 6.2% and a state unemployment rate of 5.4%, the restaurant would make the following journal entry (assuming no employee had earned more than the FUTA maximum) to record payroll taxes:

Payroll tax expense	$9,003	
FICA tax payable		$4,973
Federal unemployment tax payable		
($65,000 × 0.8%)		520
State unemployment tax payable		
($65,000 × 5.4%)		3,510

The debit to payroll tax expense ($9,003) is simply the total of the three credits to the liability accounts.

It is important to emphasize that we have discussed two separate and distinct entries: One to record the payroll and the other to record the payroll tax expense. The only connection between the two entries is the credit amount of FICA tax payable; it should be the same in both journal entries. Also, note the cost of employees to the employer: In the example above, the employer incurred gross wages of $65,000 plus additional payroll taxes of $9,003 for a total payroll cost of $74,003.

Many employees do not realize what their employment actually costs the restaurant. In the example above, there is a 14% difference between the gross wages of employees and the total payroll cost to the employer (excluding the cost of any additional benefits the employer provides). Since fringe benefits and payroll taxes can be costly, restaurants may use independent contractors rather than hire employees to perform certain services. Suppose, for example, that an independent contractor could provide a service such as night cleaning or repair work for the restaurant. If the employer hired this independent contractor, the restaurant would not have to pay applicable payroll taxes. The IRS rules for determining employee versus independent contractor status are detailed and very strict.

Employee or Independent Contractor?

Because of the significant tax implications involved in deciding whether a person is an employee or an independent contractor, the IRS has developed a variety of tests to address this issue. In 1992, the Supreme Court listed 12 factors to be considered when determining a worker's status.[17] The Court noted that *each* factor must be considered; none by itself is decisive. These factors are noted in Figure 11.6. When in doubt, restaurant managers should seek the counsel of a professional qualified to judge the status of any worker in question.

Tip Reporting Procedures

Many restaurant employees, especially servers and bartenders, commonly receive tips from guests. There are both federal and state regulations on tip reporting, and the process of tip reporting can be complex.

Certain provisions of federal and some state laws allow employers to apply a tip credit against the minimum wage of their tipped employees. In this way, the employer can reduce the amount of gross wages paid to the employees. Assume that the minimum wage is $5.15 per hour and that the state in which the restaurant is located allows a 40% maximum tip credit. Under these conditions, the employer could apply a credit of $2.06 (40% of $5.15) toward the hourly wage of tipped employees. The employer must first ensure that the actual tips received by the employees were not less than the maximum allowable tip credit. If this is the case, the employer would comply with the law by paying employees a minimum of $3.09 per hour ($5.15 − $2.06).

Let's see how gross wages payable to a tipped employee are calculated when the actual tips received are greater than the maximum tip credit. Assume that a food server works 40 hours and reports tips of $90. Assume also that the server receives a minimum wage of $5.15 per hour and that the restaurant manager applies a maximum tip credit as calculated above of $2.06. The gross wages payable to this employee are calculated as follows:

Gross wages: 40 hours at $5.15/hour		$206.00
Less lower of:		
Maximum FLSA tip credit		
(40 hours at $2.06)	$82.40	
Actual tips received	90.00	
Allowable tip credit		−82.40
Gross wages payable by employer		$123.60

---

[17]Nationwide Mutual Insurance Company, V. Daiden, 503 U.S. 318 (1992).

Factor	Explanation
1. The restaurant's right to control the manner and means by which the product is accomplished	Indicates a worker is an employee.
2. The skill required	The more skill that is required, the more likely the worker is an independent contractor.
3. The source of products and tools	Workers who provide their own are more likely self-employed.
4. The location of the work	If the work occurs at the restaurant, this indicates the worker is an employee.
5. The duration of the relationship between the parties	The longer the relationship, the more likely a worker is an employee.
6. Whether the restaurant has the right to assign additional projects to the worker	Indicates a worker is an employee.
7. The extent of the worker's discretion about when and how long to work	The more discretion, the more likely the worker is an independent contractor.
8. The method of payment	Employees are paid by the hour or week; independent contractors are paid by the job.
9. The worker's role in hiring and paying assistants	Independent contractors hire and pay their own assistants; employees do not.
10. Whether the work is part of the regular business of the restaurant	An employee's work is part of the regular business of the restaurant.
11. Whether the restaurant is in business	Employees are more likely to work for organizations that provide services or products to the public.
12. The provision of employee benefits	Employees are more likely to receive fringe benefits.

Figure 11.6   The Supreme Court's 12 Factor Test for Employee/Independent Contractor Status

If the actual tips received by the server were less than the maximum allowed tip credit, the tips received would be subtracted from the gross wages of $206 to determine the actual gross wages payable by the restaurant.

Note that the gross taxable earnings of a tipped employee include both the gross wages payable by the employer and the actual tips received by the employee.

The Tax Equity and Fiscal Responsibility Act of 1982 (TEFRA) established regulations that govern tip-reporting requirements for restaurants. Tips reported by restaurants should be at least 8% of the qualified gross receipts of the

---

WWW: Internet Assistant

One of the most difficult aspects of payroll accounting is that of recording and reporting employees' tips. The IRS provides employers several options for complying with the law. For details on each of these options and for comparison of their features go to

http://www.irs.gov/smallbiz/restaurants/voluntary.htm

---

business. Receipts from banquets (for which gratuities/service charges are often charged automatically) do not qualify. If the tips reported do not meet this 8% requirement, the deficiency is called a tip shortfall. Then all directly tipped employees reporting less than 8% will be provided with their share of the underreported tips on their W-2 forms. Note: The IRS is notified of the "under reporting." This most likely increases the probability of a tax audit of the employee's tax return.

The 8% tip regulation does not apply to all restaurants. Cafeteria and fast-food operations where tipping is not the standard practice of guests, for example, are exempt from the regulation.

MANAGER'S 10 POINT EFFECTIVENESS CHECKLIST

Evaluate your need for and the status of each of the following financial management tactics. For tactics you judge to be important but not yet in place, develop an action plan including completion date to implement the tactic.

TACTIC	DON'T AGREE (DON'T NEED)	AGREE (DONE)	AGREE (NOT DONE)	IF NOT DONE	
				WHO IS RESPONSIBLE?	TARGET COMPLETION DATE
1. Payroll is listed on the restaurant's income statement as an expense category separate from all other labor expenses.	❑	❑	❑		
2. Managers have determined minimum staff requirements on a department-by-department basis.	❑	❑	❑		
3. An imprest payroll account is in place and monitored to ensure that it maintains a zero balance.	❑	❑	❑		
4. Managers have developed systems to deter internal payroll check fraud.	❑	❑	❑		
5. Proper overtime pay procedures and calculations are in use for both tipped and nontipped employees.	❑	❑	❑		
6. Clear distinctions are contained in job descriptions and/or other records to plainly identify salaried staff eligible for overtime pay.	❑	❑	❑		
7. Separate journal entries are made to record payroll and payroll taxes.	❑	❑	❑		
8. Current State Unemployment Tax Act (SUTA) rates are used as a credit against federal FUTA rates.	❑	❑	❑		
9. Independent contractor status is granted only to those individuals who meet all requirements for this status.	❑	❑	❑		
10. Managers comply with all current tip reporting requirements.	❑	❑	❑		

12

ACCOUNTING FOR FIXED AND

OTHER ASSETS

MANAGER'S BRIEF

In most cases, the largest percentage of a restaurant's assets is represented by its investment in furniture, equipment, building, and land. These are referred to as fixed assets (those resources that are expected to benefit the restaurant for at least one year). In this chapter you will learn how these assets are accounted. You will see, for example, that they are managed differently from current assets (those whose benefits will be realized in less than one year).

Restaurant managers seeking to acquire fixed assets often have the choice of purchasing or leasing them. The decision to buy or lease affects the manner in which the asset is accounted for, and this is carefully explained in this chapter.

A key concept that must be understood when accounting for many types of fixed assets is that of depreciation. Simply put, depreciation is a method by which the fixed asset's value is reduced as its long-term ability to generate income for the restaurant is reduced. In this chapter, the two most commonly used approaches to depreciation are explained, as are the procedures for computing depreciation values using each approach.

When a restaurant manager decides to dispose of a fixed asset, regardless of any value it may have, the accounting procedures used to record this disposal are related to the depreciation methods previously used. In this chapter, the disposal of fixed assets is thoroughly reviewed, as are the procedures for recording the asset's sale (or, if appropriate, its scrapping). In some cases, one fixed asset is traded in for another newer or better asset. When this exchange happens, it must be accounted for properly, and this chapter shows how.

Lastly, the chapter describes "other assets" (those not accounted for elsewhere in the balance sheet) in detail.

A restaurant's assets are of two types: current assets and noncurrent assets. Current assets are expected to be converted into cash within one year. Noncurrent assets are expected to have a life of greater than a year. The four major categories of noncurrent assets include fixed assets, deferred expenses, noncurrent receivables (amounts owed to the restaurant by owners and officers that are not due within 12 months), and "other assets." Both fixed assets and other assets are discussed in this chapter.

FIXED ASSETS

Fixed assets include both assets that are depreciated (buildings and equipment) and others that are not depreciated (land). Fixed assets constitute the largest percentage of the total assets of a restaurant.

Overview

The *Uniform System of Accounts for Restaurants* uses the following classifications for fixed assets: land, buildings, cost of improvements in progress; leaseholds and leasehold improvements; furniture, fixtures, and equipment (FF&E); and uniforms, linens, china, glass, silver, and utensils.

Expenditures for fixed assets are capital expenditures rather than revenue expenditures. **Revenue expenditures** are those expenditures a restaurant makes for which the benefits are expected to be received within a year or less. Examples include wage and utilities expenses. **Capital expenditures** are expenditures for which benefits are expected to be received over a period greater than one year. (When a restaurant is built, its owners expect to realize the benefits over many years.) Capital expenditures must not be recorded as revenue expenditures because of the impact these entries have on the income statement. If a capital expenditure with a life of ten years is recorded as a revenue expenditure, all of the expense will be recorded in one year instead of spread over ten years. This would distort the restaurant's income statements for all ten years. (Net income for year one would be understated; net income for years two to ten would be overstated.)

> **REVENUE EXPENDITURES**
> Expenditures made by the restaurant for which benefits are expected to be received within one year.

> **CAPITAL EXPENDITURES**
> Expenditures made by the restaurant for which benefits are expected to be received over a period greater than one year.

Occasionally, a restaurant may purchase an item for an immaterial amount that is technically a capital expenditure but treat it as a revenue expenditure. An example is the purchase of a $20 calculator.

The purchase of fixed assets should be recorded at cost, which should include all reasonable/necessary expenditures needed to bring the asset in operating condition. Examples of expenditures to be included are items such as freight charges, sales tax, and installation charges. Charges not considered reasonable/necessary may include repairs due to damage in handling or a traffic ticket incurred by the delivery driver.

Recording Purchases

How is a fixed asset's purchase recorded? Assume a restaurant purchased kitchen equipment at a list price of $50,000 with terms of 2/10, n/30 (2% discount if paid within ten days; net amount due in 30 days). The restaurant can pay within the cash discount period. Also assume that sales tax of $2,000, freight charges of $600, and installation costs of $500 must be paid by the restaurant. It purchases a two-year maintenance contract for a total cost of $2,000. The cost to be recorded is determined as follows:

Equipment list price	$50,000
Less 2% cash discount	(1,000)
Net price	49,000
Sales tax	2,000
Freight charges	600
Installation charges	500
Cost of equipment	$52,100

The maintenance contract is not added to the equipment cost and depreciated over the asset's life. Instead, the $1,000 for the next 12 months is recorded as a prepaid expense; the $1,000 payment for the second year is recorded as deferred insurance (another asset).

When land is purchased, all reasonable/necessary expenditures to buy the land are included in the purchase price. These include property taxes paid, title opinions, surveying costs, brokerage commissions, and any excavating expenses that are required.

CAPITAL LEASE   A lease agreement of long duration, generally noncancellable, in which the lessee (restaurant) assumes responsibility for property taxes, insurance, and maintenance of the leased property.

Sometimes a restaurant leases an asset under an agreement requiring it to record the lease as a **capital lease.** Then the leased asset is recorded as an asset on the lessee's books and is included under furniture, fixtures, and equipment as "leased asset under a capital lease."

LEASEHOLD IMPROVEMENTS   Renovations/remodeling done on leased buildings/space before opening for business.

When a restaurant leases a building, it often must make extensive improvements to walls, ceiling, lighting, etc. These are called **leasehold improvements.** The cost of the leasehold improvements will be amortized over the remaining life of the lease or the life of the improvement, whichever is shorter. For example, assume that a restaurant leases a building for ten years and spends $50,000 on improvements that have a five-year life. It would amortize $10,000 of the cost of the improvements each year for five years.

Amortization of leasehold improvements	$10,000	
Leasehold improvements		$10,000

Cost of improvements in progress is another fixed asset reported on the restaurant's balance sheet. This represents all labor, materials, advances on contracts, and interest on construction loans incurred in the current construction of property/equipment.

Uniforms, linens, china, glass, silver, and utensils is a unique fixed asset account found on a restaurant's balance sheet. This asset is important to control. If these items are carelessly discarded, for example, expenses will increase and net income will decrease. This category of fixed assets will be discussed in greater detail later in this chapter.

DEPRECIATION

Property and equipment are expensed over their useful life in a process called **depreciation.**

> **DEPRECIATION** The reduction in the net book value of a fixed asset.

Overview

The total amount of depreciation that can be taken equals the cost of the fixed asset minus its salvage or scrap value. The manager does not write a check for "depreciation," so it is different from most other expenses: It is a noncash expense. While depreciation is not a fund of cash set aside by the restaurant, it does save cash for the restaurant subject to income taxes, because it provides a tax shelter by reducing taxable income. Property and equipment are typically shown on the books at their **net book value,** which is determined when the accumulated depreciation to date is subtracted from the cost of the asset. (Accumulated depreciation is a contra-asset account and carries a credit balance.)

> **NET BOOK VALUE** The cost of a fixed asset minus its accumulated depreciation.

> **STRAIGHT-LINE DEPRECIATION** A method of depreciation that distributes the expense evenly over the estimated life of the fixed asset.

> **DOUBLE DECLINING BALANCE DEPRECIATION** An accelerated method of depreciation that ignores the salvage value of the fixed asset and results in a greater amount of depreciation in the early years of the life of the fixed asset.

Methods of Depreciation

Two basic methods used to depreciate fixed assets are **straight-line depreciation** and **double declining balance depreciation** (an **accelerated method of depreciation,** since it results in the highest charge in the first year, with lower and lower charges in successive years.)

ACCELERATED METHOD OF DEPRECIATION A method of depreciation that results in higher depreciation charges in the first year; charges gradually decline over the life of a fixed asset.

SALVAGE VALUE The estimated market value of a fixed asset at the end of its useful life.

An important concept affecting depreciation is the **salvage value** of the asset. This is the estimated value of the fixed asset at the end of its useful life. The straight-line method takes salvage value into account; the double declining balance method does not.

Straight-line (SL) depreciation is the simplest depreciation method: The same amount of depreciation is taken on the asset in each year of its life. To compute the annual depreciation, take the cost of the asset less its salvage value and divide by the estimated life of the asset. For example, assume that dining room furniture costs $34,000, has a salvage value of $4,000, and a life of five years. The annual depreciation under the straight-line method would be $6,000 per year:

Cost of equipment	$34,000
Less salvage value	4,000
Depreciable cost	$30,000 ÷ 5 years = $6,000 annual depreciation

Total depreciation over life: $6,000 × 5 = $30,000

The *double declining balance (DDB) depreciation* method is more complicated to calculate but has the benefit of higher levels of depreciation, with resulting reduced taxable income levels during the early years of the equipment's life. To use the DDB method:

- First determine the straight-line (SL) rate.

$$\text{Straight-line rate} = \frac{1}{\text{Number of years}}$$

- Second, multiply the SL rate by 2 to determine the DDB%.

$$\text{DDB\%} = 2 \times \text{SL rate}$$

- Third, multiply the undepreciated amount of the fixed asset by the DDB% to determine the annual depreciation expense.

Depreciation expense $=$ DDB% $\times$ Undepreciated amount

Note: The DDB method ignores the salvage value (except that the total depreciation over the fixed asset's life should not exceed its cost — its salvage value).

An example will illustrate the calculation of depreciation using the SL and DDB methods: Assume a restaurant purchased a new point-of-sale device for $4,000. Its estimated useful life is eight years, with a salvage value of $400. Annual depreciation for years one through eight for the two methods is shown in Figure 12.1. Notice that the DDB yields the greatest amount of annual depreciation for years one through three, while the straight-line method results in the greatest amount of depreciation for each of the last five years.

Year	SL	DDB
1	$(4,000 - 400) \div 8 = \$450$	$1/8 = 12\frac{1}{2}\%; 12\frac{1}{2}\% (2) = 25\%$ $4,000 (0.25) = \$1,000$
2	$450	$(4,000 - 1,000)(0.25)$ $= \$750$
3	$450	$(3,000 - 750)(0.25)$ $= \$562.50$
4	$450	$(2,250 - 562.50)(0.25)$ $= \$421.88$
5	$450	$(1,687.50 - 421.88)(0.25)$ $= \$316.40$
6	$450	$(1,265.62 - 316.40)(0.25)$ $= \$237.30$
7	$450	$(949.22 - 237.30)(0.25)$ $= \$177.98$
8	$450	$(711.92 - 177.98)(0.25)$ $= \$133.48$
Total Depreciation	$3,600.00	$3,599.54

Figure 12.1   Annual Depreciation with Straight-Line and Double Declining Balance Methods

---

WWW: Internet Assistant

Maintaining up-to-date depreciation values for fixed assets is important but can be complicated and time consuming. To assist in this process, inexpensive computer programs have been developed that conform to all Generally Accepted Accounting Principles and at the same time speed calculations. To view a demonstration of one such program, go to

http://www.depreciationworks.com

or for another go to

http://www.onesquared.com/software/depreciation.htm

Both the straight-line and DDB methods are acceptable for depreciation of fixed assets. The method selected by the restaurant manager should be the one that best reflects the decline in value of the fixed asset being depreciated. The Generally Accepted Accounting Principle (GAAP) of consistency (see chapter 1) requires that the method selected for use with a specific fixed asset should continue to be used over the life of that asset. It is, however, acceptable to use different methods of depreciation for different fixed assets. For example, a building may be depreciated with the straight-line method, while the DDB can be used for one or more items of kitchen equipment.

UNIFORMS, LINENS, CHINA, GLASS, SILVER, AND UTENSILS

Restaurants use a variety of methods to charge uniforms, linens, china, glass, silver, and utensils to operations, including:

- Consider these items part of fixed assets and physically count and reflect the total cost of the items on hand.
- Capitalize the initial stock of these items and then expense the cost of the items later bought and placed in service.

Both methods have merit; however, for uniformity, the following method is preferable: Capitalize the cost of the initial stock of these items. Then depreciate this capitalized cost over a period not to exceed 36 months and expense replacements when they are placed in service. Reserve stocks of these items should be considered inventory until they are placed in service. The total accumulated depreciation should appear as a separate line item. This amount is then subtracted from the total fixed asset line to determine net book value of fixed assets.

Assume that a restaurant purchased an initial stock of uniforms, linens, china, glass, silver, and utensils for $15,000 cash on November 30, 20XX. The restaurant has chosen to write off the stock over 30 months. On December 15, replacement items were purchased for $1,000 but not placed into service. The journal entries from November 15 until December 31, 20XX are recorded below:

Uniforms, linens, china, glass, silver, and utensils	$15,000.00	
Cash		$15,000.00
Inventory—uniforms, linens, china, glass, silver, and utensils	$ 1,000.00	
Cash		$ 1,000.00
Depreciation expense—uniforms, linens, china, glass, silver, and utensils	$ 500.00	
Accumulated depreciation—uniforms, linens, china, glass, silver, and utensils		$ 500.00

On December 31, 20XX, the restaurant's income statement would include $500 of depreciation expense for uniforms, linens, china, glass, silver, and utensils. The balance sheet would include the following:

Under Current Assets:		
Inventory—uniforms, linens, china, glass, silver, and utensils		$ 1,000
Under Fixed Assets:		
Uniforms, linens, china, glass, silver, and utensils	$15,000	
Less: Accumulated depreciation—uniforms, linens, china, glassware, silver, and utensils	$(500)	$14,500

DISPOSAL OF FIXED ASSETS

Sometimes a restaurant removes fixed assets from its books because the assets are being scrapped, sold, or traded in. If a fixed asset is scrapped and has been fully depreciated, both the asset and related accumulated depreciation must be removed from the books. Assume a dish machine with a cost of $40,000 and a salvage value of zero was fully depreciated. The following entry would be made:

Accumulated depreciation	$40,000	
Dish machine		$40,000

If the dish machine is scrapped before being fully depreciated, a different entry is made. Assume that the same dish machine costing $40,000 has been depreciated to the extent of $30,000. The journal entry would be:

Accumulated depreciation	$30,000	
Loss on disposal of asset	10,000	
Dish machine		$40,000

The loss on the disposal of this asset would be closed into the income summary account at the end of the next fiscal period.

Sometimes fixed assets are disposed of through a sale resulting in a gain or loss. Suppose the dish machine had a net book value of $6,000 based on a cost of $40,000 and an accumulated depreciation balance of $34,000. If it is sold for $8,000, the journal entry would be:

Cash	$ 8,000	
Accumulated depreciation	34,000	
Dish machine		$40,000
Gain on disposal of asset		2,000

The gain of $2,000 is the difference between the selling price of $8,000 and the book value of $6,000.

Assume the same facts concerning the $40,000 dish machine, except it is sold for $4,000. Since it has a net book value of $6,000 and is sold for $4,000, a loss of $2,000 would result. The journal entry would be:

Cash	$ 4,000	
Accumulated depreciation	34,000	
Loss on disposal of asset	2,000	
Dish machine		$40,000

EXCHANGE OF FIXED ASSETS

A fixed asset such as a truck might be exchanged or traded in for a similar asset. Assume that a $30,000 truck is exchanged along with $32,000 cash for a new truck with a list of $33,000. At the time of the exchange, the old $30,000 truck has accumulated depreciation of $28,000; it has a book value of $2,000. Although the book value is $2,000, the restaurant is receiving only $1,000 on the trade-in; there is a loss of $1,000. The entry to record the exchange is:

Truck—new	$33,000	
Accumulated depreciation	28,000	
Loss on disposal of asset	1,000	
Cash		$32,000
Truck—old		30,000

Now assume the restaurant is given $5,000 on the trade-in and must pay only $28,000 for the new truck. The journal entry would be:

Truck—new	$30,000	
Accumulated depreciation	28,000	
Cash		$28,000
Truck—old		30,000

The Financial Accounting Standards Board (FASB) has stated that no gains are to be recorded on exchanges. Instead, the gain is to be reflected in the value of the asset acquired. Two points should be noted about the above entries:

- The Generally Accepted Accounting Principle of conservatism states that losses but not gains should be recorded.
- Tax reporting rules differ from financial reporting rules. When reporting for tax purposes, neither gains nor losses are recorded on exchange of similar assets.

OTHER ASSETS

The "other assets" category is reserved for those items that cannot be included in any other grouping in the restaurant's balance sheet. The most typical (and those included in the Uniform System's format) are for:

- *Amount paid for goodwill.* This is the excess of the purchase price beyond the asset's approved value. It exists when expected future earnings exceed the normal rate for the restaurant industry. Goodwill is only entered into the restaurant's books when the restaurant is purchased.

- *Cost of bar license.* In those states that restrict the number of licenses to sell alcoholic beverages, an existing license must often be purchased.

- *Rental deposits.* Deposits of cash or marketable investments may be required as security for a building being leased and to assure compliance with other rental agreement terms. Other examples of deposits include those for utility services such as water, gas, and electricity.

- *Cash surrender value of life insurance.* This is insurance that is carried on the lives of officers, partners, or key employees when the restaurant is the policy's beneficiary. The policy's cash surrender value should be accrued as an asset reflecting the increase in the cash surrender value as the life insurance premium is paid.

- *Deposit on franchise or royalty contract.* Deposits for these purposes are stated separately in the "other assets" section of the restaurant's balance sheet.

MANAGER'S 10 POINT EFFECTIVENESS CHECKLIST

Evaluate your need for and the status of each of the following financial management tactics. For tactics you judge to be important but not yet in place, develop an action plan including completion date to implement the tactic.

TACTIC	DON'T AGREE (DON'T NEED)	AGREE (DONE)	AGREE (NOT DONE)	IF NOT DONE	
				WHO IS RESPONSIBLE?	TARGET COMPLETION DATE
1. Expenditures for fixed assets are recorded as capital expenditures rather than as revenue expenditures.	❑	❑	❑		
2. The recorded value of newly purchased fixed assets includes the asset's original cost plus taxes, shipping, installation, and any other applicable costs.	❑	❑	❑		
3. Any leased asset is recorded as a "leased asset under a capital lease."	❑	❑	❑		
4. Leasehold improvement costs are amortized over the life of the improvement or the life of the lease.	❑	❑	❑		
5. Managers have, if necessary, received professional advice about the use of straight-line or double declining balance methods for computing depreciation for applicable fixed assets.	❑	❑	❑		
6. Net book values of all property and equipment are kept current using the depreciation method selected by managers with outside professional input as necessary.	❑	❑	❑		
7. Where practical, managers capitalize the initial cost of china, tableware, uniforms, etc.	❑	❑	❑		
8. Replacement costs for china, tableware, uniforms, etc. are considered an expense in the month they are placed into service.	❑	❑	❑		
9. The sale or exchange of a fixed asset results in an adjustment in the appropriate accumulated depreciation and/or fixed asset account.	❑	❑	❑		
10. All "other assets" owned by the restaurant are clearly indicated on the restaurant's balance sheet.	❑	❑	❑		

13

CASH AND REVENUE CONTROL

MANAGER'S BRIEF

One of a manager's most important responsibilities is to protect the restaurant's assets from theft and fraud. A restaurant can be an easy victim of these crimes, so internal control systems that maintain the security of its assets are critical. This chapter describes the essential elements of an effective control system and suggests how these components can be implemented and maintained.

Maintaining asset security is a process that includes bonding employees, requiring mandatory vacation periods, limiting access to theft-prone assets, training, separating duties, and more. Each of these key control components and a discussion of why they are essential is presented.

One of the most vital and certainly the most visible of assets in any restaurant is the cash generated daily. Unfortunately, cash can be very tempting. You will learn procedures for safeguarding cash from the time it is received from the guests until it is deposited in your bank account. Also included in this section is information useful in maintaining sound accounts receivable and accounts payable systems.

A complete revenue control system requires four major steps. It is necessary to verify product sales, guest charges, and revenue receipts and deposits. This chapter will show how you can manage each step to help ensure the safety of your restaurant's revenues. Regardless of the operation's size or the method of payment used in your restaurant (that is, whether the guest pays a cashier, the guest pays service staff who pay the cashier, or the guest is billed later) you will learn about tools helpful for safeguarding the restaurant's physical assets and revenue.

Restaurant managers need an effective system for controlling cash and revenues. These controls are very important, because restaurants typically have hundreds (or more) daily cash sales transactions and many employees who handle cash. This chapter will review basic procedures important in the control of cash and revenue.

FRAUD AND EMBEZZLEMENT[18]

> **FRAUD** Deceitful conduct designed to manipulate someone into giving up something of value by (a) presenting as true something known by the fraudulent party to be false or (b) concealing a fact from someone that may have saved him/her from being cheated.

Fraud and **embezzlement** occur all too frequently in restaurant operations. Fortunately, there are numerous ways restaurant managers can reduce opportunities for such thefts to occur.

Factors Encouraging Fraud and Embezzlement

At least three factors are necessary for fraud and embezzlement to occur:

- *Need.* Economic and/or psychological motives can encourage restaurant employees to steal. While some managers attempt to study their employees' "lifestyles" to determine whether selected staff members

[18]The first five sections of this chapter are based upon: Raymond S. Schmidgall, *Hospitality Industry Managerial Accounting,* Fourth Edition, (Lansing, Mich., 1997).

may steal, a better approach is to develop systems that reduce theft opportunities and that
make it difficult for employees to "beat the
system."

> **EMBEZZLEMENT Theft of financial assets including cash.**

- *Opportunity.* Managers might best discourage theft by implementing systems and procedures to reduce opportunities for employees to steal.

- *Failure of conscience.* Sometimes thieves rationalize stealing to justify taking someone else's property. Some staff members might believe that "almost every dollar the restaurant takes in is profit. I deserve more money (the restaurant pays me a low wage), so no one is hurt, and I benefit!" Employees often don't realize how low a percentage of revenue profit actually is. Effective managers can at least have an indirect influence on this factor. For example, they can create an organizational culture that makes it difficult to rationalize theft as acceptable. Implementation of internal control systems that apply to everyone (managers as well as employees) is one example. In many cases, restaurant managers have benefits and "perks" that go with their jobs, which some hourly employees do not enjoy. These benefits may include automobile allowances, free on-duty meals (and in some cases alcoholic beverages while entertaining clients), personal use of telephones, and wholesale purchasing privileges. Some hourly employees observing these benefits may get the impression that the "company" deserves to absorb some theft, because it must be doing well to offer managers these types of benefits.

Of the factors noted above, managers have the most influence over theft opportunities. Procedures presented throughout this chapter focus on preventing them.

Restaurants Are Vulnerable to Theft

Restaurants have some general operating characteristics that make them more vulnerable to theft than many other businesses.[19] These include:

- numerous cash transactions
- many jobs requiring low skills

---

[19]*Internal Control: A Fraud-Prevention Handbook for Hotel and Restaurant Managers* (Ithaca, NY, 1991).

- many positions with perceived low social status

- items of relatively high value that are commonly used/available

- availability of products that employees must otherwise buy

The increased use of credit cards has reduced the number of cash transactions in many restaurants. Still, cash is often exchanged between guests and employees. Numerous cash banks available over several cashier shifts create potential problems as well. The use of relatively unskilled employees in low-paying positions with little social status contributes to high turnover rates, which can also influence the internal control environment.

Many restaurants are small, and even large restaurants are often organized into several (or more) small revenue outlets (such as a restaurant, several bars, and perhaps take-out stations). Any economies of scale that normally assist large operations with efficiencies and control are usually lacking in a restaurant. These are among the characteristics of restaurants that create a strong need for effective internal control systems.

OBJECTIVES OF INTERNAL CONTROL

The American Institute of Certified Public Accountants (AICPA) has a long-standing definition of internal control: "Internal control comprises the plan of organization and all of the coordinate methods and measures adopted within a business to safeguard its assets, check the accuracy and reliability of its accounting data, promote operational efficiency and encourage adherence to prescribed managerial policies."[20]

This definition indicates that internal control relies on a plan of organization and the use of methods/measures to attain four objectives. (These methods/measures will be discussed later in this chapter.)

We begin our discussion by addressing effective organizational plans. These should be written in a form all restaurant employees can understand. When possible, the plan should separate cash-fund, custodial, and accounting

[20]American Institute of Certified Public Accountants, Committee on Auditing Procedures, Internal Control—Elements of a Coordinated System and Its Importance to Management and the Independent Public Accountant (New York, 1949).

functions to help prevent fraud and assist in the provision of accurate and reliable accounting information.

The four AICPA objectives for internal control noted above should be explained:

- **Safeguard assets.** This objective addresses the protection of assets from losses including theft, the maintenance of resources (especially equipment) to ensure efficient utilization, and the safeguarding of resources (especially inventories) to prevent waste and spoilage.

- **Check accuracy/reliability of accounting data.** This objective addresses the checks and balances within the accounting system designed to ensure the accuracy and reliability of information. Dependable data is needed for reports to owners and government agencies (and other outsiders); it is also needed for the managers' internal use. Restaurants of all sizes will benefit from the use of the Uniform System of Accounts.[21] Accounting information is most useful when it is timely; reports for managers must be prepared regularly and promptly.

- **Promote operational efficiency.** The restaurant's training programs and procedures, along with effective supervision, promote operational efficiency. For example, when cooks are properly trained and supervised, food costs are lower. The use of mechanical and electronic equipment can improve efficiency. Point-of-sale (POS) devices in restaurants can relay orders from server stations to preparation areas and increase staff efficiency.

- **Encourage adherence to prescribed managerial policies.** Most restaurants require hourly-paid employees to clock in and out personally; one employee cannot do this for another employee. Locating the time clock for easy managerial observation may encourage workers to follow the policy.

The above objectives may seem to conflict at times. For example, procedures for safeguarding the restaurant's assets may be so detailed that efficiency is reduced. Requiring multiple signatures to withdraw products from inventory may reduce theft, but the policy may require so much time that increased labor

[21]*Uniform System of Accounts for Restaurants,* Seventh Edition (Washington, D.C., 1996).

costs exceed potential losses. Perfect controls, even if possible, are often not cost-justified. Managers must evaluate the costs of implementing controls against their benefits. Managers are efficient when there is a proper balance of costs and benefits.

ELEMENTS OF EFFECTIVE INTERNAL CONTROL

The objectives of internal control discussed above can only be attained if effective methods and measures of control are implemented and consistently followed. For example, to safeguard cash, a restaurant may need a safe to hold cash between shifts, or it may require bank deposits when the amount of cash on-site totals, for example, $2,000. Before discussing the details of internal control systems, general characteristics of an effective system should be noted. These principles of internal control are essential to all effective systems used by a restaurant.

Leadership

Leadership is critical to the restaurant's internal control system. Effective policies must be developed, clearly communicated, and consistently enforced. Each level of management is responsible for ensuring that applicable control procedures are adequate. Exceptions to policies should be minimized and justified.

Restaurant managers who are true leaders select outstanding employees and then train and empower them to help establish objectives and provide specific input on the development of control procedures. Leaders work hard to continuously improve control procedures and do not get sidetracked by concerns about "how we have always done things" or "what is the easiest way."[22]

Organization Structure

CHAIN OF COMMAND The formal organization structure that indicates how communication and authority flows throughout the restaurant.

Most restaurants are divided into several departments, such as production, service, beverage, and perhaps accounting/finance, human resources, and purchasing. Employees must know and follow the **chain of command.** Policies should reinforce the restaurant's for-

[22]Readers interested in learning more about effective hospitality industry leadership techniques are referred to: R. Woods and J. King, *Managing for Quality in the Hospitality Industry* (East Lansing, Mich., 1996).

mal organizational structure by requiring staff members to discuss complaints or suggestions with their immediate supervisors. This reduces confusion and will likely result in greater efficiency. Note: Situations involving management fraud are exceptions to this rule. Then employees must be able to communicate with the higher levels of management and/or with internal auditors.

Each position in the restaurant should have a written job description (a detailed list of duties). A procedure manual should tell how a job or duty should be performed.

Effective Procedures

Effective procedures help to create an environment that lends itself to internal control. Examples of such procedures include:

- *Bonding employees.* One procedure restaurant managers may use to protect against fraud and embezzlement is the **bonding** of employees whose jobs include the handling of assets.

> **BOND(ING)** An insurance agreement in which an insurer guarantees payment to an employer in the event of a financial loss caused by the action of a specific covered employee.

- *Mandatory vacation policy.* Employees holding positions of trust are required to take an annual vacation. Other employees can then perform the absent employee's duties. (If an absent employee has committed fraud, the temporary staff member may discover this so that management can take corrective action.)

- *Code of ethics.* Some restaurants require managers to comply with a code of ethics that prohibits illegal acts.

Assigned Responsibility

When possible, responsibility for a specific activity should be given to a single individual. Then the staff member can be given a set of standard operating procedures and expected to follow them. When responsibility is given to one person, the manager knows where to start looking if a problem is identified. Note: When employees are held responsible for their assets or actions, they need conditions that allow them to carry out these responsibilities. For example, a cashier should be solely and fully responsible for the cash bank. To ensure this, no one except that employee should have access to the bank. There should be no sharing of the bank and no sharing of responsibility for it.

Limited Access

Only employees needing access to theft-prone assets such as cash should be allowed to handle such assets. The cash bank example above illustrates this principle.

Competent Staff

COLLUSION A theft method in which two or more people work together to defraud the restaurant.

Competent and trustworthy personnel are the most critical element in an effective internal control system. It is difficult to design systems of internal control that prevent **collusion.** Careful selection, training, and supervision are vital. Managers must hire people with potential and train them properly. This includes communicating what the jobs are and how to do them and following up to assure that training is effective. Employees must also understand how their jobs relate to the restaurant's mission and goals.

Finally, employees must be properly rewarded for work performed. This includes compensation and praise for a job well done and promotions when a person is ready and a position is available.

Separation of Duties

Separation of duties occurs when different personnel are assigned accounting, asset responsibility, and production activities. Duties within the accounting function should also be separated. The major objective of separating duties is to prevent and detect errors and theft. Consider a restaurant: A server takes a guest's order and records it on a guest check. A cook prepares the guest's food order based on a copy of the guest check. The food was issued from storage by use of an issue requisition submitted earlier based upon estimated sales. The guest receives a copy of the guest check and pays the cashier. The cashier records the sale after checking the server's accuracy. In this example, the functions of order taker (sales), cook (production), storekeeper (custodian of assets), and cashier (accounting) are separated. This helps safeguard assets and promotes operational efficiency.

Additional separation of duties may further enhance efficiency. For example, the production area of a large restaurant may employ many people, including chefs, sous chefs, preparation assistants, and others. Tasks within the accounting department are divided among personnel to ensure proper checks and balances. For example, different personnel maintain the **general ledger** and the

cash receipts journal. Cash reconciliation is prepared by personnel other than those accounting for cash receipts and/or disbursements.

Unfortunately, it is not possible to separate duties in small restaurants that do not have specialized accounting and general management positions. The last section of this chapter offers suggestions about the minimum cash/revenue-handling duties that should be assumed by the manager of a small restaurant.

> **GENERAL LEDGER** The book of accounts from which financial statements are prepared.

> **CASH RECEIPTS JOURNAL** An accounting record that is used to summarize transactions relating to cash receipts generated by the restaurant.

Approval Procedures

Managers must authorize every business transaction. Authorization may be either general or specific. General authorization occurs when all employees must comply with selected procedures and policies when performing their jobs. For example, servers must sell food and beverage products at the prices listed on the menu. In addition, a guest may pay for purchases with a credit card. If the purchase is authorized by the issuing company, the cashier may accept it and process the payment without any other authorization.

Sometimes, managers require that certain transactions receive specific authorization. For example, the per guest charge for a unique banquet function may require the restaurant manager's or owner's approval; the transaction cannot be completed without this written authorization.

Adequate Records

The recording of transactions is essential for effective internal control. Examples of documents that record transactions are guest checks, credit card vouchers, and bank deposit slips. Documents should be designed so they are easy to complete and to understand. Multiple use forms help minimize the number of forms needed by the restaurant. For example, a guest check can have three parts: The original copy is the guest's bill, the second copy communicates the order to the cook (bartender) and the third copy can be retained by the food (beverage) server.

Prenumbered forms help facilitate control. They should be prepared when the transaction occurs to minimize errors. For example, if coffee is ordered, it should be put on the guest check immediately — not when the server "has time." This reduces the chance that the coffee sale will be omitted from the guest check.

Written Manuals

Each job within the restaurant should be defined in writing. A procedure manual should list the details of each position, including how and when to perform each task. This will encourage consistent job performance, especially for new employees who may be uncertain about job tasks. Written manuals also make it easier for someone to help out during a regular employee's absence.

Physical Controls

Physical controls are necessary to safeguard assets. They include security devices such as safes and locked storage areas. Mechanical and electronic equipment can authorize and record transactions to safeguard assets.

Budgets and Internal Reports

Budgets and internal reports are necessary for an effective system of internal control. Budgets help to ensure that financial goals are attained. If actual performance does not meet budget plans, corrective action can be taken. (Chapter 9 discusses operating budgets in detail.)

Other reports can alert managers to potential operating concerns. These include reports prepared daily (sales receipts reports, for example), weekly (weekly unit sales reports), monthly (income statements and statements of cash flows), and annually (cumulative income statements and balance sheets).

Performance Checks

Performance checks help to ensure that all of the elements in the internal control system are functioning properly. They must be independent (a person doing an internal verification must not be the same person responsible for collecting data initially). In large restaurants, internal auditors who are independent of both operations and accounting personnel and who report directly to top management are used.

Smaller restaurants may use external auditors, who verify financial statements, study accounting control systems, and test these systems to determine how extensive the remaining audit will need to be. (The stronger the system of internal control, the more dependable it will be and, all other things being equal, the less extensive audits will need to be.)

The independence of audit checks is ensured with the separation of duties. For example, when possible, a bank reconciliation should be done by personnel who are independent from those who account for cash receipts and disbursements.

BASICS OF INTERNAL CONTROLS

Each restaurant must develop control methods that meet its needs. Some of the basics of internal control that should ideally be incorporated into these methods are discussed in this section.

Cash Control

Cash is the most vulnerable of all assets. Commonly used cash control procedures include:

- All bank accounts and staff members who sign checks must be authorized by the restaurant manager.

- All bank accounts should be reconciled monthly; reconciliations should be reviewed by the manager.

- The staff member who reconciles bank accounts should receive bank statements (including canceled checks, if applicable) directly from the bank. Those who sign checks or have other accounting duties relating to cash transactions should not reconcile the bank accounts. Reconciliation should include the examination of signatures and endorsements and the verification of the accuracy of cash receipt and disbursement records.

- The manager (small restaurant) or accountant (larger restaurant) should be responsible for cash. If the accountant is responsible, the manager should review cash transactions to provide a check on the accountant's performance.

- The custodian of the cash must take annual vacations, and his/her duties should be assumed by another employee.

- Cash banks and petty cash funds should be counted at unannounced intervals by the manager. Special attention should be given to noncash items such as IOUs and accommodation checks (those cashed for guests to provide guests with cash).

- Disbursements from petty cash funds should be supported by cash register tapes, invoices, or other documents. This supporting data should be verified when funds are replenished and should then be canceled to prevent duplicate payment.

Cash Receipts.   Use of the following procedures can help in the internal control of cash receipts:

- The accounting for and physical control over cash receipts should be established when the cash is first received, whether by the cashier/hostess or through the mail. For example, only one person (cashier or bartender, for example) should have access to a specific cash bank; incoming mail receipts should be initially listed by an employee independent of both the general cashier and anyone with specific accounts receivable responsibility. (This establishes an independent record that can be checked against daily bank deposits and the general ledger posting to accounts receivable.)

- A restrictive endorsement such as "For Deposit Only to Seashore Restaurants Account" should be placed on checks when first received to guard against fraudulent use of these cash receipts.

- Employees responsible for accounts receivable should not handle checks or currency.

- Cash received should be given to the manager (accountant) as soon as is practical. Cash receipts should be deposited daily and intact. They should not be mixed with other cash funds used to pay invoices or other expenses, or to cash accommodation checks.

- The general cashier or subordinates should not be responsible for the following activities:
  —preparing/mailing city ledger statements
  —posting accounts receivable records or balancing detail ledgers with general ledger control accounts
  —posting the general ledger
  —authorizing rebates, allowances, discounts, or writing off uncollectible accounts
  —preparing cash disbursements or reconciling bank accounts

General instructions for those taking cash receipts from guests include:

- The cash drawer must be closed after each sale.

- Any overrings must be circled and initialed on the register tape at the time of occurrence.

- Cash registers must be locked and keys removed when unattended.

- Cash sales must be rung up when made.

- Cashiers may not have briefcases, handbags, purses, cosmetic bags, etc., at their work place.

- The manager should be told at once about any cash register problem.

- Cashiers should verify the amount of cash banks when they receive and sign for them and should not be allowed to count the banks after that time.

- When possible, purchases should be rung up separately to allow the register to total the sale.

Cash Disbursements. Procedures to help ensure a strong system of internal control over cash disbursements include:

- When practical, all disbursements should be made by check. (An exception is petty cash disbursements.)

- Checks should be prenumbered and used in numerical sequence. A check protector imprinting device can be used to enter the amounts on the checks to deter anyone from changing the check.

- Checks drawn in excess of a minimum amount should contain two signatures; checks written under this may require only one signature. Before signing a check, carefully review supporting documents to ensure that documentation is properly audited and approved. Check signers should not be responsible for preparing checks or for blank checks (unless the check signer is the restaurant manager).

- When a mechanical check signing device is used, only the employee authorized to use it should have the key (code). The restaurant should maintain an independent record of the number of checks processed through the device. (That number should be reconciled with the numerical sequence of the checks used.)

- Vouchers, invoices, and other documents supporting cash disbursements should be canceled by stamping them "PAID" when the check is signed to prevent duplicate payments if the document is later detached from the check copy.

- Signed checks and disbursement vouchers should not be returned to the check preparer; they should be routed to another employee for mailing.

- Only authorized check preparers should have access to blank checks. Voided checks should be mutilated to prevent reuse.

Accounts Receivable

Accounts receivable are promises to pay the restaurant. Segregation of duties is needed to prevent employees from pocketing cash received in payment of accounts receivable. Control procedures for accounts receivable include:

> **REMITTANCE ADVICE A document accompanying a cash payment from a guest that indicates to what the payment pertains.**

- Postings to accounts receivable for cash received should include **remittance advice** or a listing of checks received. Control totals for postings should be made independently of accounts receivable employees by the general ledger clerk to the accounts receivable control account. In a small property the same person probably performs both tasks; this is a weakness in the control system of a small restaurant.

- At the end of the month, the total of guest accounts should be reconciled with the independently determined balance in the general ledger control account. This provides protection against manipulation by the employees responsible for accounts receivable. A failure to separate cash handling and accounts receivable may facilitate lapping. Lapping occurs when an accounts receivable clerk steals cash received on an account, then posts cash received the next day on a second account to the first account. For example, assume that guest A pays $100 on his or her account, and the accounts receivable clerk steals the $100. The following day, guest B pays $150. The accounts receivable clerk takes $50 for personal use and credits guest A's account for $100. (Now the accounts receivable clerk has stolen $150.) This activity may continue for a long time when duties are not separated. However, if the accounts receivable clerk is required to take a vacation, it should be detected when another accounting employee fills in.

- Noncash entries to receivable accounts, including writing off an uncollectible account, should be done by an employee (manager) who does not handle cash and who is not responsible for maintaining accounts receivable.

- Clerical employees should not routinely adjust accounts receivable.

- An adequate system of internal reporting is needed. Periodically, accounts receivable should be aged, and special collection efforts should be made on overdue accounts. The trend of accounts receivable balances in relation to credit terms should be tracked.

- All collection efforts should be carefully documented; uncollectible accounts should be written off only with the manager's approval.

Accounts Payable

Internal control procedures for accounts payable include:

- Suppliers' invoices should be routed directly to accounts payable personnel; purchasing personnel should not handle or approve invoices.

- Control over vendors' invoices is needed when they are received. A voucher system (see Figure 13.1) may be used. A voucher system uses prenumbered vouchers prepared from suppliers' invoices and recorded in a voucher journal. Invoices should be reviewed for possible cash discounts, and discounts should be taken if cash flow permits.

- The terms of sale, prices, and list of items received on invoices should be checked against applicable purchase orders and receiving reports. All amount extensions and totals should be checked. The person auditing the suppliers' invoices should initial these documents.

- All vouchers, invoices, and supporting documents should be canceled when paid.

- Only accounting personnel not responsible for the general ledger should maintain the accounts payable subsidiary ledger (which should be reconciled monthly with the general ledger control account for accounts payable).

- A monthly trial balance of accounts payable should be prepared for the manager's review.

- Suppliers should be paid on a timely basis in order to maintain good supplier relationships.

Accounts Payable Voucher   **Voucher Number 7321**

Pay to: **Date**   **Date**
Address: **Paid**   **Check**

No.

Date	Description	Amount	Discount % Amount	Other Deductions For	Other Deductions Amount	Net Amount			Account	Amount

Entered on voucher   Total charges_____
Recorded by _____   Less Discount_____

Prepared   Approved for   Posted   Other Deductions _____
by _____ Payment by _____   by _____   Amt. of Check _____

Audited
by _____

Figure 13.1   Voucher Used in Voucher System

<hr>

REVENUE CONTROL: A FOUR-STEP PROCESS[23]

Sophisticated revenue control procedures are not practical for small restaurants with only a few employees, because a proper segregation of duties is not possible. The owner/manager is the most critical control element in a small restaurant.

In its simplest form, revenue control and security is a matter of matching products sold with revenues received. An effective revenue security system ensures that the following happens in the restaurant:

Product sales = Guest charges = Revenue receipts = Revenue deposits

Revenue Security Concerns

The potential for guest or employee theft or fraud exists in all of these areas. To illustrate possible problems, assume you own a chain of ten dessert shops: You

[23]The remainder of this chapter is adapted from: Jack Miller, et al., *Food and Beverage Cost Control,* Second Edition (New York, NY, 2002).

sell pies of many varieties for $2.00 per slice or $15 for a whole pie (eight slices). You also sell coffee for $2.00 per cup. Assume Figure 13.2 details your sales on one day for one of your ten stores.

If you have an effective system to control revenue, you should have total receipts (revenue) of $1,400 for January 1 at this unit. If, at day's end, you have only $1,300 in actual revenue, a security problem exists, perhaps not in the control of products but in the control of receipts.

There are several reasons why you might be short in revenue; they can involve external or internal threats to revenue security.

External Threats

Your property could lose revenue because some guests try to defraud the restaurant. Perhaps a guest **walks** or **skips** the bill (guest check).

> **WALK (SKIP) To consume a product and leave a restaurant without paying the bill.**

Revenue loss from walks/skips can be substantial. To help reduce this type of guest theft, consider the steps in Figure 13.3 on page 310.

A second form of guest theft involves fraudulent payment. This includes passing counterfeit money, writing bad checks, and using invalid credit or debit

---

Unit Name: _____The Pie Parlor #6_____   Date: _____January 1, 20XX_____

Item	Number Sold	Selling Price	Total Sales
Apple Pie			
Slices	60	$ 2.00	$ 120.00
Whole	11	15.00	165.00
Pumpkin Pie			
Slices	40	2.00	80.00
Whole	14	15.00	210.00
Cherry Pie			
Slices	75	2.00	150.00
Whole	5	15.00	75.00
Peach Pie			
Slices	25	2.00	50.00
Whole	10	15.00	150.00
Coffee	200	2.00	400.00
Total			**$1,400.00**

Figure 13.2 Sales Record

1. If guests order and consume food prior to receiving payment, instruct servers to present the bill promptly when guests have finished.

2. If the restaurant has a cashier in a central location, assure that the cashier is available and visible at all times.

3. If each server personally collects for guest charges, assure that the servers return to the table promptly after presenting the bill to secure payment.

4. Train employees to observe exit doors near restrooms or other areas that can provide opportunities for guests to exit without being easily seen.

5. If an employee sees a guest walk/skip, a manager should be notified immediately.

6. When approaching a guest who has left without paying, ask if the guest has inadvertently "forgotten" to pay. (Usually the guest will then pay the bill.)

7. If a guest refuses to pay or flees, note the following on an incident report:

   - number of guests involved
   - amount of the bill
   - physical description of the guest(s)
   - vehicle description, if applicable, with license plate number, if possible
   - time and date of the incident
   - name of the server(s) who served the guest(s)

8. If the guest successfully flees, the police should be notified. In no case should your staff members or managers attempt to physically detain the guest.

Figure 13.3   Steps to Reduce Guest Walks/Skips

CREDIT CARD A card, usually issued by a financial institution, which requires the cardholder to pay for goods and services purchased sometime *after* the card is used.

DEBIT CARD A card, usually issued by a financial institution, which allows the financial institution to remove funds directly from the cardholder's account *at the time the card is used* to purchase goods or service.

cards. A **credit card** obligates users to pay their credit card companies for the goods and services charged on the card. A **debit card** covers purchases using funds that are transferred from the user's bank account to the entity issuing the debit card.

The number of stolen and fraudulent credit cards in use today is high. The manager should check the validity of a credit or debit card before accepting it for payment. To enhance your chances of collecting from credit/debit card companies and to reduce the risk of fraudulent card use, insist that your staff follow the steps in Figure 13.4.

Some restaurants that accept personal checks use a verification service. Such services do not actually certify that there are sufficient funds in the bank.

1. Confirm that the name on the card is the same as that of the individual presenting the card for payment. Use drivers' licenses or other acceptable forms of identification.

2. Examine the card for obvious signs of alteration.

3. Confirm that the card is valid (not expired or not yet in effect).

4. Compare the signature on the back of the card with the one used by the guest paying with the card.

5. The employee processing the charge should initial the credit card receipt.

6. Carbon paper, if used, should be destroyed.

7. Credit card charges not yet processed should be kept in a secure place to limit the possibility of theft.

8. Do not issue cash in exchange for credit card charges.

9. Do not write in tip amounts for the guest unless the "tip" is a mandatory service charge (and that fact is communicated to the guest).

10. Tally credit card charges on a daily basis. Assure that the above procedures have been followed. If not, corrective action should immediately be taken.

Figure 13.4   Credit and Debit Card Verification Procedures

Rather, they notify the manager if that specific checking account or individual has had difficulty in the past in covering checks written on the account. These services will also reimburse the restaurant for approved checks that are subsequently dishonored by the paying bank.

Another method of theft is used by the **quick-change artist**. For example, a guest who should have received $5 in change may use a confusing routine to

> **QUICK-CHANGE ARTIST   A guest who attempts to confuse the cashier in order to receive excessive change.**

WWW: Internet Assistant

Theft and fraud involving the use of credit and debit cards is becoming increasingly common. Managers must take action to ensure that this illegal activity is not committed by either guests or employees. Credit and debit card issuers also want to reduce theft. For suggestions from two of the largest card issuers on fighting credit and debit card thievery, go to the following Web sites

http://www.usa.visa.com/business/merchants/fraud_basics_index.html

http://www.mastercardintl.com/merchant/accept.html

secure $15. Train cashiers well and instruct them to notify a manager immediately if there is any suspicion of attempted fraud.

Internal Threats

Most restaurant employees are honest; some are not. Managers must protect revenue from any dishonest employees. Cash is a major target for dishonest employees. Cash-handling personnel do not generally remove large sums of cash at one time. Rather, they typically use a variety of techniques to steal a small amount at a time.

One common server theft technique involves an omission on the guest's order. If, in our Pie Parlor example, a guest ordered pie and coffee, but the pie sale is not recorded, a piece of pie will be missing, but no record of sale will be made. The server might have chosen to charge the guest and keep the revenue, or might have attempted to build favor with the guest by not charging for the product. (Theft of this type is especially prevalent in bars.) All sales must be recorded when a system that matches products sold to revenue received is in place. Complete revenue control involves developing the checks and balances necessary to ensure that the value of products sold and the amount of revenue received are equal.

To understand how server theft could occur, a manager must know the different options for recording sales. In the least effective option, no record is made of the sale at all. Guests are simply told how much they owe by the server.

GUEST CHECK   A written record of what was purchased by the guest and how much the guest was charged for the item(s).

Obviously, this approach is ineffective. A second and improved approach is to require a written **guest check** recording each sale. The use of guest checks is standard in the industry, but dishonest employees can abuse them. If, for example, a guest at the Pie Parlor orders peach pie and coffee, and the service person collects the revenue for these products, in some operations the same guest check could be used one hour later for another guest who orders peach pie and coffee. The server could then keep the money from the second sale. To prevent fraud of this type, a system must be in place to make sure each check is used one time only. Hard-copy guest checks should be recorded by number and then safely stored or destroyed.

Another method of fraud also involves the use of guest checks. The server gives the proper guest check to the guests, collects payment, and destroys the guest check but keeps the money. In this case, the manager finds the money in the cash register to equal the sum of the guest checks, but the actual amount of product served does not equal that indicated on the guest checks. For this reason, many managers use a **precheck/postcheck system** for guest checks. In a precheck/postcheck system the server records the order (prechecks) on a guest check. Kitchen/bar personnel cannot issue products to the server without a precheck guest check. When the guest pays the bill, the cashier recalls the prechecked total, and the guest pays that bill. In this case, products ordered by the guest and issued by the kitchen/bar should match the items and money collected by the cashier. Today, precheck/ postcheck systems are sold as a component of nearly all **point of sales (POS) systems.**

> **PRECHECK/POSTCHECK SYSTEM**
> A system in which the server records the order (prechecks) on a guest check. Kitchen/bar personnel cannot issue products to the server without a precheck guest check. When the guest desires to pay the bill, the cashier recalls the prechecked total (postchecks), and the guest pays that bill.

A variety of components are available for designing a good guest check control system. These include management-issued guest checks, multicopy guest checks (carbonless paper), and guest checks generated by computerized POS systems. In all cases, the goal is the same: to reduce server theft by the proper recording and collecting of all product sales.

> **POINT OF SALES (POS) SYSTEM**
> A system for controlling the restaurant's cash and product usage involving a computer processor and, depending on the size of the operation, additional computer hardware, communication devices, and/or software.

Sometimes honest mistakes are made. This often occurs when service personnel must total guest checks by hand. Simple errors in addition and subtraction can cost the restaurant dearly. Service personnel should not total guest checks without use of a POS system, cash register, adding machine, or calculator.

Many operators use a computerized system to record product sales, tally guest check totals, and compare money collected with what should have been collected. Even sophisticated systems hold the potential for employee fraud. Consider the precheck/postcheck POS system that requires a server to enter a password before allowing that server to precheck items. A dishonest server who discovers another server's password could use that password to defraud the restaurant and blame the fraud on the unsuspecting server.

Cashier/Bartender Theft

In some restaurants, servers act as their own cashiers; in others, server and cashier functions fall to different individuals. Regardless, whenever a cashier is responsible for collecting money, several areas of potential fraud exist. The cashier may collect payment from a guest but destroy the guest check that recorded the sale, or the cashier can fail to ring up the sale while pocketing the money. Managers must be able to identify missing checks and match guest check totals with those of cash register sales.

Restaurant employees can defraud guests with techniques such as:

- charging guests for items not purchased and keeping the overcharge
- changing the totals on credit card charges after the guest has left or imprinting additional credit card charges and pocketing the cash differences
- misadding legitimate charges to create a higher-than-appropriate total and keeping the overcharge
- shortchanging guests when giving back change and keeping the extra change
- charging higher-than-authorized prices for products or services, recording the proper price and keeping the overcharge

In all but the most outdated cash register systems, the totals of guest checks rung on the machine during a predetermined period are mechanically tallied so managers can compare sales recorded by the cash register with the money actually contained in the cash register. For example, a cashier working a shift from 7:00 a.m. to 3:00 p.m. might have recorded $1,000.00 in sales. If no errors in handling change occurred, the cash register should contain $1,000.00 plus the amount of the beginning cash bank. If it contains less than this amount it is said to be **short;** if it contains more than this amount, it is said to be **over.** Cashiers rarely steal large sums directly from the cash drawer, but managers must investigate all cash shorts and overs. Some managers believe that cash shortages (but not overages) need to be monitored. Consistent cash shortages may be an indication of employee theft or carelessness

SHORT This occurs when the cash drawer contains less money than expected.

OVER This occurs when the cash drawer contains more money than expected.

and should be investigated. Cash overages, too, may be the result of sophisticated theft by the cashier; the victim may be the restaurant or the guest.

If the cash register has a void key, a dishonest cashier could enter a sales amount, collect for it and then void (erase) the sale after the guest has departed. Then, total sales would equal the amount of the cash drawer. If the guest check was destroyed, the remaining guest check totals, cash register total revenue figures, and cash drawer would balance. Managers should insist that all cash register voids be performed by a supervisor or be authorized by managers. Since cash registers record the number and often the time at which voids are performed, these tallies should be monitored.

Another method of cashier theft involves the manipulation of complimentary meals or meal coupons. Assume that, at your Pie Parlor, you have distributed coupons for a free piece of pie. If cashiers have access to these coupons, they can collect money from guests without a coupon and then add the coupon to the cash drawer while removing revenue equal to the coupon's value. Alternatively, the cashier can declare a check to be complimentary after the guest has paid the bill. Then, the cashier would remove revenue from the register in an amount equal to the "comped" check. This fraud can be prevented by denying cashiers access to unredeemed cash value coupons and by requiring special authorization from managers to "comp" guest checks.

It should be clear from these examples that managers must have a complete revenue security system to ensure that all products sold generate revenue. Even good revenue control systems present the opportunity for theft if managers are not vigilant or if two or more employees collude to defraud the operation. It may not be possible to prevent all types of theft, but a good revenue control system can help to determine if a theft has occurred. Then managers must investigate and take appropriate actions.

Employees may be bonded to help protect against employee theft. As noted earlier, bonding involves purchasing an insurance policy against the possibility that an employee will steal. If a bonded employee is involved in theft, the restaurant will be reimbursed for the loss by the bonding company. While bonding will not completely eliminate theft, it is relatively inexpensive and worth the cost to require that all employees who handle cash or other forms of revenue be bonded. It is also advisable to verify a potential employee's funds-handling experience in prior jobs.

Developing the Revenue Security System

An effective revenue security system will help managers accomplish the following:

- verification of product issues
- verification of guest charges

- verification of revenue receipts
- verification of revenue deposits

Each of these tasks must be included in a total revenue security system. Every restaurant uses a different method to sell products and to account for revenue. We can, however, address any restaurant's revenue control system with respect to these four key points and how they relate to each other. Ideally, a product would be sold, its sale recorded, its selling price collected, and the funds deposited in the restaurant's bank account in a single step. Rapid advances in technology including "smart" cards are making this a reality for more restaurants each day. An example from the grocery industry helps illustrate how this works:

A grocery store customer uses a bank-issued debit card when buying a frozen dinner. The cashier uses a scanner to read the bar code printed on the dinner. The following happens:

- The amount the shopper owes the store is recorded in the POS system and the sale itself is assigned a tracking number (verification of product issued/sold).
- The sale amount is displayed for the guest, who confirms its correctness; a receipt is printed (verification of guest check accuracy).
- The store's POS system records the amount of the sale as well as the form of payment used (verification of revenue).
- The shopper's debit card number is attached to this specific sales tracking number and a transfer of funds takes place from the shopper's account to that of the grocery store (verification of deposit).

Note: Although it is not part of the store's revenue control system, something else also occurs: The inventory level for the frozen entrée is reduced by one unit; at a specific order point the store may be alerted that an order must be placed with a supplier (or an order might be electronically placed).

Not all restaurants can duplicate all phases of this system. Managers should, however, adapt the technology they currently use to develop a good revenue control system. They must design the control system *first* and then decide which aspects of the system are best computerized. Computers do not *bring* controls to a restaurant, but they can assist in making control systems work faster and with less human effort.

Managers must have a thorough understanding of how the revenue security system works and what is required to maintain it. Consider Faris, who owns a restaurant with a small cocktail area and 100 guest seats in the dining room. Total revenue exceeds $1 million per year. When he started the restaurant, he did not give much thought to the design of his revenue control system. Now he spends more time in a second restaurant and needs both the security of an adequate revenue security system and the ability to review it quickly to evaluate the sales levels of both restaurants. Faris has begun to develop a revenue security system using the formula noted earlier:

Product sales = Guest charges = Revenue receipts = Revenue deposits

He knows that computer systems are available, but he does not wish to overspend on a system in terms of either money or time. He wants a control system that will achieve his goals. The first goal is to verify product sales.

Step 1: Verification of Product Sales. The key to verification of product sales is to follow one rule: *No product shall be issued from the kitchen or bar unless a permanent record of issue is made.* This means that the kitchen (bar) should not fill any server's request for food (beverage) unless that request has been documented. In some restaurants, this takes the form of multicopy, written guest checks. In other cases, order information is sent to the production area by computer. (The order is viewed by the production staff on a computer terminal, or the computer prints a hard copy of the order for the production staff.) The software then maintains the permanent record of the request.

In the bar, the principle of verifying all product sales is even more important. Bartenders should never issue a drink unless that order has first been recorded on a guest check or in the POS system.

This rule regarding product issuing is important for two reasons. Requiring a permanent, documented order ensures that there is a record of each product sale. Also, this record can verify proper inventory usage and product sales totals. Faris enforces this rule by requiring that no menu item be served from the kitchen or bar without a written record of the sale. To do so, Faris implements a precheck/postcheck system to match product sales with sales receipts. The precheck portion also fills the requirement that no menu item be issued from kitchen or bar without first documenting its sale.

If his verification of product sales system is working correctly, Faris will find that:

$$\text{Documented product requests} = \text{Product sales}$$

Step 2: Verification of Guest Charges. When the production staff distributes products only in response to a documented request, it is critical that those documented requests result in guest charges. It makes little sense to enforce the verification of product sales step without also requiring staff to ensure that guest charges match these requests. This concept can be summarized: *Product sales must equal guest charges.* There are numerous ways this can be achieved. Consider Faris, who could use a manual guest check system or a computerized POS system.

If he uses manually completed guest checks he must ensure that product sales equal guest check totals. If they do, all issued products will result in correct charges to the guest. If guest checks are used, the numbers on the checks are of no value if checks are not tightly controlled. Each check must be accounted for, and employees must be held responsible for each check they are issued so a dishonest employee does not present a guest check for payment and then destroy the check and keep the money.

Use of manual guest checks can be time consuming. A POS system simplifies this task and saves time by creating a unique transaction number for each server request. A documented request for products generates a guest check matched to that request. Guest checks cannot be "lost" on purpose, because the POS keeps a record of each transaction and records employee attempts to order a product, receive it from the kitchen or bar, and then "void" (subtract) the charge from the guest's bill.

When properly implemented, this second step of the revenue control system results in:

$$\text{Product sales} = \text{Guest charges}$$

Regardless of whether Faris uses a manual guest check system or purchases a POS system, he now has two major revenue control principles in place. The first is that no product can be ordered from the kitchen or bar unless the order is documented; the second is that all guest charges must match product orders.

With these two systems in place, Faris can deal with many problems. If, for example, a guest has "walked," the kitchen will have a duplicate of the order. Managers will know which products were sold, which server sold them, and, perhaps, information such as the time of the sale, the number of guests in the party, and the revenue value of the products. The precheck system Faris uses also ensures that employees do not attempt to write an item on the guest check and charge the guest a higher or lower price. A periodic audit of checks is necessary to help detect such fraud.

Step 3: Verification of Revenue Receipts. **Revenue receipts** are the actual revenue received in payment for products served. For Faris, this means all revenue from his restaurants and lounges. If his revenue security system is working properly, he will know the following:

REVENUE RECEIPTS The actual revenue received in payment for products served.

$$\text{Guest charges} = \text{Revenue receipts}$$

Verifying sales receipts is more than counting cash at the end of a shift. In fact, cash handling is only one part of the total sales receipt verification system. Faris wishes to ensure that the amount of cash, checks, and bank card charges in his cash register at the end of a shift matches the dollar amount of his guest checks at the end of the shift. (Then he will have accounted for all sales receipts, since he has controlled for both product sales and guest charges.)

Faris recognizes an essential principle: *Both the cashier and a supervisor must verify sales receipts.* While this will not prevent collusion between the two employees, it is important that sales receipt verification be a two-person process.

There are four basic payment arrangements used by most restaurants:

- ■ *Guest pays cashier.* In this situation losses occur primarily because of guest walks. This system works best in quick-service and cafeteria settings where a guest does not actually receive the order until the bill is paid. It works less well in a table service restaurant, where a cashier may be too busy to notice whether an individual who has consumed a product has paid the bill before leaving. Under this system cashiers could also collect funds, destroy a guest check, and claim a guest has walked without paying the bill.

- *Guest pays service personnel who pay cashier.* In this situation, the server presents the bill to the guest, accepts payment, and takes the payment to the cashier for processing. Under this system, the guest's change is returned by the service personnel along with the receipt. An advantage of this system is that it is more difficult for guests to leave without paying, since it is easier for servers to watch their own tables than for a cashier to observe the entire dining room. A second advantage is that the guest need not stand in line to pay the bill during a busy period. A disadvantage is that guests may have to wait to settle their bill if servers do not notice when they are finished with their meal.

  From a control perspective, it is a good practice to separate the processes of ordering products and delivering them and totaling the guest check and collecting payment. This system makes it more difficult to defraud the restaurant.

- *Guest pays service personnel, who have paid cashier.* This method of payment is popular in some restaurants and beverage operations. Each server begins the shift with a predetermined cash bank (which either is his/her own or which is issued by the manager). When the kitchen or bar fills guest orders, service personnel *purchase* these products using their own bank. The server then collects final payment from the guest. Servers are responsible for the total of their bank, since all food and beverages were purchased at the time they were issued.

  This system is not under direct management control. Employees can defraud guests and guests can walk without managers' knowledge. Also, employees may resent this system because it makes them personally responsible for guest walks.

- *Guest is direct billed.* In some situations, creditworthy guests are invoiced for the value of the products they have consumed. Invoices must accurately reflect all guest charges. Consider Faris, who agrees to provide a banquet. The guest guarantees a count of 90 guests, but 100 guests actually attend. The guest should be billed for 100 meals, and payment by the guest should reflect that. This done, the principles of revenue control are still in place; that is, guest charges should equal revenue collected.

- *Special revenue collection situations.* In some cases, variations on the four payment systems occur. Consider a drink coupon—often sold in hotel reception areas for use at cocktail receptions. These coupons should be treated as if they were cash. The individuals who sell the coupons should not be the same as those dispensing the beverages. Collected drink coupons should equal the number of drinks served.

  A second special pricing situation is the reduced-price coupon. Coupons are popular and can take forms such as 50% off a specific purchase, "buy-one-get-one-free" promotions, or a program where a guest buys a number of meals and gets the next one free. In all of these cases, the coupon should be treated as cash.

With guest charges reconciled to sales receipts, Faris moves to Step 4 of the revenue security process.

Step 4: Verification of Revenue Deposits. Only managers should make the actual bank deposit of daily revenue. The deposit slip may be completed by a cashier or other clerical assistant, but the manager should be responsible for monitoring the deposit. This concept can be summarized: *Managers must personally verify all bank deposits.* This involves the verification of the contents of the deposit and matching bank deposits with actual sales. If, for example, Faris deposits Thursday's sales on Friday, the Friday deposit should match the sales amount of Thursday. If it does not, a loss of revenue has occurred after the cashier has reconciled sales receipts to guest charges.

Embezzlement occurs when money, in rightful possession of an employee, is diverted by the employee through a fraudulent action. Embezzlement is a crime that can go undetected for a long time, because the embezzler is usually a trusted employee.

Falsification of bank deposits is a common method of embezzlement. To prevent this activity:

- Make bank deposits daily, if possible.

- Ensure that the individual making the daily deposit is bonded.

- Establish written policies for completing bank reconciliations (comparison of monthly bank statements vs. daily deposits).

- Review and approve bank statement reconciliations each month.

- Employ an outside auditor to examine the accuracy of deposits annually.

If verification of sales deposits is done correctly and no embezzlement is occurring, the following holds:

$$\text{Revenue receipts} = \text{Revenue deposits}$$

By following these steps, Faris has completed the revenue security system. Its four key principles follow:

- No product shall be ordered from the kitchen/bar unless a permanent record of issue is made.

- Product orders must equal guest charges.

- Both the cashier and a supervisor must verify revenue receipts.

- Managers must personally verify all bank deposits.

It is possible to develop and maintain a completely manual revenue control system. Each of the four major components of the revenue control system can be implemented without the use of a computer or even a cash register. In today's world, however, this approach is wasteful of time and suspect in accuracy. The amount of information needed to effectively operate a restaurant grows constantly. Guest dining choices, vendor pricing, inventory levels, payroll statistics, and revenue control are just a few concerns that involve data collection and manipulation. Fortunately, new technologies can easily and quickly assemble the data needed to make good management decisions. A restaurant manager should not expect a computer to "bring" control. It may, however, take good control systems and add speed, accuracy, or additional information.

To improve a revenue security or any other cost control system, a computerized system will be of immense value. If a restaurant has no controls, and if a manager is not committed to the control process, the computer will simply become a high-tech adding machine used to sum up guest checks and nothing more. Properly selected and understood, however, technology-enhanced systems can be a powerful ally in the cost control/revenue security system.

WWW: Internet Assistant

A variety of software programs are available to help integrate all of a restaurant's financial activities. One of the most popular is Great Plains, offered by Microsoft. The popularity of Great Plains is due in part to its integration with the equally popular Microsoft Excel and Word programs. To view the financial management tools Microsoft offers small business owners, including restaurants, go to

www.greatplains.com/smallbusinessmanager/default.asp

CASH AND REVENUE CONTROL PROCEDURES FOR SMALL RESTAURANTS

Many of the cash and revenue control procedures discussed in this chapter assume that several accounting-related positions are set up to enable duties to be separated. Small restaurant operations do not have this luxury. It becomes the responsibility of the owner/manager to perform key duties to overcome potential weaknesses in the internal control system. What, at minimum, should the owner/manager do? These critical duties are outlined below[24]:

- *Cash receipts:* Open all mail each day, list cash receipts, and keep a copy of the list; deposit all cash every day, compare the deposit with the bookkeeper's cash receipts debit, and reconcile cash receipts with cash register data.

- *Cash disbursements:* Sign all checks and review and cancel all supporting documentation; use only prenumbered checks—account for them when signing checks; total the check disbursements periodically; compare the total to the bookkeeper's cash credit and prepare the bank reconciliation.

---

[24]Adapted from: Raymond Schmidgall, *Hospitality Industry Managerial Accounting,* Fourth Edition (Lansing, Mich., 1997).

- *Revenue control:* Keep all cash registers locked; remove cash register tapes when not in use; compare cash register tape totals with daily cash debits and cash deposits.

- *Payroll:* Examine the payroll worksheet (or payroll journal) to note employees' names, gross pay, hours worked, deductions, and net pay; add the payroll and compare the net pay with the cash credit and distribute payroll checks.

- *Accounts receivable:* Review aging of accounts receivable (if applicable); personally resolve any disputed account balances.

- *General tasks:* Review all general journal entries; employ and bond a competent, trustworthy bookkeeper. If possible, use an independent auditor to conduct an annual audit; periodically conduct limited surprise audits of cash and accounts receivable.

MANAGER'S 10 POINT EFFECTIVENESS CHECKLIST

Evaluate your need for and the status of each of the following financial management tactics. For tactics you judge to be important but not yet in place, develop an action plan including completion date to implement the tactic.

TACTIC	DON'T AGREE (DON'T NEED)	AGREE (DONE)	AGREE (NOT DONE)	IF NOT DONE	
				WHO IS RESPONSIBLE?	TARGET COMPLETION DATE
1. Managers distribute an employee manual to all employees detailing penalties imposed for theft of the restaurant's assets.	❑	❑	❑		
2. All active bank accounts are reconciled monthly and reviewed by the manager.	❑	❑	❑		
3. Managers count cash and petty cash banks at unannounced intervals.	❑	❑	❑		
4. All checks received are dated, and the notice "For Deposit Only" is stamped with the restaurant's name when each check is accepted.	❑	❑	❑		
5. Cash revenues are recorded and cash drawers are balanced at the end of each shift or at least once daily.	❑	❑	❑		
6. Cash drawers are locked and keys are removed any time the drawer is left unattended.	❑	❑	❑		
7. Checks used to pay restaurant bills are numbered, used in sequence, supported by proper documentation, and reviewed by someone not responsible for preparation of the checks (unless that person is the manager).	❑	❑	❑		
8. No food or beverage products are issued from the production area without a written guest check or its equivalent.	❑	❑	❑		
9. Guest checks are numbered, issued, and used to verify revenue totals on a daily basis.	❑	❑	❑		
10. Employees have been trained about and use techniques to help detect and reduce theft and fraud by customers.	❑	❑	❑		

RECOMMENDED READING

Friedlob, G. Thomas and Franklin J. Plewa. *Understanding Balance Sheets.* New York: John Wiley & Sons, Inc., 1996. An excellent and inexpensive book if you are interested in learning more about balance sheets and how to understand them.

McVety, Paul J., Bradley J.Ware, and Claudette Lévesque. *Fundamentals of Menu Planning, 2nd Edition.* New York: John Wiley & Sons, Inc., 2001. The ability to develop and properly price a menu is an important one. This is an excellent book that thoroughly discusses this topic as well as other price-related menu development concepts.

Miller, Jack E., David K. Hayes, and Lea R. Dopson. *Food and Beverage Cost Control, 2nd Edition.* New York: John Wiley & Sons, Inc., 2001. This book is an excellent resource with up-to-date information on the latest foodservice technology including a discussion on procedures to analyze income statements and make necessary operational corrections to improve profits.

INDEX